YOU HAVE BEEN WATCHING...

THE AUTOBIOGRAPHY OF DAVID CROFT

BOOKS

To my wonderful wife Ann
and to the wonderful family we have produced

Published by BBC Books, BBC Worldwide Limited, 80 Wood Lane, London W12 0TT

First published 2004. Copyright © David Croft 2004
The moral right of the author has been asserted.

ISBN 0 563 48739 9

Commissioning editor: Ben Dunn
Project editor: Sarah Emsley
Copy-editor: Steve Dobell
Designer: Ann Thompson
Production controller: Christopher Tinker

*BBC Books would like to thank the following for providing photographs and for permission to
reproduce copyright material. While every effort has been made to trace and acknowledge all
copyright holders, we would like to apologise should there have been any errors or omissions.*

All photographs courtesy of the author or copyright BBC except for section 2, page 6:
Press Association.

Set in Meridien.
Printed and bound in Great Britain by CPI Bath
Colour separations by Radstock Reproductions, Midsomer Norton

Contents

Thanks

To Ben Dunn, Sarah Emsley and David Cottingham for their help and guidance in the preparation of this book, to Billy McCranor and the staff at our home for 'minding' me while I wrote it, and – above all – to the Richard Stone Organisation for representing me with great care for over 50 years.

Special Thanks

To the hundreds of actors and actresses, camera and lighting crews, costume, make-up and scene crews and designers, and all my assistants and secretaries, who are not named but who have all made my life so rewarding – and such enormous fun.

Introduction

It was a fair cop. I should have seen the signs – there were plenty that I might have noticed if I hadn't gone around in a dream world. In the first place there was Ann. After being married to her for forty-something years I should have detected the subtle unease in her manner. One day whilst we were in Portugal she had been unusually keen to get me out of the house and down to the market in Cabanes to get the shopping.

Then there was the car that the BBC sent to take me to what I believed was to be a meeting about Australian rights. Usually I get what they optimistically call a 'VIP' car. It is always liberally strewn with cigarette butts, the door is tied on with hairy string, and it is driven by a man who doesn't know his Arsenal from his Eltham. This car was a large, gleaming Mercedes. The driver was in uniform and wearing a chauffeur's hat. And why was he driving so slowly? Even an old diesel taxi passed us. 'It's murder on the road these days,' he said. 'Cameras, police cars, everything. I can't afford to lose my licence – it's my living.' This was followed by a hushed conversation on the car phone. I could only catch the odd words like 'early' and 'five minutes'.

As we turned right into the main entrance of the BBC the barrier went up as though we were expected. They can't have recognised me – they never do. The second barrier went up as if by magic and we were climbing the rise to the main entrance. A couple of 5K lamps were providing a pool of light, so somebody was filming something. Through the windscreen I could see something suspiciously like Jones's butcher's van. Now even I began to take notice. Bill Pertwee, dressed as the air raid warden, was running towards the car with his hand held up and he was shouting, 'What are you doing here? Stop! Stop!' Suddenly Clive Dunn in a straw hat was opening the side door and I was being pulled out by Pike. Now I could see a camera being pointed my way and Michael Aspel, carrying a big red book under his arm, was saying, 'David Croft, OBE – this is your life!'

I mumbled something stupid like, 'Well I never', and then, before I knew what was happening, a production manager was whisking me past the grinning receptionists and down the corridor towards the dressing room. There was barely time for a couple of puffs on my nitrite spray to ward off the likely arrival of an angina attack before they sat me down and the production manager was popping a cork and doling out a glass of champagne – not my favourite drink but very welcome nevertheless.

There was no time to collect my thoughts. The production manager had been specially selected to prattle on endlessly to stunned victims of this programme. I should know. I had directed a dozen of them in the early

1960s when I was being punished by Tom Sloan, head of light entertainment, for not getting on with Benny Hill. Mercifully the lad excused himself and, with a plea to me not to peep outside because I might see some of the people who were going to be on the show, he left me alone for a few minutes. A couple more puffs and a few moments to think.

Who would they get and how far back could they go? Not as far as school. I hadn't seen or heard of anyone from cold, windswept Durlston Court in Swanage for years. Oh yes, there was the lovely, viciously witty John Frankau, also a television producer, but surely he was in China or somewhere? Perhaps they'd got Adamson – Sir Campbell Adamson – with whom I shared a study at Rugby. I could still see him as he was when I met him on that first night. I arrived at school very late because of the snow and was taken to the dormitory, and he was standing there in his shirt tails with no trousers. We were introduced by Johnston, the housemaster, and we gravely shook hands. He was a possible.

Ann might have dug out a couple from the army. She had met red-headed Joe Postlethwaite from Glasgow, one of my Bofors gun-layers when I was in North Africa. But did she know about his mate Peter Wyper, a big, blonde, dour paviour or big Frank Lock, the loader, who used to play full-back for Charlton? And what about Sergeant Barber, a wonderful, strong-willed man who fought with the International Brigade in Spain but would never talk about it? Surely they wouldn't find that humourless Scottish bastard Major Wilson who told me I wasn't officer material? Less than three years later I was turning down the offer to be a lieutenant-colonel. I don't suppose he ever knew that. If he was there, at least I would have a chance to tell him.

Perhaps they had got some of my mates from the Barmouth Officer Cadet Training Unit before I was commissioned. Maybe Barry Stewart-Fisher, the impeccably turned-out Czech lawyer, who arrived at our tent at Sandhurst with a 15-cwt truck full of kit and proceeded to off-load it so we had no room to sleep. Or the other member of the trio – Johnny Spittal, a down-to-earth plumber from Birmingham who, like Barry, had a prodigious appetite for the sugar-coated pancakes we could get if we doubled to the end of the deserted prom at Barmouth after we had done an exhausting day's training.

But what about Cliff Adams and the BBC Show Band singers? The money for those sessions provided the wherewithal I needed in order to stay in London while making the transition from being an actor to being a writer and producer. And what about all the television shows?

And what about… And what about…

Another glass of champagne and a brush of the usual brown stuff from the make-up department and I am standing all alone behind the familiar set of *The Life*. And now they are playing the music. A frantic gesture from the production manager, another couple of puffs of the nitrite – this would be a rotten moment to have a heart attack and keel over – and I am on…

1
Is This My Life?

Mother wanted a girl. The evidence cannot be contradicted. It is there for the whole world to see. One glance at the snapshots of the time says it all. The long, curly golden locks, the powdered complexion, the camp knitted two-piece suit. They all wanted a girl. The doctor held up ugly little me by the heels and said, 'I'm afraid it's another boy' – as if it weren't obvious. My brother Peter, aged six, took one look, said 'Damn' and left the room in a huff. Olive Rawdon, Mother's friend and lifetime companion, kept her counsel as usual. Olive had arrived on the scene some 12 years earlier at the age of 13. Mother, who had reached the advanced age of 14, had left school, as one could in those days, and had set up a stage academy where she taught singing, dancing and acting. Olive arrived to play the piano. She was supposed to stay for a fortnight. In the end she became paid companion, nanny, confidante and general factotum and stayed for 80 years, which shows the advantage of keeping your counsel. She didn't talk a lot.

The scene of this early emotional family disappointment was a bungalow by the harbourside at Sandbanks, near Poole in Dorset. The year was 1922. The precise time and date – 11.15 a.m. on 7 September. Mother had been starring in a revue called *The Peep Show* at the London Hippodrome. At that time she was known as Annie Croft and she was billed second only to top comic Lupino Lane. She said that being pregnant with me cost her £1,500 in lost salary. That was a lot of money in 1922.

Father was Reginald Sharland. He was starring in the same show but his name was further down the bill. Mother took care of that. A keen relation once thoroughly investigated the family of Sharland. Grandpa was a well-respected draper who supplied knick-knacks and knickers to the respectable people of Southend. He was also, it turned out, well practised in dalliance with the opposite sex – a skill that was passed on a generation or two. It was obviously simpler before the First World War to be a well-practised and undiscovered dallier with the opposite sex. Telephones were a rare luxury. Thus, no little busybody could ring up, anonymously if necessary, and say, 'I think you ought to know that your husband is carrying on with that hussy at number 17.'

Such events frequently remained undiscovered until the will was read and the hussy at number 17 collected a shilling or two for services rendered. These days a man has only to take a couple of paces down the hotel corridor and the *Sun* features it on the front page.

I think the keen relation was desperately seeking connections with a king or a prince or at least a lord. He was disappointed if so. Not even an MBE showed up. The Sharlands were extremely ordinary and had been extremely ordinary since records were first kept, apart from a great uncle who wrote for *Punch* and was a 'confirmed bachelor'.

Reginald Sharland is described on my birth certificate as 'Theatrical Actor'. Since the BBC didn't start operations until November of that year he couldn't have been called a 'Wireless Actor'. I suppose he could possibly have been labelled 'Silent Film Actor' except that he had not at that stage been in a film. Theatrical Actor conjures up visions of an operatic cloaked figure entering through a cloud of smoke and declaiming something portentous in stentorian tones. This was not Reginald Sharland's style at all. He was handsome with a brilliant smile, a charming manner and a not very true baritone voice. Theatrical Actor he was not. I put the description down to an excess of zeal for accuracy on the part of the registrar.

Mother had a more complicated background. In the year 1892, at the age of six weeks, she was adopted by a grocer named Michael Croft and his wife Emma. They ran a corner shop in Hessle Road, Hull. A crude adoption letter came to light when Emma died in 1948, naming little Annie as Gertrude Mulgrave, daughter of Frederick Mulgrave and Elizabeth Davis. All this seems straightforward enough, but ask anyone in Hull who was alive at the time and they would tell you that Annie was the love child of Edward VII and Muriel Wilson of Tranby Croft. The Prince of Wales, as he then was, frequently visited the Wilsons who were extremely wealthy. Arthur Wilson owned a shipping line, an enormous house in Grosvenor Place (which is now the Irish Embassy), and a huge villa set in four acres on Cap Ferrat in the south of France. It was at Tranby Croft that the notorious gambling scandal involving the Prince of Wales occurred.

It is said to be on record somewhere that during his interesting life Edward sired 67 illegitimate offspring, so it was easy to believe that he sprang a 68th after dallying with young Muriel. On the other hand, she would have been only 17 when Annie was born, which makes the ageing Prince a distinctly dirty old man. In his defence, Muriel was by all accounts a 'goer', given to pranks and adventures, so it is not hard to imagine that she took part in a 'prank too far'. Be all that as it may, rumour was definitely rife in Hull and it had the effect of causing Annie to think that she was a considerable cut above everybody else. From the earliest age she walked like a star, talked like a star and behaved like a star. She *was* a star.

The year 1922 was a good one to be born in as far as the Croft/Sharland family was concerned. Money was plentiful. Father had a Wolseley open tourer, shortly to be replaced by a roomy Delage saloon. I led a cosseted life for my first two years. In truth, after a few weeks' lying in a make-up basket on the floor of the number one dressing room of the London Hippodrome, I was more than cosseted. There are photographs of me sitting happily in the Poole Harbour mud – a stout Glaxo-fed baby clad from head to foot in woolly vest and pants, a shady hat pulled well down, with face barely visible in case my delicate skin should be exposed to the British sun. When not thus occupied, I am to be seen in even more layers of wool lying in a large pram thoughtfully lent by Lupino Lane. The pram had been recently vacated by his son Laurie – an even larger and probably more cosseted child.

Lupino Lane was the principal comedian in *The Peep Show* with Mother and Dad at the London Hippodrome. Lupinos abounded in the theatre at that time. Apart from Lupino Lane, who was a cousin to the rest, there was Stanley and Barry and Mark and Ida, to name but a few. The Lupinos called themselves 'The Royal Family of the Greasepaint' and were proud to trace their ancestry back to the great clown Joseph Grimaldi. Stanley had the distinction of being the funny one. He had that heaven-sent gift of appearing to be inhabiting a comic world of his own as soon as he stepped into the limelight. As with Tommy Cooper and Eric Morecambe, the audience started laughing at the mere sight of him.

Lupino Lane, on the other hand, would go to endless lengths to be funny. As a result, he was addicted to stage traps – to disappearing through the stage and appearing a split second later through a handy grandfather clock. He made his first entrance in *The Peep Show* by being propelled out of a dustbin. This was strategically placed over a small lift trap in the stage operated from below by four sturdy stagehands using ropes and pulleys. At the given signal the lads would simultaneously heave on the ropes and 'Nipper', as Lupino Lane was called, would be projected out of the dustbin. One memorable night, early in the run of the show, an over-zealous stagehand found the dustbin lid to be rather loose. 'This won't do,' he said to himself, and gave it a good screw down. The signal was accordingly given to the men on the ropes, and Nipper was projected head first into the immovable lid and knocked unconscious. Mother, who was sitting on stage in a fire engine at the time, waiting for her cue to ask Nipper to save her child from a nearby inferno, was left to improvise a scene based loosely on the theme 'Will somebody save my little boy from the fire?' with only the knocking of the reviving but entrapped Nipper to punctuate the drama.

By the time I was struggling to walk, we had moved to a comfortable house at 29 Finchley Avenue in Finchley, London. It was a newly built four-bedroom house with a large garden surrounded on three sides by fields. The number 143 bus to Hendon stopped on the other side of the road. If you had it in mind to go to Finchley, the bus stop was right outside the front door. The butcher and the grocer came round every day for the orders, which were conveyed to us on the same day by a whistling errand boy on a bicycle. Coal – always Derby Brights because that was the best – was delivered by the ton by a man covered in coal dust and his patient horse. The Gas, Light and Coke Company used a similar form of transport but a cleaner labourer to deliver coke for the hot-water boiler, which in turn would deliver not very hot water to the solitary bath. Mr Soper, the gardener, came every Friday and, according to Mother, sold her back the plants he had just removed from the garden, and Dr Gleed, a cheerful man with a black moustache, wearing a frock-coat and wing collar, could be summoned at a moment's notice by means of the candlestick telephone. Ethel the maid lived in, wore a neat black uniform with a white apron and received 15 shillings a week, while Olive presided at the gas stove and kitchen sink.

Brother Peter went to school in his chafing grey flannel shorts at Garsington House, half-way up the hill opposite. He was the only person who knew how to operate the wireless set, which took up a large amount of space in the dining room. It had been presented to the parents in return for giving interviews on the original BBC radio station 2LO and was a most imposing piece of machinery. Three cabinets – each two and a half feet long, a foot square and bristling with dials and knobs – were placed one on top of the other and wired to a horn speaker and a couple of substantial batteries. Inside the cabinets, visible through half a dozen wire mesh-covered holes, numerous valves glowed brightly or dimly according to how far you turned the rheostat controlling the voltage. Another half-dozen precisely engraved dials selected the wavelength. The signal came down a wire that was threaded through ceramic insulators, having come up the side of the house and across the garden from beyond the garage, where it was attached to a 30-foot pole. All this palaver culminated in one squeak-ridden station giving the fatstock prices and the Gersham Parkinson Quintet. On one memorable occasion it produced a barely audible commentary on Sir Alan Cobham's triumphant landing on the Thames following his solo flight from Australia. Olive and I listened with heads glued to the speaker and were suitably impressed.

Early recollections are hazy and condensed, and for me this mid-1920s era remains a mixture of fox fur, Chanel Number 5, cloche hats, traffic jams caused by horse-drawn carts, roads strewn with manure effectively flattened by car tyres, rice pudding and Father sitting in a hide armchair reading *Winnie-the-Pooh*, which had only just been published.

By the time I was five, the theatre had begun to insert itself into my mind. This was probably because it was the main topic of conversation and visitors to the house would be mainly theatrical types. The caller who styled himself 'Uncle Billy' is the one who stands out. Uncle Billy, or Billy Merson to give him his full, top-of-the-bill theatrical name, was another less than hilarious comic. The main thing that he had going for him was the fact that he was short and had a sad, spaniel-like face and an air of offended dignity. In those days these attributes served to place him in the leading comedian category. By the time I encountered him he had decided to become an impresario and was to be found in front of the Shaftesbury Theatre clad in white tie and tails, which made him a ridiculous Norman Wisdom-like figure.

He was a frequent visitor to the house at Finchley. Invariably, upon encountering little me, he would produce a two-bob bit and say, 'Do you know what this is? It's a poo tilling shiece.' I suppose that I was expected to go into peals of mirth at this, but even at the age of five I knew a bad gag when I heard one and steadfastly remained stumm.

Nevertheless, Uncle Billy generously provided me with a box on the few occasions when I was allowed to see *My Son John*, a musical in which he was appearing with Mother and Father at the Shaftesbury Theatre. The one occasion when he failed in this duty resulted in my first ever appearance in front of an audience. This time I was taken to the side of the stage – O.P. or 'stage right' side, I remember it well. Molly, Mother's loyal Irish dresser, stood with me there and since I seemed enchanted with the whole atmosphere of musical theatre, left me on my own while she prepared Mother's next change.

The parents were performing a number that went, 'Oh love's a game, it is sweet I declare, and it ought to be taught in the schools.' Having completed what in those days was called 'the vocal refrain', they went into the dance. By the time they got into their stride I decided to join in. Needing support for the more agile parts of the chorus, I advanced a pace or two and grabbed the tabs (curtains), thus giving the audience a view of first a foot, then a leg, followed by the major part of a four-year-old boy. The reaction from the matinee audience was instant hilarity, which I enjoyed for a full few seconds before I was whisked away by the red-faced Molly.

Following this production, I suspect that my parents suffered a slight career lull, and I also suspect that it was about this time that cracks began to appear in the marriage. However, if there were any rows or arguments they most certainly did not take place in front of the kids and apart from Mother sitting on the back seat of the Delage and sloshing Father round the ear with a hot-water bottle – the rubber sort, not the pottery – all appeared serene.

The parents had a very good offer to go to Australia to the J.C. Williamson theatres with the Rogers and Hart musical *The Girl Friend* so, leaving behind the house in Finchley and my adored but notorious postman-eating wire-haired terrier called Caesar, we embarked from Tilbury on the P&O liner *Moldavia*.

The journey to Australia took six weeks. As far as I was concerned, the first few days were taken up with being seasick through the Bay of Biscay. After that, shipboard life settled down to a well-ordered routine. Children, which meant me accompanied by Olive, were separated from the adults at all mealtimes. The grown-ups seemed to spend most of their days on deck reclining on roomy wooden loungers wrapped up in rugs, and most of their evenings playing auction bridge. Early every morning some natives known as Lascars, shouted at not very politely by the ship's officers, scrubbed the decks with soft soap, which usually made me sick again. When we stopped at a port, hordes of the same Lascars – I don't know to this day what country they came from – would toil up the gangways carrying sacks of coal for the engine bunkers. We stopped and took trips at Port Said, Aden, Bombay and Colombo. I don't recall much about our fellow passengers. The Liptons – the tea people – were supposed to be aboard. Little did I know then the despair that the sight of just one of their little yellow labels dangling forlornly from a teapot would engender in me as I travelled all over the world in later years. If only I could have told them to print instructions on the other side of the label saying 'Put four of the bloody things in and boil the kettle', I could have achieved something worthy of a peerage.

The next big feature for me was being seasick right through the Australian Bight. It seemed to go on all the way from Perth to Sydney, which is lot of throwing up for a small boy.

In Sydney we had a glorious flat on a hill above Elizabeth Bay, with fine views over the most spectacular harbour in the world. It also gave a grandstand view of awesome lightning and thunderstorms that are one of the specialities of that part of the world. Olive was terrified but for some reason her fear was not communicated to me and I revelled in the great flashes of forked lightning and the deafening crashes of thunder. This makes all the more surprising my reaction to the flashes used by the press photographers who gathered whenever Mother and Dad appeared. These came from a T-shaped device that was held aloft by the photographer's assistant and went off with an enormous 'Whoosh' and a 10-foot blinding flame that made me jump out of my skin. Knowing it was about to happen I would dive behind the nearest adult body, so I suspect that pictures of me in Australia are pretty thin on the ground.

The opening night of *The Girl Friend* was the first I ever attended. The house was packed and Olive and I stood at the back of the dress circle. What was upsetting for me was that in the action of the piece Mother, having unwisely alighted from the rear end of a stage train in order to sing the odd duet with Papa (which in this case was 'Mountain Greenery', where you may recall *God paints the scenery*), supposedly sprained her ankle on a handy railway line, whereupon the siren sounded and the train started to move off. At the last minute all was well because Papa – 5 foot 7 – grabbed Mama – 5 foot 6 – and carried her unsteadily to the train to continue their journey.

At the end of the show came an unforgettable event. The cast lined up to take their curtain call and the 'rag' went up a number of times to enthusiastic applause. Then the director, George Highland, came on from the side and took centre stage. He was a portly figure with white hair and very bushy eyebrows. He held up his hands in a bishop-like gesture and the audience fell respectfully silent. 'Tell me,' he said. 'Tell me,' he declaimed again. 'Is it a success or not?' Australian audiences were not used to making snap judgements of this nature, so a silence worthy of the Cenotaph ceremony continued unbroken for an age. Sensing a theatrical debacle, some brave person in the fourth row of the stalls tentatively clapped his hands together. Slowly this spread to the rest of the audience and the situation was saved, but ever since I have had a sinking feeling in the pit of my stomach whenever anyone steps forward on a first night to make a speech.

The England cricket team led by Herbert Chapman came to Sydney about this time. Father was a keen cricketer so we spent a lot of our leisure time with them, usually on a launch belonging to a tough, short Aussie called Charlie Messenger. On one occasion he took us past the Heads, which is the entrance to the harbour and leads to the open sea. Once outside the shelter of the Heads, one encounters seas that have been practising being rough for two or three thousand miles. As far as I was concerned they had the art of turning small boats on their end to absolute perfection. The girls did a lot of screaming, as girls used to do in those days, which in different circumstances can be rather attractive. I was sick.

The object of this foolhardy caper was for Charlie to catch a shark, which he duly did on a very large hook attached to piano wire. This being accomplished we headed for the harbour. I would have heaved a sigh of relief but I had no sighs left. Once inside the harbour somebody bet Charlie that he couldn't ride astride the still lively shark. I am not sure who offered the bet but I think it was Leo Franklyn who was the comedian out of *The Girl Friend* (in this case he was thoroughly professional and funny but he finished up in Brian Rix's company playing endlessly in farces at the Whitehall Theatre in London.) It was almost certainly Leo because the bet was for a fiver and he didn't throw his money about. Charlie dived into the water and, amid many more screams from the girls who were practically hoarse by this time, straddled the shark. The said shark, which was a grey nurse and measured 14 foot, hadn't been broken to this sort of bronco treatment and thrashed about in protest. Shark skin has all the smoothness of a kitchen grater, so Charlie's thighs bled a lot, and that attracts other sharks, so he was pulled aboard amid more shrieks and screams. Charlie won his fiver but if he pulled one of the shriekers that night I doubt if he could do much about it.

On another occasion we went up one of the creeks of the Parramatta River with a lot of the Australian team aboard. We landed for a picnic and a team of British and Australian world-class cricketers took on a team of local kids who were playing with a petrol drum for a wicket. They are probably boasting about it to this day. At one point I was standing in front of Arthur Mailey, the Australian googly bowler, who sent me down a few balls, so now I am boasting about it too.

The Girl Friend was followed by *Hit the Deck*, but there was no suitable part for Father, which must have been another blow for the marriage. The shows moved to Melbourne where we lived in a smart block of apartments known as Mewden Mansions. Our pad was next to that of Dame Nellie Melba. Olive and I used to creep to our front door and open it the better to hear her early morning practice. Among the classical works we often heard Dame Nellie yelling a stream of obscenities at her long-suffering maid – a 'recital', as far as I know, unrecorded. The parents went with the shows to New Zealand and played the main towns and such smaller towns as Rotorua and Wanganui. These latter were one-night stands. Olive, Peter and I stayed in Melbourne because Peter had to go to school.

Having played all the possible dates, and no other show being available, it was decided that we would quit Australia. Mother, Olive, Peter and I set sail on the P&O ship *Narkunda* for London. Father decided to try his luck in Hollywood because talkies were just starting and he was exceedingly photogenic.

It was the parting of the ways. Dad stayed behind to catch a later boat to California. When I last saw him he was on the quayside at Sydney, waving to Mother and me, the gently weeping Olive and my hysterically tearful brother Peter. I never clapped eyes on him again.

2
Schools – Private of Course

The return journey to England was uneventful. I was seasick in the same bays, bights and oceans as on the outward journey only in reverse order. On arrival, Mama was determined to live in style. It was rumoured that she was at this juncture worth £35,000, which was a sum not to be sneezed at in 1929 and would be a nice windfall even today. As 29 Finchley Avenue was still being let, she rented a luxurious furnished apartment in Piccadilly while rehearsing for a new show called *Dear Love*, presented by Jack Waller at the Palace Theatre. In this she played opposite Tom Burke, a rather scruffy but robust Welsh tenor from the world of opera. Mother had a very true, sweet voice but the prospect of duets with a renowned opera singer daunted her not a little. She therefore took lessons from a fashionable Welsh singing teacher called Gwynne Davies, who had his studios at his large house in Chiltern Street. Apart from having other star pupils such as the actress Evelyn Laye, he was well known for his ability to shove a full-sized grand piano around the room using only his stomach muscles, which he did once a day in order to demonstrate the power of his diaphragm. Many years later, after leaving the army, I took lessons with Gwynne in the same studios, by which time the same grand piano, which he still played atrociously, was well overdue for its MOT.

By now I had achieved the ripe old age of seven years and two months and, apart from being picked up and kissed by a multitude of chorus girls, had received no education whatever. (Incidentally, I loathed being picked up and kissed by chorus girls and regarded it as a totally unacceptable invasion of my privacy, although I was unfortunately unable to express this at the time and could only look truculent and do a little impolite struggling). I was therefore dispatched to Arnold House in St John's Wood to repair my shortcomings on the academic side. Arnold House was a fashionable day school that was presided over by the short but formidable Miss Hanson and boasted such notable pupils as Hughie Green, Laurie Lupino Lane and Peter Howes, son of the comedian Bobby Howes. Its uniform was, and still is, a bright red blazer with green edging and, of course, chafing grey flannel shorts.

Before embarking on an account of my brief schooldays it is worth pointing out that I was, and still am, completely incompetent athletically. Brother Peter was invariably in the first 11 at soccer and cricket and in the first 15 at rugger. He also wiped the floor with the opposition at running and jumping over things, and was a leading light in the school swimming events both above and below water. He returned home every holiday from his prep school in Tonbridge loaded with silver trophies of various sizes, which strained our mantelpieces to breaking point. My single achievement throughout my entire school career was represented by the smallest EPNS silver cup ever manufactured – a vessel that would not have been adequate to house an acorn – which was presented to me for impersonating Jack Hulbert singing 'The Sun Has Got His Hat On' in an end-of-term talent competition. However, my shortcomings on the games fields were no handicap at Arnold House, where our principal recreation was to play an organised game of 'witches and fairies' on nearby Primrose Hill. On the other hand, I remember Miss Dawson, my well-loved form mistress, saying to me, 'Come on, David, you little slacker,' so perhaps I failed to excel even at that.

Living in Finchley and starring at the Palace Theatre clearly provided a transport problem, and the solving of it presented one of the more exciting features of life at the time. Mother acquired a limousine. This was the sort of car you could see in gangster films of that period, in which hoodlums would lean out of the side windows of such cars yelling, 'I'll fill you full of lead, you rat,' and would proceed to carry out the threat with drum-fed tommy guns. The car had a lever in the rear passenger compartment that could be pulled up to divert the exhaust gases through a radiator that heated the back of the car to sauna-like temperatures.

The heater came into its own when Mother and I did a cinema commercial for somebody's flour. Mother, in an attempt to appear domesticated, volunteered to provide the dough for the bread-making portion of the film. Olive duly kneaded the mixture and placed it in one of those traditional brown bowls that one uses for that sort of thing. When we set out the bowl was placed in the rear of the car and the heater was activated so the lump continued to rise. The process continued under the warmth of the studio lights. I was given direction during the action by a chap with a megaphone who frequently pleaded with me not to look at the camera while climbing on to the sideboard to steal a slice of cake. The cake, which was 'one Mother made earlier', had suffered a drying-out process under the warmth of the same studio lights and it took a brave professional effort on my part not to spit it out. I still have the film.

Our chauffeur at this time was Archie Cork, who had worked for a well-known actor manager called Arthur Boucher. Cork was a decided success and stayed with us for many years as friend, surrogate father, prop handler and stage extra. A more suitable car was bought. This was an Austin 16 which was large and comfortable, except that it did not have a heater. Warmth was provided by hot-water bottles, fur coats and rugs. It had two important assets – a temperature gauge sticking out on the bonnet, which warned when the radiator was about to boil over, and a sunshine roof. At every opportunity I would stand beside Cork on the front passenger seat with my body sticking out of the roof of the car and adopt a position later to be used by Hitler, Mussolini and, I believe, Haile Selassie. Nobody seemed to mind.

With two hungry boys to educate through boarding school Mother was understandably concerned about the future. This brought her into contact with a lady named Nell St John Montague, who described herself as a society clairvoyant. Nell was a striking figure. She was tall and thin with very strong, startling features made the more startling by the liberal use of dark, almost black Pola Negri-type eye make-up. Costume-wise she was firmly anchored in the early 1920s, with flowing chiffon garments enhanced by many rows of long necklaces. The whole was topped with a cloche hat. Her room was festooned with glass 'witches' bowls' of various colours which hung from the ceiling, while on her shoulder lurked a very bad-tempered monkey which was wont to hiss and spit at her clients. Nell was a wonderful source of society gossip, and her customers would emerge from her lair very satisfied with their future prospects. She was well aware that people who paid good money wanted to hear good news, and this she provided plentifully. However, her efficiency as a soothsayer was, it transpired, fatally flawed. Some years later she failed to foretell the arrival of a large landmine bomb which exploded with such violence that no trace of Nell, her witches' bowls or for that matter her bad-tempered monkey was ever found.

Another place from which Cork the chauffeur and I would wait patiently for Mother to emerge was, of course, the hairdresser's. This was invariably Maison Jack. Jack had a French accent but probably hailed from Bethnal Green, while his principal asset was his most wonderfully subservient manner. He would bow and practically crawl around his salon saying 'Yes, madame' and 'Of course, madame' and occasionally 'Would madame care for another cup of tea?' His most frightening piece of equipment was his massive hairdryer. This was about the size and shape of a cinema projector, and had a long elephant trunk connecting it to the wet head of the person needing drying. It was gas fired like an oven. Jack would light it with a taper to avoid incinerating his fingers, and it would then give out a continuous roar to which was added the formidable sound of an electric fan. From then on all conversation, whether subservient or not, would cease. Jack too was a good source of gossip, but not while the dryer was in play.

Dear Love came to an end after a respectable run and was replaced by *The Maid of the Mountains*. This began as a touring production and was my first encounter with the touring life. Olive, the lifelong friend, was never allowed to dress Mother in the theatre. This function was carried out by Molly, her fiercely loyal Irish dresser. She had a very exacting task. When I toured with Mother at the outset of the war some years later she had cut down the required luggage to 27 cases, necessitating two taxis to and from every station. For *The Maid* there was no need to moderate her needs. Among the paraphernalia deemed essential to Mother's comfort were two Louis Vuitton cabin trunks for personal clothes, a large square basket for hats, a large flat basket containing dressing-room essentials such as dressing-table cloths, trays, kettle, tea service, inhaler with baize cover and bottle of medication to go in it, glasses for hospitality, gin, whiskey and sherry, eggs – because Mother would drink a raw egg in sherry before every performance – and window curtains, quite apart from theatre make-up. To top all this, a 5-foot tin bath was included because the eponymous Maid was from some strange gypsyish Balkan country, the female inhabitants of which sported all-over tans. The resulting heavy make-up had to be washed off every night, and even the number one dressing room was rarely equipped with more than a small basin and a cold tap.

The musical and variety theatre was at this time still the major scene of entertainment. Mother attracted crowds of 20 or 30 fans who would wait outside the stage door after every performance. They had to wait quite a long time after *The Maid* owing to the aforementioned bath routine which had to be undergone before emerging in front of the patient public. During the holidays, I toured with her on a couple of occasions. When playing York we stayed a few nights in Whitby at the palatial home of Fred Pỳman, a self-made millionaire and shipping tycoon. He gave large house parties for up to 30 guests and every lady was given a substantial piece of jewellery. On Sunday after lunch the guests would gather in the drawing room and sit on armchairs and sofas near the large grand piano to hear Fred give his solo. He had an excruciating voice, which was obvious to everyone, including the pianist, who made wry grimaces and knowing winks behind Fred as he sang – very often his own compositions – while the guests tried to stifle their giggles.

By this time I too had acquired a voice. It was not one of those sweet choirboy voices that can be heard once or twice in every generation singing 'Oh for the Wings of Dove'. It was a strong, tenorish sound that tended to surprise the listener. I had also reached the age when you only have to hear a song a couple of times to know it for the rest of your life. I kept this particular talent well under wraps, but Mother was proud of it and would never fail to start the process of persuading me to sing. I would routinely resist for minutes on end because I truly hated performing in public. After the tenth repetition of 'Oh, go on – just for me' the rest of the party would of course join in and it was then less embarrassing to sing than to continue the fight. On this occasion at Fred Pyman's house I bellowed 'Who Cares?', Tom Burke's solo from *Dear Love*, which brought very enthusiastic cheers and applause. (I was good.) This was followed by Mother's solo from the same show, a plaintive ballad which began 'Some day I'll reach that land of love-in-a-mist' and which I concluded, leaving not a dry eye in the house. Some years later, on my first day at Rugby, I was passing a group of senior boys and hoping not to be noticed – generally the best policy on your first day at a public school – when suddenly a voice rang out, 'Hey – you're Sharland aren't you?'

Thinking it best to admit my identity, I wittily replied, 'Yes'.

'I saw you at my uncle's house in Whitby. You sang "Love in a Mist".'

Since the earth steadfastly refused to swallow me up, I again said 'Yes' and fled.

I was too young to be continuously touring with Mother, so odd holiday periods were spent with Olive at Grandma's little semi-detached cottage at 5 Khyber Road, Parkstone, near Bournemouth. Grandma was widowed when Mother was little more than a child. She then married a man named Drury, who was a pilot on the Humber estuary and was by all accounts a celebrated inebriate, as were several of his colleagues. I later visited Hull, expecting to see the banks of the river littered with

Drury hulks, but it seemed comparatively clear. Perhaps they had some very strong tugs to cover up his mistakes. He died at an early age and the twice widowed Emma Drury went to live in Bournemouth to be near her sister Polly, with whom she quarrelled continuously until Polly's dying day. The house was gas lit, so I was introduced to the world of gas mantles, washing in a china bowl or the kitchen sink, bathing once a week with water heated in the clothes copper, and turning the handle of the great wooden-rollered mangle on wash day.

Grandma Drury, who came from Hull, spoke with a homely Yorkshire accent and called a spade a spade. Khyber Road was an unmade-up cul-de-sac and a friendly sort of lane. Thus Grandma had 'neighbours', a feature of life unknown in Finchley, where one only spoke to the people next door in the event of fire or world war. Grandma revelled in neighbours. At the top of the road stood Yeatman's, who took care of the hire car and funeral service for the district. From time to time Grandma would fall out with Mr Yeatman and award her funeral to the Co-op, and then give it back to Mr Yeatman when she fell out with the Co-op.

For the sum of £5 a year Grandma rented a canvas beach hut on the prom in nearby Alum Chine. This was a 40-minute walk away beyond some pine woods, and made for a magical wander through the tall trees on pine needles that gave off a wonderful heady scent. The hut was equipped with an oil stove to boil the kettle, deck chairs, buckets and spades, swimming costumes and all the paraphernalia needed for a day on the sands. It was heaven for a small boy.

One of the great features of the holidays was the frequently falling Grandma. This happened on average twice a day and was completely undramatic. We would be walking gently along, there would be a quiet swish followed by an 'Ooomp', and we would look behind to see the prone Grandma, usually shaken by uncontrollable low-key laughter until she was helped to her feet again. A piece of tissue paper would be more than enough to initiate the tumble, but she never bruised or scratched herself.

Other holidays were spent with Olive's sister Ivy and their mother. If I was called upon to cast Ivy, the part would have to be played by Su Pollard. She was like her in every detail – an irrepressible, fun-loving extrovert – and was the leading light in the local dramatic society. She had been the youngest member of Mother's acting academy in Hull.

Brother Peter was by this time at Haileybury, an uncomfortable public school where he was, as usual, being earmarked for first 11s and swimming teams. I was now ten years old, and it was clearly time for me to go to boarding school too because that was the track taken by all middle-class boys whose families could find the necessary cash.

Considering the enormous trouble that middle-class parents take today to select suitable schools for their offspring, it is remarkable to remember how haphazardly choices were made in 1931. I recall Lancing School in Sussex being considered and its prospectus duly inspected, but none of the contenders were actually visited or interviewed. Possibly this is because Mother discovered that an old army chum of Dad's had opened a school in Swanage, Dorset, named Durlston Court. The chum was Pat Cox, who at the age of 17 had been a junior officer in the Durham Light Infantry and who had shared a tent with my father in Rugely Camp during the First World War. Dad had gone so far as to write a short verse for him, which went as follows:

A favourite occupation 'twas of Pat's
Reading Balzac
By a candle
In the lats.

He had then got himself into the Guards, was wounded in the backside and later scraped a degree at Cambridge. A lunch at the Savoy confirmed that he was young, enormously enthusiastic and had an infectious giggle that was accompanied by a percussive rush of air through his back teeth. My entry was confirmed, and Mother and I found ourselves at Rowe & Co of Bond Street, who were the Rolls-Royce of school outfitters. Here, aided by an elderly shop assistant who knew the uniform of every school by heart, we purchased all the goods necessary to send a ten-year-old to boarding school. These included a mackintosh, an overcoat, woolly gloves, a blazer, a grey cap with circular bands of white, lots of pairs of flannel shorts, long trousers, stiff Eton collars and a straw boater for wearing on Sundays, football boots, shirts, scratchy woollen underwear and socks for every occasion, 12 handkerchiefs, a wooden tuck box, a trunk and countless Cash's name tapes, which Olive sewed on to every article, including my toothbrush and sponge.

All this was assembled, packed and consigned 'Luggage in Advance' and sent to the station via Carter Patterson's horse-drawn cart for the princely sum of two shillings, the railway ticket having been purchased a week or so previously. At Waterloo, met by the ever-cheerful Pat Cox, we joined the parents of half a dozen other new pupils. It was Pat's custom to reserve a carriage for the London boys, and he personally conducted us to a reserved compartment. All too soon, the whistle was blown and, amid much steam and smoke and puff-puffing, we embarked upon the first great lone adventure of our lives. It would have been a tearful farewell but, as we all knew, boys don't cry. Girls and French boys might cry but British boys – never. The main part of the journey I knew well having been many times to Bournemouth. The last part past Holton Heath, the site of a cordite factory during the First World War; Wareham, with the spectacular, craggy ruins of Corfe Castle; and then the single line to Swanage was all new to me. We got off the train at the end of the line and, clutching our overnight cases, walked with the rest of the boys through the little town of Swanage and up the steep hill past St Aldhelm's Church to the turreted Durlston Court.

The building had started life in the mid-Victorian era as a large private house. After it had become a school, Edwardian and 1920s' additions were made in order to house more pupils and to confuse the draughts. Cox's wife and family lived in part of the ground and first floors. The classrooms were on the rest of the ground floor and the dormitories were on the second and top floors. Three-foot central heating radiators had been put into most of the rooms, except on the top floor, but thanks to the usual inadequate boiler and the relentless east wind, they simply served to take the draughts from the very cold or freezing mark to the temperature at which good white wine should be consumed.

On arrival we were given a quick tour of the school, which was confusing because one classroom devoted to the enlightenment of small boys looks very like another. A brief meal was served, which was the forerunner of nearly six years of the sort of undistinguished and frequently inedible food that it was the custom to dish up in schools at that time. After dinner there was a rather frightening period when we were left alone to find shelter from the older pupils, who screamed and rushed around the corridors as if they had some great and urgent satanic mission to complete – which they hadn't.

Then came evening prayers, including that hymn which goes 'Lead kindly light amid the encircling gloom' (of which we were well aware by now), continues with 'The night is dark and I am far from home' (which was all too obvious) and concludes with 'Lead Thou me on'. 'He', on this occasion, led me on to an eight-bed dormitory where we all climbed into our stiff new flannel pyjamas and prayed, kneeling beside our beds, that our parents would realise the mistake they had made and come to rescue us next morning. Morning came and, to the great disappointment of eight small boys, not one single parent turned up in answer to our eight earnest, God-destined entreaties. So boarding-school days started and were to carry on, in my case, for six years.

Boarding preparatory and public schools were designed mainly to produce candidates to run the not inconsiderable empire that Great Britain controlled at this time, and in the main they did a very good job. All around the walls of the dining room at Durlston were inscribed the names of former pupils and the public schools they had gone on to. There was a liberal sprinkling of double-barrelled names such as Ludlow-Hewitt, Lee-Warner, Hill-Smith and Pridham-Whipple, which gave the list a strongly middle-class character. The fact that there were no 'Sirs' or 'Lords' reinforced the middle-class feel of it all. Nobody had gone to Eton or Harrow. A number of the best had gone to the Royal Naval College at Dartmouth. Those who had muffed the difficult selection process and exams for the navy had gone to Pangbourne where they would be destined to become officers in Britain's very large merchant navy. The rest had finished up at places like Shrewsbury, Bradfield, Oundle, Fettes and Charterhouse, from where many had proceeded to the Imperial Service College, the Palestine Police, the Indian Army or Indian Civil Service, or the West African Rifles.

We learnt the school song, which informed us that the school had been founded in 'Nineteen hundred naught and three / When Edward was king o'er land and sea / O'er Durlston Hill with its bay below – the place where the breezes always blow' (it added with commendable honesty not normally found in such works).

We also learnt the school motto, which was engraved in Latin on the school crest and read 'Erectus non elatus'. We were gravely informed that this, loosely translated, meant 'Erect but not boasting about it'. It was not until many years later at the age of 20, when I was enveloped in a mosquito net in an improvised lean-to shelter in North Africa at four o'clock in the morning, about to go on guard in the gun-pit, that I suddenly saw the funny side of this and burst into peals of laughter, to the surprise and alarm of the rest of the gun crew.

At Durlston our general welfare and health, which were good – bugs and disease being incapable of survival at such low temperatures – were looked after by the caring, mousy Miss Lawton and her warm-hearted young sidekick Miss Lupton. On the rare occasions when any of us had a temperature, we were packed off to a room which was known as 'The San'. Nobody had asthma and allergies had not been invented. Every morning some of the boys who were more cosseted by their parents were given a large, sticky spoonful of sweet-tasting Virol or Radio Malt. What the radio had to do with it was a mystery because the wireless had not progressed very much past the Gersham Parkinson Quintet. Jack Payne and his dance orchestra were just about in vogue, as were Gillie Potter and John Tilly, the latter an ex-pupil of Durlston, but 'radio' was a bit of a buzz-word at the time.

The staff, led by Pat Cox and his two partners Ellis and Fawkus, were pleasant and efficient. Pat Cox took Latin and French, which he spoke with the most appalling Edward Heath accent with plentiful pleas not to pass his pronunciation on to Mr Tolson, who spoke it quite well. Maths was taken by a tall, hearty young master called Anderson, who appeared every day wearing only slacks and a collarless flannel shirt with the sleeves rolled up. It required not a little fortitude on his part to stand in a chill classroom clad in this fashion. We were well wrapped up in woolly vests, pullovers and jackets. He had lost his two front teeth playing rugger, which added to his carefree, piratical appearance. I think it was because of him that I acquired the above-average ability in arithmetic that later got me into Rugby. He also taught us two little poems that have stood me in good stead:

Mr Anderson said with a smile
Seventeen sixty yards in a mile.

And also

Mr Anderson likes to drink beer
Three hundred and sixty-five days in a year.

Parents were only allowed a couple of one-day visits in a thirteen-week term, with a two-day visit for sports day in the summer, so one got a definite feeling of isolation. Nevertheless, Pat Cox had devised a routine that made every hour of the day a crowded one. We were taught to

27

play rugger. I learnt very quickly that if I was in receipt of that odd-shaped ball, the best thing to do was to throw it away – backwards. If I hung on to it and ran I would swiftly find myself face down in the mud, which was never a favourite position of mine. Being of a stocky build, I found myself in the second row of the scrum. I was thus required to put my head between the muddy thighs of two of the occupants of the front row, which I found very bad for the ears and on the whole rather unhygienic. In looser situations I would dither rather in the manner of Private Godfrey. On top of all this discomfort, we invariably seemed to play in a biting east wind and drizzling sleet or rain. Nevertheless, in spite of these conditions we all managed to shout weakly with feigned enthusiasm and pretend that we were enjoying the whole ghastly experience. I suppose it was character building, but I still couldn't say which aspect of my character was thus built. We also learnt cricket, which I knew well enough, and the rules of soccer, a game I have never found in the least stimulating.

Perhaps I should record at this juncture a rather distressing medical condition that developed, I suppose, somewhere about the age of seven or eight. Someone, I presume Olive, discovered a pronounced lump in the David Croft crotch. The frock-coated Dr Gleed was summoned – we never went to see him, he always came to see us. Having examined the mysterious lump he pronounced that it was a rupture and that the only way of eliminating it was by surgery. Mother was not a believer in surgery. Brother Peter was operated on for the removal of his tonsils and adenoids and the consequences had been distressing to all concerned, especially Peter, who reportedly survived on only ice cream for eight days.

Incidentally, virtually all middle-class boys had their tonsils and adenoids removed at the age of 12 or 13 as a matter of course. It was fashionable. I have never been very clear what function adenoids actually perform in the everyday running of the body, and I have not heard of them or their removal for forty years or so, but in the 1930s out they all came. Except for mine, which are still with me.

Mother having vetoed surgery, I was yanked round to one of those mysterious shops that dispensed 'surgical appliances'. There, in the privacy of a well-curtained back cubby-hole, I was fitted for a 'surgical appliance'. This was a rather wide rubber belt that was fitted firmly round the waist and attached by pressing two holes on to two

SCHOOLS – PRIVATE OF COURSE

projections on an inflated rubber lump that fitted not very cosily over the rupture, which was thus pushed back into the place from whence it came. To prevent the damned thing from riding up, a further strap led from somewhere at the back near the spine, over the buttock, round under the crotch to be secured to another small projection on the inflated rubber lump. A few years later this device was replaced by a more robust affair made in spring steel liberally padded and secured by small leather straps. I wore this every day until I was 16 when, the lump having failed to show for a year or so, I pronounced myself cured. You would expect that nasty little boys, on discovering this contraption, would leap round the dormitory brandishing it in the air and using it as an aid to miming headphones, wireless aerials and fairground hoopla sideshows. No nasty little boy ever touched it. Perhaps they knew where it had been for the last few months. Occasionally somebody in the third row of the scrum, having nearly had his ear torn off, would yell 'What the hell's that?' but, on receiving the reply 'My truss!', would make no further comment.

Durlston Court had a pretty large staff. There was an enormous, heavy-browed houseman who cleaned our shoes and tried to keep the changing room clean. Housemen were known by the boys – snobbish little gits – as Blogs. Fortunately we were polite enough to him when in his hearing. This one was Blog Harman. At least I was able to perpetuate his name in *Are You Being Served?*

Beds were made, dormitories cleaned and meals served by anonymous maids. I never knew the names of any of them. Once a week Cox would trot out his 16-millimetre silent projector and show an evening film. Charlie Chaplin and Laurel and Hardy were in the repertoire, but the favourite was a detective serial called *Sexton Blake*. This gave a great opportunity for the boys to raise the roof with hisses, boos and cheers, and it was the highlight of the week. From time to time members of the private school lecturing circuit would descend on us. One such was Grey Owl, who purported to be a Red Indian but was in fact a complete phoney named Archie Belany from Hastings. He gave a great performance, however, and we all lapped it up. A member of Shackleton's expedition to the South Pole was another well-cheered lecturer. An outstanding success among the boys was a deep-sea diver, who appeared with the full diving suit, lead boots and brass diving helmet and was fed air by two boys turning a large wheel to activate the pumps. Not being in the water, he blew up like a Michelin man, which caused such hysterical hilarity among the boys that the pump operators ceased pumping, so the diver nearly passed out. All the lecturers brought slides to be projected on the school lantern which was operated, on a signal from a hand-held clicker, by a reliable, much envied senior.

On Sundays we made our own beds and then struggled with studs and stiff Eton collars to ready ourselves for chapel at St Aldhelm's, a name I used for the church in *Dad's Army*. In order to look neater and tidier for this occasion, we all lined up for Miss Lupton to sprinkle our heads with water and tame our unruly locks with a brush and comb. Although the church was only two or three hundred yards away, we 'crocodiled', as was the custom for schools at the time. Quite soon I got into the choir, which meant a smaller 'crocodile' but the same Eton collars. The choir wore gowns and surplices, as did Pat Cox, whose tuneful baritone drowned out our pre-pubescent piping. Later, Pat would climb into the pulpit and deliver the sermon. On Sunday afternoons, we donned overcoats, gloves and scarves and walked as a mob on the windswept cliffs of the Purbeck Hills. Only the very sick were excused.

The boys were by and large a benign lot. Bullying was rare. I must already have acquired a certain verbal dexterity for I clearly remember telling one boy – the elder of a set of twins who later went to Pangbourne – that if he attempted to hit me I would make him look such a fool at our table at lunch that he'd wish he hadn't been born. To my surprise, he backed off. Tony Hancock had left the school just before I arrived. The mistress in charge of the junior school told him that if he didn't sit up straight and hold his head up, he would grow up to be a round-shouldered old man. She was right. John Frankau, the son of cabaret comedian Ronald Frankau and later a very talented TV producer, came as a junior just before I left. I remember him as a small, ferret-like boy. It was not done for senior boys to talk to small, ferret-like junior boys, so I didn't.

During the Christmas term we always performed a Gilbert and Sullivan operetta. In my time, these included *The Pirates of Penzance*, *The Mikado*, *Iolanthe* and *The Gondoliers*. Pat used his evening music session to teach the ensemble music to the whole school. Auditions were held for the principal roles. I copped Ko Ko in *The Mikado*. After much preparation, the first performance arrived. I gave my 'Tit Willow' to the best of my ability and at the end there was a brief moment of dead silence. I thought I must have screwed up somehow, but then the little theatre burst into thunderous applause. It is a very potent drug. I was hooked for life.

Looking back I have every reason to be grateful to Pat Cox. He taught us to be honest, truthful, loyal and polite – in fact totally unsuitable to enter into commercial activity of any description. Thanks to his leadership my days at Durlston were as happy as one could expect them to be, considering that I was away from a very comfortable home. But I couldn't wait to grow up and leave. I had experienced applause.

At this stage, Mother's career took a revolutionary turn. She was very much at the top of the tree as a musical comedy star but roles that she fancied were not materialising. Noël Coward, for instance, was not one of her admirers and consequently Evelyn Laye had pipped her to the post in *Bitter Sweet*, and Gertie Lawrence was well established as a favourite of his in both the musical and straight theatre. Mother had also become very choosy as far as vehicles for her talent were concerned, so she decided to go into management and produce her own shows. It is hard to exaggerate what a bold step this was. A lone woman in the role of theatre actress/ manager was an unheard-of thing in those days and, as far as I know, has not been heard of since. She decided to present Oscar Strauss's opera *The Chocolate Soldier*, the role of Nadina being tailor-made for her talents. She duly canvassed all her rich friends, such as Fred Pyman, and a few poor ones as well, such as Grandma Drury, to finance Anne Croft Ltd. She rented a three-bedroomed flat as an office at the top of 122 Shaftesbury Avenue overlooking the stage door of the Shaftesbury Theatre.

This transformed the school holidays as far as I was concerned. Nothing was quite as exciting as the 'get in' on Sunday night when all the scenery, costumes and props were unloaded into a new theatre, followed by the band call on Monday morning. To help her, Mother had an intensely loyal band of colleagues, helpers and assistants. First among these was Ernest Irving, the musical director who later became the director of music at Ealing Studios. The sheer delight in his eyes as he conducted the Oscar Strauss score that he loved with his knobbly arthritic hands is a sight that will always stay with me. It was at about this time that Moss Empires, the owners of most of the larger theatres in England, were deciding to modernise their halls by installing microphones and amplifiers. This was a complete anathema to Ernest. However, he quickly found the antidote in the form of a medium-sized pair of electrical pliers. Having protested the presence of the new equipment, and having been informed that under no circumstances could it be turned off, even for an Oscar Strauss light opera, he would carefully sever the cables of the new installation before the first performance. And when the local theatre manager came round after the opening and declared with a smile on his face, 'There! Wasn't that a big improvement? I told you it would be all right,' Ernest would happily agree that he had never heard sound quite so good in any theatre.

Manager and stage director was the harassed and worried Gordon Rennie – harassed because of his many responsibilities and worried because his soprano wife played Mascha in the show and was by no means Mother's favourite artiste. Backstage was the carpenter, prop man, general factotum and fixer-upper Bill Finch, who was a cockney, Private Walker type who could do anything and, if need be, anyone. In the office was Miss Willis, a short, determined young lady who could type like a maniac and take down Mother's long letters in fast, accurate shorthand.

The touring contract required that a certain minimum number of artistes should appear on the stage in ensemble chorus songs and at the end of the show. In fact, everyone was co-opted to make up the quorum including Cork, the chauffeur, and Miss Willis disguised in heavy beard and moustache as a rough Bulgarian soldier, in her case a short one.

Another loyal and ever-present follower was Kitty Folloy, who had an extremely robust, top soprano voice and a face like a truck – an old truck. She was tactically placed right behind Mother so that she would not attract attention but, when necessary, she could belt out a top C to reinforce Mother's efforts at the same note or, in the event of flu or some such affliction that would not respond to the aforementioned inhaler, act as a vocal substitute so Mother had merely to open her mouth wide and look triumphant.

All went well during the early days of Mother's embarkation into management. For a month or two she was taking goodly sums to the bank every week, but disaster soon struck. The country was in a shaky state economically and, on 21 September 1931, the chancellor of the exchequer announced that Great Britain was no longer on the Gold Standard, following which the pound fell and the Great Depression slowly took a grip. Takings at the theatres fell dramatically. The hundreds that were being taken to the bank became twenties and fifties, sometimes paid in and sometimes taken out.

In spite of all this Mother decided to take the show to London – to the Shaftesbury Theatre, the scene of my first ever appearance on a stage – and a very good cast was assembled. Mother masterminded all the preparatory stages, negotiating contracts for actors and the theatre and dealing with costume design and construction. In the part of Bumerli she cast Horace Percival. He was one of those lucky people who seem to be a friend of the whole world. He had an impish sense of humour and was marvellous company. He played many characters in the famous radio show *ITMA* during the war, and I encountered him a lot in my early career. The show had a modest but fairly successful run. After that, Mother took the show to the music halls, which were offering good terms. *The Chocolate Soldier* became a twice nightly attraction with two matinees. This was achieved by playing the show in two acts instead of three and making a lot of cuts to dialogue and music.

Mother managed to sing the score with liberal help from the inhaler and by downing an egg in sherry before each performance. She compromised by taking the top C in 'My Hero' only in the second house, while Kitty Folloy was called upon more often to fill in during the chorus numbers. When possible, at the end of the week during my holidays we would pile into the car and get well rugged up while Cork drove us home, stopping at a fish and chip shop on the way out of town.

Several other family things happened about this time. Mother decided that the marriage was over and she should get a divorce. Nell St John Montague, the clairvoyant, was consulted and, having gazed into her crystal ball, agreed that it was indeed over, whereupon she introduced Mother to a distinguished lawyer whose imposing name was John B. de Fonblanque and who operated from an appropriately imposing house in Lincolns Inn Fields. The law took its course and in due time the ties were legally severed. JB became a lifelong friend and spent frequent nights at Finchley, though I am sure the creaking noises heard along the corridor during his visits were due either to settlement of the building or mice. Meanwhile, my brother Peter, having hit the age of 16, became bored with Haileybury and Mother, having left school at 13 herself, allowed him to leave and join Dad in Hollywood.

Dad, by this time, had landed a few small parts in movies for RKO such as *East Meets West* with George Arliss, and had starred in a second feature called *The Fire Walker*. In this he played a British Army officer who had been slightly traumatised by shell blasts in the First World War and had finished up in some jungle outpost as a district officer. The movie, unsurprisingly, made no lasting impact on the Hollywood scene, so Father turned his attention, with enormous success, to radio. He created a character called the Honourable Archibald Chislebury, who led a Wooster-like life in California with a Japanese Jeeves named Frank Watanabe. He wrote and appeared in this on KNX, the then NBC station, sponsored by Grayco Shirts for five nights a week at peak time for five years – until Pearl Harbor. Next morning Dad was off the air, all the Japanese were interned and the USA was in the war.

Back at the Finchley ranch, I contrived to grow yet another lump. This one appeared, not at the right side of the crotch but at the rear of the left ear. Once more Dr Gleed was summoned: he pronounced that it was a 'mastoid' and that the only cure was surgery. Once more Mother's aversion to the surgeon's knife surfaced and, a little illogically, she sent for Mr Scott Stevenson who was the leading ear, nose and throat surgeon in the country. Before he arrived Mother decreed that a fair-sized Spanish onion should be put in the oven and part baked. After half an hour or so it was taken out and cooled, and the sticking out bit was inserted into my ear hole, fitting rather well. A relay of onions followed while Scott Stevenson, frock-coated of course, sped towards Finchley from Harley Street by fast Rolls-Royce.

I heard him arrive at the front door and hasten up the staircase but unfortunately, lying on my right side to balance the onion in my left ear, I was had my back to the door so I was unable to see his face as he entered. It was probably the one and only time that a distinguished Harley Street consultant has been confronted by such an exotic example of folk medicine. 'What in heaven's name is this!' I heard him say, whereupon the warm, slightly soggy onion was removed from my ear and a more conventional clinical examination ensued. There was then a subdued conference outside the bedroom door during which Scott Stevenson explained the seriousness of the situation and the necessity for immediate surgery, but Mother would have none of it. Faced with the continuation of the Spanish Onion Therapy, the eminent surgeon returned to my bedside and proceeded to do his best with a pair of tweezers. There followed a few seconds of agony, and I of course yelled, whereupon Mother rushed into the room and said, 'What are you doing to my child?' in a melodramatic but genuinely concerned voice, by which time the offending growth had been somehow lanced. For ten days or so I lay on my left side while my ear, without Spanish onion, drained on the pillow, and I have never had the slightest trouble with it to this day.

3
A Brief Encounter with Rugby

Mother squeezed the juice out of *The Chocolate Soldier* on the number one touring dates and played most of the worthwhile number two dates, but it was evident that there was no substantial money to be made while paying a heavy royalty for a well-established musical with an Oscar Strauss score. There followed touring productions of *Prudence* and a bright musical called *Happy Weekend* with Eric Fawcett, who later became a successful television producer and with whom I worked in the early days of commercial TV at Rediffusion. It was in this show that I met a unique little man called Arthur Stanley. Arthur stood all of 5 foot 3 with wild unkempt hair protruding from the side of his bald head and from his ears and nostrils for good measure. His real name was Arty Goldstein. Coming to the conclusion after the First World War that being Jewish would be no help to him at all in his future career, he changed his surname to Stanley. He was a very talented lyric writer and had written the lyrics of *Happy Weekend*. He later helped me enormously when I earned my living as a lyric writer. He endeared himself to me forever, having penned the lines:

> *My wireless installation*
> *Can pick up any station*
> *But passes Brompton Road by way of Variation.*

During this rather fallow period, Mother began to plan her own original musical and she acquired the rights to an old farce called *The Strange Adventures of Miss Brown*. She had the book adapted by a couple of authors called Worton David and Alfred Parke, and the music written by Colin Wark and Hubert David. She bought the songs outright for £10 each, which was an extremely tough deal, £10 not being a large sum even in those days. For me, the preparation of the show made a wonderful new diversion for the holidays. I found that if I kept exceedingly quiet I could sit in on the writing sessions while a new musical was being created, the music played and the dialogue tried out. Mother was very much a hands on producer. She evolved a system of producing a draft script with scissors, sticky tape and GripFix, a paste-like glue that came in a small metal pot with a built-in brush and that smelt very strongly of almonds. The result was an article like an elephant's loo roll. The latest draft would be cut and rearranged then either stuck on to foolscap paper with GripFix, or attached together with a long roll of transparent, sticky paper that had to be licked. I frequently supplied the lick. New material could of course be added with pen and ink. I used the same system for the stage play of *'Allo 'Allo*.

Preparation of the music and book proceeded, much to my delight. This was to be no ordinary production. The show, called *Tulip Time*, was set in a country not unlike Holland called Vanderlew. Dutch windmills were to be built over the stage boxes. The orchestra pit was done away with and a rocky, step-like structure was to be built, with the musical director at the bottom of the steps and the drummer at the top and a grassy bank to conceal the entrance of the musicians. At the front of the theatre there was to be a giant windmill, and the box office was to be incorporated into another smaller windmill. Nothing like this had been seen before, and the opposition from the Alexandra Theatre in Hull, which had been selected for the opening, was very formidable. The news that the peasant chorus in the opening were to wear Dutch caps caused considerable mirth, which I did not understand at all.

The cast was to be young and preferably made up of the sons and daughters of distinguished actors and comedians. Not only would they be talented but, as Mother was well aware, they would come considerably cheaper than well-established actors. Thus we acquired Betty Baskomb, daughter of pre-First World War star A.W. Baskomb, Leslie Laurier, son of early film actor Jay Laurier, Jean Capra, daughter of the distinguished cellist, and Joan Fred Emney, the daughter of old Fred Emney and the sister of the portly Fred Emney whom I used many times in *Hugh and I*. Max Adrian, who played for me in *Up Pompeii!* was cast as the young butler. Freddie Carpenter, who gave me my first chance as a writer and song writer for *Aladdin*, one of his brilliant pantomimes for Howard and Wyndham in Edinburgh, came back from Broadway to produce the dances. The faithful Ernest Irving decided that the score was scarcely his cup of tea, so a young musician named Jack Borelli, whom Ernest described as 'a sliding fiddler', was recruited to front the Vanderlew Orchestra. Jack was a good showman and played a flamboyant violin solo, but was inclined in the more emotional bits to slide his finger up the fiddle until he triumphantly reached the right note – hence Ernest's dismissive description of him. Finally, Peter was brought back from Hollywood to play the juvenile lead, the dashing young pilot Karl Heissen.

Not content with one production in Hull for that Christmas, Mother embarked on another project to be staged in the city at a forbidding Victorian building known as the Royal Institute, in aid of the Lord Mayor's Hospital Sunday Fund. This epic was called *Sonnie Christmas* and was based on the premise that Father Christmas was getting very old and decrepit and had decided to hand over his thriving business to his son Sonnie. It was to be played by children or very young actors. Following an embarrassingly successful appearance as the Lord Chancellor in Pat Cox's school production of *Iolanthe*, I was elected to play the leading comedian. The music was taken from the shows that Mother had written for various productions she had staged at her drama school before the First World War.

Tulip Time opened to a moderate success, but the crowds were not impressed by the offspring of the stars and, on the whole, stayed away. *Sonnie Christmas*, after a gala opening in front of Archie Stark, the mayor, suffered the same sort of fate.

In an endeavour to recoup some of the capital spent on *Tulip Time* in Hull, Mother tried to get a few provincial dates for the show. R.H. Gillespie, the boss of Moss Empires, was not impressed with the young cast on offer, so insisted that Mother should have a principal part since she was still a box-office draw. Gillespie had not seen the show and was unaware that the only leading part available was that of Angela Brightwell. Angela was supposed to be an innocent young schoolgirl who, early in the show, sat on the grassy bank and, while Jack Borelli played his emotional sliding fiddle, sang:

> *The world is gay*
> *Both night and day*
> *When you're only seventeen.*

Mother was in her early forties at the time and her figure, while not exactly matronly, could not be described as sylph-like. In addition, the leading man she played opposite was her 18-year-old son Peter. Word must have got back to London, for the tour was a very short one. Between the recession-hit tours of *The Chocolate Soldier* and the expensive try-out of *Tulip Time*, the coffers of Anne Croft Ltd were now dangerously low. Nell St John Montague was consulted and she introduced Mrs Ray Turner Marshall, who was an exceedingly eccentric and moderately wealthy lady of fifty or so. Her most noticeable idiosyncrasy was her mania for cleanliness. She permanently wore white gloves, but this did not prevent her from washing her hands every half-hour or so. Dogs had to be shut away securely before she entered the house, and she shrank against the wall rather than come into contact with me. However, Mother managed to find a very hygienic cheque book for her to sign, as a result of which a London production of *Tulip Time* was planned.

Bruce Sievier, a very talented lyric writer, was co-opted to brass up the score. He had an endearing habit of rocking with laughter at his own work, which enlivened the creative process enormously. He was a former RAF pilot, and one of his lyrics, to be sung by 12 uniform-clad airmen, had the lines:

We glide and then we swoop
And dive into a loop
As across the sky
We proudly fly
At a hundred miles an hour
The backbone of each power.

These words came back to me only five years later in 1940 as I watched the Battle of Britain from Primrose Hill, with the planes flying across the sky at well over 350 miles an hour.

Funds were getting very low by now so I was hurriedly taken away from Durlston Court and, as soon as the show was rewritten, 29 Finchley Avenue was shut and we all went to live in the office at 122 Shaftesbury Avenue. I was swiftly enrolled with Mr Bird, the tutor of Balcombe Street, because the common entrance exam was looming ahead and I was deemed unlikely to pass. I had been entered for Rugby and, for good measure, Eton and Harrow many years previously. Living at the office was a totally new experience. We were on the top floor. Mother had a largish, attic-like living room with a turret window overlooking the old Shaftesbury Theatre, the fire station next door to it and, further down the road, the stage door of the Palace Theatre. A new, mild-mannered and patient secretary called Miss Bowman had a small office at one end of the flat. There was a very small kitchen and two bedrooms at the other end.

I slept in one room with Mother, Peter had the other bedroom and Olive slept in the office. Catering was limited so Mother sent out to various restaurants such as Kettners, who would deliver meals on very ornate silver trays, or Genaro's – now the Groucho Club – or De Hems, the oyster bar round the corner. Near at hand were the Criterion and the Trocadero, and the massive sweet trolleys that both restaurants boasted were the height of gastronomy as far as I was concerned.

The flat at 122 Shaftesbury Avenue hadn't got a lot going for it – at least not for a 12-year-old boy. The office was always busy, so there was only the bedroom for me, my homework and whatever I found to do to pass the time. Aside from attending the despairing Mr Bird, who saw no reason why I should get into Rugby, a couple of times a week I went to the Wigmore Hall to visit Myers Foggin, who tried patiently to improve my skills on the piano. It wasn't very convenient to use the piano in the flat for practice, so I would wander along to Weekes Studios, where I would add my scales to the cacophony of London's aspiring musicians at two shillings an hour. Dotted around the district were a few 'news cinemas' where I could spend the odd hour for one shilling. Behind the flat were Lisle Street and Gerrard Street, both liberally strewn with aged prostitutes who had no hesitation in saying 'Hello, darling' to a bewildered 12-year-old who had not been introduced.

Somewhere along the line, Mother took the ever-faithful Ronnie Linton with her to play the piano while she sang and auditioned *Tulip Time* to the formidable impresario Sir Oswald Stoll. The hugely popular Jack Buchanan had just had a rare flop at The Alhambra Leicester Square with a circus-based show called *The Flying Trapeze*. Mother took her courage in both hands and, telling Ronnie on no account to stop playing, sang the whole show to Sir Oswald and enthused him with the idea of having windmills all over his historic theatre and of playing *Tulip Time* twice nightly with a top price of 10 shillings. No musical had ever played twice nightly in London, but the theatre in general was in a parlous state, with a dozen or so houses dark. The usual price for a musical was 25 shillings, and Sir Oswald agreed to give it a go. The result was that Mother found herself co-presenting the show with the great Sir Oswald Stoll – a unique achievement for a woman.

Mother was given a suite of offices at The Alhambra, which included the boardroom overlooking Leicester Square. The boardroom was the size of the average country house ballroom, and Mother was in her element.

She would sit at a large desk at the far end, at least a 30-pace walk from the entrance, with Miss Bowman in an adjacent office.

Tulip Time opened with great success. The show was spectacular, fast moving and funny, and the public flocked to it. My enduring memory is of the dinner party at the Savoy after the first night. There were about 16 people at a long table. Mother was at the head of the table and I was at the other end. At the conclusion of a long, hilarious evening the head waiter brought the bill. It was passed from one guest to another and having gone round the table a couple of times finished up in front of the well-lit chap on my left. He looked at it a couple of times, tore it into confetti-sized pieces, threw it in the air and declared, 'Look everyone – it's snowing!' The head waiter was not amused and there then ensued one of those embarrassing scenes when the best mathematician present divides a large sum by 16 and all the men pass up £5 notes.

To everyone's amazement, not least mine, I passed the common entrance exam into Rugby. I was second from bottom on the list, and the letter indicating my success contained the footnote, 'Could something be done about his handwriting?' Nevertheless, I was in. For the record, nothing was ever done about my handwriting which was, and still is, appalling. That December we thankfully returned to 29 Finchley Avenue, which was redecorated to receive us, and Cork the chauffeur returned to the payroll.

Rowe & Co of Bond Street were not the only suppliers of uniform for Rugby, so we engaged the services of Peter Robinson, who were now one of the competitors for that particular trade and a lot cheaper. Rugby schoolboys were formally attired in black coats, striped trousers and stiff collars on Sundays. On weekdays, rules were relaxed to the extent that we wore grey flannels. House caps and Sunday straw boaters were bought at the school outfitters in Rugby town. Driven by Cork we accordingly set out, in our modest Austin 12, on a snowy January day to take me to Rugby. The A5 was still a narrow winding road that only very occasionally broke into three lanes. The snow really began to belt down, so we arrived at Sheriff House three hours late, when all the boys were preparing for bed.

This was Mother's first sight of Rugby and her first meeting with Mr Johnston, the housemaster. Sheriff House was built in 1932 to a very good specification by a talented architect. Cork went swiftly to the kitchen, which he pronounced good and an amazing improvement on brother Peter's Haileybury, which seemed to have been built for the maximum discomfort of all concerned. Johnston was the best kind of British schoolmaster, with a strong, no-nonsense character. His charming, practical wife shared the running of the house, as was usual in those days, and was unpaid, which was also usual. Housemasters' wives were quite cynically exploited in this way. I was taken up to my dormitory, which was a large, centrally heated room with 12 beds, parquet flooring and rafters high above, and there I was introduced to my fellow pupils – all in their shirt-tails without trousers.

Next morning there was a knock at the door which was then opened by the house 'Boy' – a tolerant, thin 45-year-old – who announced that it was 'Quarter past seven, gentlemen', and the day began. At eight the whole house assembled around the oak-panelled walls of the dining hall for a Rugby custom known as CO. This was short for 'Call Over', the school term for roll call. We were the usual mixed-looking bunch of schoolboys varying in age from me – 13 and 4 months – to the head of house who was 18 going on 19. I would have been much more impressed had I realised that around the walls were ranged three future bishops (Rodger of Oxford; Bickersteth of Bath and Wells; and Sebag-Montefiore of Birmingham), future judges Ackner, Waddilove and Mars Jones, several future consultants (Buchanan, Batty-Shaw and Badenoch) as well as my study mate Campbell Adamson, who became director general of the CBI and chairman of Abbey Life.

The boys at Sheriff House were on the whole an amiable lot and there was virtually no bullying, which is hardly surprising with all those bishops and judges floating about. It was declared to be a 'non-beating' house, which meant that neither the staff nor the senior boys were permitted to cane anybody. Most of us settled down quite quickly. Campbell Adamson and I shared a study, which was a minute room with just enough space for two desks, two small easy chairs and a couple of cupboards for our books.

Music formed an important part of our lives. There was a skillful choir, to which I lent my as yet unbroken voice, a good school orchestra, a band in which I played my squeaky clarinet, and a large number of piano booths where we could practise. I didn't make much progress as a pianist. At Durlston and Rugby I was perhaps unlucky to have dull teachers. However, every Sunday after chapel I would visit Mr Salmon in his stable flat. In between resolving the current domestic crises with his wife upstairs, which was always done in hushed, well-mannered tones, he taught me a little about harmony and quite a lot about the theory of music and, more importantly, how to write it down. I think this was probably the most useful thing I took from my time at Rugby. Long after I left I found I had the ability to write the top line of a melody without reference to a piano, and when writing a lyric I could sketch out the rhythm pattern. Aside from that, like most kids of that age, I took little advantage of all the facilities at my disposal. I was interested only in show business.

Meanwhile, Mother set up a theatrical agency. The principal motivation for this was her acquaintance with John Corfield, the chief of the film-producing company British National Pictures, who had the studios at Borehamwood. Many years later the studio was adapted by entertainment mogul Lew Grade as a television studio. When the BBC bought it, many years later still, I took the largest stage to produce *'Allo 'Allo* and *You Rang, M'Lord?* Mother landed exclusive representation of British National but unfortunately John Corfield never made a movie there at that time. He confined himself to turning up for Sunday lunch at Finchley with monotonous regularity and consuming large quantities of roast lamb, beef, chicken, pork, veal and burgundy. Still searching for another show to produce, Mother and I journeyed down to Peacehaven, near Brighton. There, in a shed-like village hall, we saw an amateur production of a musical with a score written by Felix Powell, whose considerable claim to fame was the fact that he wrote 'Pack up Your Troubles in your Old Kit Bag', which was one of the best-known marching songs of the First World War. Mother detected the germ of an idea in this show, and Felix had written a tuneful score, so she took out an option to develop it as another West End musical.

So while I plodded on up the ladder at Rugby, Mother proceeded to create the successor to *Tulip Time*, which she called *Primrose Time*. During the holidays I eagerly attended all the writing sessions that I could. Arthur Stanley was engaged to write the lyrics, the wildly white-haired Felix Powell pounded the piano, and Laurie Whylie wrote the book. He was a gloomy-looking character who had the habit of brushing the dandruff off his lapels while he was talking, which he did in a particularly miserable tone of voice, but he was a funny writer. It was, of course, necessary to raise the capital for this project, and this led to some remarkable changes to our lives.

4
Looking for an Angel

During Mother's touring days she frequently received anonymous notes from an admirer who signed himself 'Cameo Brooch', the reason for this being that on more than one occasion the note was accompanied by a very nice gold-set cameo. He now wrote to her at Finchley, identifying himself as William Bey Quilliam, saying that it was about time they met face to face and inviting Mother to have dinner with him at the Savoy. The meeting accordingly took place and 'Billy Q', as he now preferred to be known, turned out to be in his middle fifties, bald-headed, portly, expansive, a very generous host and marvellously good company. Mother, detecting that he was not exactly poor, told him about *Primrose Time* and he straight away volunteered to underwrite the production to the tune of £10,000, which was roughly what musicals cost to stage in those days.

Nell St John Montague introduced another, more modest, investor, a thirty-something solicitor named Hugh Gough, who owned an estate called Brands Hatch and was happy to divvy up £500 provided a musician friend of his by the name of Austin Treliving could fix the orchestra. A production was arranged for Christmas 1937 at the Theatre Royal, Brighton. There was a part suitable for me as a young public school student and the headmaster of Rugby was accordingly approached to find out if he could bear to be without me for ten days of term just before Christmas so that I could rehearse. The Reverend Hugh Lyon, the said head, was a fair man who delivered rather tedious sermons on Sundays and wasn't known to giggle a lot. I don't think he was too clear as to which of the 650 boys he was being asked to release, but his verdict was, 'I can stomach most things but I cannot stomach that.'

Not to be defeated, Mother cut down the part so that I could rehearse for the few days between the end of term and the Boxing Day opening. This was a time of considerable family tension because Billy Q had consistently failed to produce the promised £10,000. Mother had booked the Theatre Royal, Brighton and pencilled in a few touring dates for January. Sets and costumes had been designed, the construction commissioned, and the production date was looming ahead.

At the last minute Billy Q telephoned to say that he was bringing the money round in cash and he duly arrived breathlessly up the 85 steps that led to the Shaftesbury Avenue office bearing a Gladstone bag. He dumped this on the office floor and proceeded to count the contents, which consisted of a small number of notes and a lot of shilling and sixpenny pieces. When he arrived at the final total it was something in the region of £1,378. 6s. 4d. This was followed by a confession that the police were after him for fraud, he was likely to get two years and this was all the money he had. After Mother had politely enquired if his wrong-doing had included robbing a large number of gas meters and been assured that he in fact had interests in slot machines, Billy Q departed, not to be seen again except in Wormwood Scrubs, and Mother began making frantic calls to the theatre and the people making the scenery and costumes in an attempt to cancel the whole production.

The Theatre Royal could not be cancelled that near to Christmas, so somehow the show had to go on. Capes of Chiswick, who were making the sets, agreed to cancel most of the construction work and arranged that the ever-persuasive Mother would be allowed to hire enough scenery to stage the opening weeks. Obviously the theatre receipts for the Christmas season would be good, so it was just feasible to go ahead. Mother managed to get out of the subsequent touring dates that had been pencilled in. To my infinite disappointment, I was at school during this time of monumental crisis and only learnt of it when I got to Brighton for the last few days of frantic rehearsal. We had all trooped down there and were living in a mock-Tudor house with four bedrooms on the clifftop at Peacehaven. It was a very cold December that year and the draughts in this particular undesirable residence put even Durlston Court to shame.

Cork the chauffeur, Molly the dresser, Bill Finch the carpenter and Ronnie the pianist all came on board to get the show staged. Ernest Irving did the orchestrations very cheaply and conducted the orchestra with his usual delightful enthusiasm. Charles Heslop, a good-looking light comedian, took the lead opposite Mother, and a competent cast was assembled which included the enchanting Roma Beaumont who later made a huge hit in Ivor Novello's *Dancing Years*. On the first night Charles Heslop gave me my first lesson in timing. He had a line that unexpectedly got a good laugh. I had the line that followed and of course I dived in over the audience laughter and was thus completely inaudible. 'Say it again,' hissed Charles under his breath. I said it again. It was a feed for his next laugh, which accordingly came as if nothing untoward had happened.

Primrose Time was well received and did good business at Brighton, which was just as well as there was nothing in the kitty. By now the family finances were in a woeful state and it was decided that this would be my final term at Rugby. Johnston gravely broke the news to me at breakfast one morning and tentatively pointed out that there were various funds that could be called upon to make up the shortfall. Since I knew well by this time that the shortfall would be in the region of 100 per cent, and since I couldn't wait to leave school and get on with being an actor, I told him that my mother wouldn't dream of accepting charity.

Looking back, my Rugby schooldays had few highlights and, for that matter, few lowlights. I kept out of trouble and merged into the general melee in an undistinguished manner. My fellow pupils and study mates such as Tony Batty-Shaw, John Buchanan and John Black were all good friends and became consultants at various hospitals. Campbell Adamson got himself knighted on the strength of his work at Abbey National and the CBI and became a school governor. Most of my teachers were very good indeed, but the whole scholastic world was so far removed from the life that I intended to lead that I could muster little real enthusiasm. Aside from the annual senior school play – *Richard of Bordeaux* springs to mind – there was absolutely no drama in which I could take part. The theatre was in fact frowned upon. Politics was not discussed, presumably because everyone was a Conservative and Stanley Baldwin was prime minister and there was no one among us to argue the Labour viewpoint. The abdication of Edward VIII of course made its impact. I received quite a bit of forewarning on the subject in letters from my father, with whom I now had a good postal relationship. The story broke in the American press well before it did in Britain because, unlike our press, they had no agreement to stay off the subject. On the evening of 11 December 1936, Johnston brought a portable wireless up to our dormitory and we all sat listening to the abdication speech. Johnny was obviously moved but the rest of us were mainly disappointed that a bright and 'with it' young man should have deserted us.

Public schools were always supposed to be hotbeds of homosexual activity, but I have to say that I never encountered it in any way whatsoever. Knowing the likelihood, Pat Cox at Durlston had assembled all the school-leavers at the end of term and said to us, 'If anybody tries any funny business, just you give them a jolly good root up the bottom.' I got the gist of what he was referring to, but such drastic action was never called for.

During my final term it transpired that the *Primrose Time* investor Hugh Gough had been seeing a lot of Mother – a fact she had indicated to me in her letters. They duly drove down one weekend in Hugh's SS and announced that they had experienced a whirlwind romance, were going to get married in June and wanted me to be the first to know. This seemed to be a good idea to me. Hugh appeared to be a nice enough bloke of 36 or so – some 9 years Mother's junior – and I approved of his car. He took me aside to tell me that he hoped I wasn't too shocked and indeed that I approved. Furthermore, he had heard from Mother that I was leaving Rugby that term, but if I wanted to stay on, he was sure something could be done. This didn't accord with my plans at all. I wanted out of school and into show business as quickly as possible, so I assured him that I was more than happy with the status quo. Thus, after a few cups of tea and a couple of cream buns they departed happily in a faint cloud of pale blue exhaust. I concluded the term by doing as little work as possible and in due course found myself on an express train steaming fast to Euston. I was aged 15½ and eager to start life in whatever form fate decreed.

The first priority was to check out the credentials of Hugh Gough. We accordingly went down to spend a weekend at his place in Kent. It was quite impressive. The house was a largish, three-storeyed, early Victorian affair. It sat on a hill at the end of a long gravel drive in the middle of a 450-acre estate that included Brands Hatch. Hugh was the co-owner. At this time the racing circuit consisted of a simple grass-covered oval track used every other weekend for motorcycle racing and exceedingly noisy scrambles on mud tracks through the woods. Today's sophisticated track was not built until well after the war.

Hugh lived a bachelor life here in some style. He employed a highly camp butler of about 35 called Victor, who wore a black jacket and striped trousers and had a perpetual twinkle in his eye as if about to say something rather outrageous. I think he found the prospect of confirmed bachelor Hugh getting hitched to a 45-year-old star of the musical theatre highly amusing. There was an ancient and skilled cook called Miss Polmere and a 17-year-old maid called Josie, who was the cheerful butt of Victor's wit.

Unusually, a cheque for £100 arrived from Father in a last-ditch attempt to prevent me from leaving Rugby. It was of course seriously too late, so Mother decided that rather than return it – a course of action that never even entered her head – she would put it to good use on my behalf. I was accordingly entered for a course of typing, shorthand and book-keeping at Pitman's Secretarial College in North Finchley, a course of horse-riding lessons with Colonel Lawrence at his stables in Balham, a course of singing lessons with Madame Nicholas Kempner in Baker Street, and a course of dancing lessons with Zelia Raye in Maida Vale. This kept me busy flying all over London by courtesy of London Transport. Eighty per cent of my fellow pupils at Pitman's were girls of various shapes and sizes, all about 17 years old. I found the typing classes quite hilarious. We all sat in front of the old upright typewriters in rows of eight. The keyboards were covered up with rattling tin covers to prevent us looking at the letters. The material to be typed was in front of us at eye level on a tilted wooden shelf. On the word 'Go', a gramophone would start playing a merry tune, in time to which we would plonk the keys. At the end of the line all the typewriter bells would go 'Ping' and we would all slide the carriages back and start the next line. If you fell behind it was chaos. Nevertheless, I learnt to touch-type at speed, which has been useful ever since. I never had any intention of taking dictation from anybody, so I made little progress with shorthand, and it only helped to make my spelling worse than ever. Simple book-keeping has come in handy from time to time.

Madame Kempner, the Hungarian singing teacher, was reputed to have taught the great tenor Richard Tauber at some stage in his career. She issued each of her students with a long plastic spoon more usually employed for eating iced sundaes out of tall glasses in an ice-cream parlour. While I sang 'Aaah' on various notes of the scale, she would urge me to press down on my tongue with the spoon. The principal result of this was a terrible urge to throw up. I don't think she did anything for my voice, but every time I hear Tauber I think of him singing 'You Are My Heart's Delight' with a plastic spoon shoved down his throat.

Preparations for the impending wedding went ahead. It was to be a quiet wedding, in fact almost silent, as the only persons to be present apart from the bride and groom were to be myself, to give the bride away, and Austin Treliving, to hold the ring. Hugh was anxious to be married in church, which presented great difficulties because Mother was a divorcee. Eventually a liberal-minded vicar was run to earth and Hugh went to live for three weeks in Erdington, Birmingham, to establish some sort of residential qualification. Very early on the appointed day in June, Mother and I climbed into a large Daimler, hired for the occasion, to be driven to the church. Mother wore a very attractive mauve outfit with a notably big hat, looked very good and was surprisingly nervous. During the journey she confided that she was doing this for me, to which I seem to remember replying, 'Thank you very much.' We ultimately arrived at the vast Victorian parish church, where awaited the dark-suited Hugh with his best man. The organ played 'Here Comes the Bride' and Mother and I launched ourselves up the aisle through the cavernous and echoing nave to the altar. The service proceeded without music, which was a blessing because there was no choir or congregation to sing. When the vicar said, 'Who giveth?' I duly said, 'I do.' Austin Treliving delivered the ring, the registration documents were signed and we were all off back down the aisle again to the triumphant organ notes of 'The Wedding March' and into the waiting Daimler without benefit of photographer. As quiet weddings go, it should be in the *Guinness Book of Records*.

By now, in the absence of adequate backing for *Primrose Time* and with no prospect of work in cabaret, finances were past the critical stage. The house at 29 Finchley Avenue was put on the market and a low offer accepted. Hugh said he would keep everything going somehow, but Mother would have none of it. She tried to open a few doors for me and persuaded the band leader Jack Hylton to give me an audition. I proceeded to a cine-variety theatre in Balham where he was closing the programme with his orchestra and Bruce Trent as the vocalist. The finale featured 'The Posthorn Gallop', with one of Jack's less successful racehorses at full gallop on a moving platform in the background. So that I could be heard through a mike system I sang 'The Day Is Ending Little Drummer Boy' in the empty theatre after the show. Jack was kind and said he would do his damnedest to find me something, but he never rang back. With Bruce Trent in the band he scarcely needed a 16-year-old light baritone. I auditioned for a small part in a tour of *No, No, Nanette*, but when asked to dance to a fast chorus of 'I Want to Be Happy', made a complete hash of it. The producer, who was a small-time comic, said, 'You're not very good, are you?' and I had to agree with him. I tried to join Radio Luxembourg, to which end I was given a one-night spot in a West End cabaret club called the New Manhattan Club. I sang a couple of numbers and went off to tepid applause.

From then on, things took a turn for the better. Peter landed the small part of John Mills's batman in the film of *Goodbye Mr Chips*, starring Robert Donat and Greer Garson. This included a flashback scene between the 12-year-old John Mills, played by Terry Kilburn, and the young batman as a butcher's boy, played by me. The film was shot at the vast MGM studios at Denham. Victor Saville was the producer and Sam Wood the director – both legendary achievers. However, Sam Wood's talent seemed to be based on the ability to mutter 'Let's go again' without giving any indication of what was unsatisfactory about the previous take. Thus a two-minute, three-handed scene involving about six set-ups averaged 25 takes and lasted for two days. Donat was infinitely patient and courteous – unless anybody got in his eye-line, in which case he 'blew'. Screens were erected to avoid this dire eventuality, so the shooting galloped along at the pace of a crippled snail. The speed wasn't helped by the meticulous care of the brilliant young lighting cameraman Freddie Young.

It struck me as quirky that the young public schoolboy should be played by Terry Kilburn, the not particularly talented son of a bus conductor, while the butcher's boy should be played by a 15-year-old fresh out of Rugby, but I was not one to quibble. With a lot of dubbing of other parts in the picture I got four or five days out of it and made £20. This legendary film is now regarded as one of the all-time greats and never fails to bring tears to the eyes. It also represents not only the beginning of my film career but also the middle and end of it.

At this time I was introduced to two young men – Derek Glynn and Felix de Wolfe – who were just starting an agency called G&W Direction. They got me an audition with the BBC for the National and the Empire Programmes. Some time later I received a letter saying I had passed as being suitable but they had no work to offer. Fate decreed otherwise because a young producer named Roy Speer was preparing the radio version of a film musical called *Charing Cross Road* that had starred John Mills. By some miracle I landed a leading part in this, playing a hopeful young actor who, later in the script, became a drunken failure played by Hugh French, a handsome leading man who went on to become a big-time Hollywood agent. I had a couple of numbers to sing and a fair amount of dialogue. I was over the moon. The papers ran articles about me as 'the BBC's youngest juvenile'. The broadcast was staged at St George's Hall, which was next to Broadcasting House on Portland Place. The cast included Mother's former leading man Horace Percival, who metaphorically held my hand during rehearsals, and a full orchestra of twenty-five or so conducted by the legendary Charlie Shadwell. The BBC being a very formal organisation at that time, I telephoned Roy Speer the night before the transmission to find out if I should wear a dinner jacket for the show. He said a lounge suit would be quite sufficient, but in the event the announcer did in fact wear a dinner jacket. The broadcast passed off without a hitch and I was elated.

Meanwhile, on the home front, Whiteley's moved us to Kingsdown Park, Brands Hatch. We had been at number 29 for 14 years. Not a stick was sold. They moved the whole shooting match, including most of the costumes and the orchestrations for *Primrose Time*. The effect on Hugh's house was bizarre. We finished up with two principal bedrooms – Hugh's and Mother's – plus two drawing rooms – one with Mother's Chinese and English furniture plus grand piano at the back of the house, and another with Hugh's Parker Knoll suite and pianola at the front. There were also two dining rooms – one with Hugh's real Chippendale and priceless grandfather clock at the front, and another with Mother's Dutch oak with heavy hide chairs adjoining. It made the house look rather like Harrods.

From the earliest days the marital relationship was not what you would call a hit. One bone of contention was Hugh's insistence on getting our food supplies via a rather beautiful but sadly unprofitable Palladian hotel that he owned in Shooters Hill. He used a large firm of wholesale hotel grocers and thus we had huge 7-lb jars of strawberry jam which Mother insisted – rightly – were entirely devoid of strawberries. We were used to Scott's Little Scarlet Strawberry, which was loaded with them. Hugh countered this by ordering raspberry. Mother referred to the Sunday joint of beef as a 'bit of old kelt' and insisted on carving it herself because she said that when Hugh carved he cut the meat so thin you could read *The Times* through it. I suppose

I was finally aware of large dark clouds on the horizon when she started referring to him as 'that sanctimonious, Bible-banging bastard'. It was about this time that she began to hit the gin and tonic rather harder than usual. In a gallant attempt to raise a little dough for the kitty, she agreed to help further a musical written by Adrian Beecham, the nervous son of Sir Thomas, for a fee of £300. It was to be called *Joyzelle*, and a pantomime writer and part-time comic called Rex London was engaged to write the book and lyrics.

I fulfilled the function of secretary and wrote endless letters, assisted by a dictaphone that had been purchased some years previously. This was a most elegant machine made in three substantial steel sections, all on wheels. The dictating bit consisted of a thin, silvery trunk with a tortoiseshell mouthpiece. To dictate you used your thumb to depress a lever that transferred your words to a revolving wax cylinder, rather after the fashion of the earliest Edison talking machine. The secretary – I, that is – had a separate machine with a foot control and earphones. He – I – could press one foot lever to hear the dictator – Mother – and the other to go back ten words or so if the diction was muffled or scrambled. Yet another precision machine was a sort of lathe that shaved the cylinder clean for further use.

In my ample spare time I walked the dogs in the bluebell-swathed woods, collected butterflies and wondered at the thousands of rabbits that covered the race track like a moving carpet. Hugh owned a parrot that he had recklessly taught to whistle 'The Wedding March', which the wretched animal proceeded to do throughout the weeks of the deteriorating marital scene.

A very cold Christmas arrived, during which we were to be seen huddled round the drawing-room fire surrounded by all the screens owned by the joint households and wearing coats and scarves. This was accompanied by *Finlandia* on the pianola and 'Tell Me Dear Flower Your Secrets Tell' played by Hugh on the flute. Men who play the flute have to do things to their upper lips so as to shoot air and spittle into the little hole in one end and produce the required sound. I apologise to all flute players, but this makes them look distinctly nerdish. Hugh was no exception to this unfortunate rule.

Spring came, the primroses blossomed and the marriage didn't. Nor for that matter did my slender career, save for one broadcast for the radio producers Freddie Piffard and the great Roy Plomley for whom I played a young New York hoodlum in a half-hour playlet called 'Gals, Gats and Gangsters' in a series named *Hurrah for Hollywood*. By this time *Joyzelle* had progressed to a stage at which Adrian Beecham wished to play his work to his father. The three of us therefore proceeded to Sir Thomas's very grand and beautifully furnished apartment in a block of flats in Hampstead, overlooking London. We were entertained to tea and cakes, following which Adrian proceeded to play the score while Mother and I sang the songs. After a very short time the visibly pained Sir Thomas said, 'Adrian – please!' and swept his son aside. He then sat himself at the full grand piano and proceeded to play the music faultlessly from the piano copy while Mother and I continued to supply the vocals. At the end he was very complimentary about Mother's voice, which he said was very charming, sweet and true. I don't recall him saying anything about Adrian's music, but in all honesty the show was not a serious contender for production and nothing further became of it. Let the record show that Adrian was also a pretty lousy pianist.

By this time the likelihood of war breaking out was growing daily. Father was anxious that I should join him in Hollywood while there was still time. He arranged a passage for me on a Holland America ship named the *Vollendam*, which was to depart from Rotterdam in a week or two on 9 September bound for San Francisco via the Panama Canal. John B. de Fonblanque fixed me up with a passport.

Hugh, meanwhile, spent more and more nights sleeping in his hotel, until he came to the conclusion that married life with Anne Croft was not for him. A couple of tearful, confrontational days followed, during which he made his position clear. He saw me while I was feeding the chickens that were scratching around his derelict tennis court and said he was sorry for the situation. In between chucking a few handfuls of grain to the unproductive hens I agreed that he was hardly to blame. He had tried, within the limits of his ability, to make the marriage work, but Mother had belittled him and handled the situation with the minimum of compromise or tact. The marriage was over.

A few days later, we were at war.

5

War – Phoney and Real

Whiteley's removals were summoned to put our furniture into storage. They were in the middle of this operation when, on Friday 1 September, Hitler decided to invade Poland. I was listening to the wireless with Whiteley's foreman when the formal voice of the polite BBC man announced the event. 'Blimey, he's kicked off,' the foreman said, and proceeded to hurry his boys to finish the job as quickly as possible.

My brother Peter was appearing in twice-nightly rep for Barry O'Brien at the London Coliseum. It was decided to close all London theatres, since nobody wanted to go anyway, so on Saturday he made for Brands Hatch. By this time the taxis refused to come out because they were too scared of bombs. I hitched a lift on a lorry to meet Peter's train at Swanley Junction, and we hitched a lift back, carrying between us his leather suitcase, which was one of the largest and heaviest known to man. Next morning Chamberlain made his 'It is the evil things we will be fighting against' speech, and we were officially at war. Olive promptly burst into tears and Mother said, 'Well, that's one thing Hugh Gough wasn't expecting,' as if the world cataclysm had been staged specifically as a sort of 'one in the eye' for the unfortunate Hugh. Half an hour later the air raid sirens sounded, Olive quickly dried her tears and dived under the stairs with a saucepan on her head, and Peter and I went out on to the front lawn with the binoculars ready to see the hoards of Nazi bombers. There then followed frantic efforts to ensure that the windows would be comparatively lightproof by the time it was dark. It is worthy of note that from now on the ever-polite BBC ceased to refer to Hitler as Herr Hitler and just called him 'Hitler'. The entertainer Tommy Handley broadcast a song called 'Who Is This Man Who Looks Like Charlie Chaplin?' so it was evident that the BBC was committed to a no-holds-barred conflict. It was about this time that my passport was cancelled, so all hopes of my going to Hollywood were abandoned.

It was hardly surprising that Mother was in a bit of a daze by now, so, after an exceedingly terse telephone call from Peter, a hire car was found by Hugh to take us to Grandma Drury's very small cottage in Bournemouth. Peter and I, keen to do something positive, volunteered to help at the Poole council buildings, and we were assigned to the billeting department. Here we answered the queries and listened to the problems of the people who, willingly or unwillingly, had given homes to the children evacuated from London. We were able to hand out blankets and bedding to those who needed them, and rubber sheets to the unlucky housewives who had copped the bed-wetters. Some of the ladies were a bit reluctant to tell their troubles to a 17-year-old, in which case I summoned one of the three or four older staff who were in the office. All this served to bring me face to face with a parade of ordinary non-show business characters, which was a hilarious and frequently touching experience.

All the windows of the Bournemouth trolley buses had been covered in dark blue transparent paint, which had the eerie effect of making all the passengers look like ghosts by day and of rendering it impossible to see if you had reached your bus stop by night. All street lights were out, the headlights of cars were covered by tin with slits that gave out no light worth mentioning, and even torches were covered with three layers of tissue paper, on top of which was a piece of cardboard pierced with a hole the size of a sixpenny piece.

The anticipated air raids didn't materialise, and the theatre was remarkably quick to react to what transpired to be the phoney war. Out of the blue in October, Mother was contacted by a Mrs Whitty who was planning a tour of *The Belle of New York*. She wanted Mother to play Cora Angelique, the middle-aged star of the music hall. On reading the script, however, Mother rightly decided that Cora was not the star of this particular piece and wrongly decided that she would rather play the 'Belle', who was an innocent young Salvation Army lass, preferably of some 21 summers. I was aware of the existence of *The Belle of New York* because my mentor Arthur Stanley had told me that when the show first hit London it was held up to him as a fine example of the work of the new wave of American lyric writers. When the curtain rose on the New York Bowery scene and the assembled chorus sang:

> *Pretty little China girlie*
> *Velly velly nice*
> *When she stay a long way off*
> *Chin chin*
> *Take a little China girlie*

Put her on the ice
Make a little China girl cough
Chin chin

Arthur left the theatre.

I was given the small part of Sheep, the young vicar who finally performs the marriage ceremony between the Belle – Mother – and Young Millionaire – 25-year-old Leslie Mitchenor. After a couple of weeks' rehearsal in a cigarette-stained room above a seedy pub in blacked-out London, we departed for the opening date at the Kings Theatre, Southsea. Loyal Molly was summoned once more to be dresser. We hadn't got a car to be chauffeured in, so we all departed by rail. I counted 27 items of luggage, and we needed two taxis to carry us to the station and, at the other end, to the astonished Mrs Raven in the back streets of Southsea, who declared that she had never seen so much luggage in all her born days. The show opened and, although the public did not feel inclined to rush through the blackout to be present, the business was not disastrous. Come Friday, the company manager presented me with 30 shillings for my week's effort. Since the chorus were receiving £3 upwards and I was after all a small part player with my name in the programme, I asked for more, and even threatened to withdraw my labour. We arrived at the next date, which was the Theatre Royal, Brighton and no additional money was offered so, my bluff being called, I walked out. I never did this again in my entire life.

This production stands out in my memory because it was then I met Leslie Dwyer, who played Blinkie Bill, a sort of Private Walker character who lived in the Bowery. Many years later, at the end of his distinguished career, he played the Punch and Judy man for me in *Hi-de-Hi!*

The show teetered on for a few weeks, playing Bournemouth, Southampton and Newcastle, where, standing at the back of the dress circle of the Theatre Royal, I heard one member of the public remark, 'She's past it, you know.' No dates being available round about Christmas, *The Belle* passed away peacefully. Mother, unfortunately, was on a percentage of the gross.

Christmas came and went with comparative normality, there being no rationing at that stage, although there was an uneasy feeling that this hiatus was not going to last. The theatres tried to return to normal.

James Shirvell, who put out tours of musicals, expressed an interest in *The Chocolate Soldier*, so we swiftly renewed our rights and I went to London to try to negotiate a favourable contract above 6½ per cent, which was the cost to us. I nervously climbed the stone stairs up to Shirvell's Cambridge Circus office and kicked off by trying to get him to agree to 7¼ per cent. At 17 I was no match for Shirvell, and I came away rather red-faced, having agreed on 6¾, which at least meant we had a small profit.

Back in Bournemouth, I organised a fire-watching rota at Khyber Road and, furthermore, set about persuading the fifteen or so residents that we ought to buy a stirrup pump for 30 shillings. Dragging two shillings each out of the neighbours required diplomacy on the Kissinger level, and the local chief warden was so impressed that he made me an air raid warden. This meant that I got a black tin hat with 'W' written on the front in white. I did not, however, go about shouting in a loud Warden Hodges voice, 'Put that light out.' Rather I would knock rather timidly at the front door and say, 'I'm awfully sorry to disturb you but you've got a bit of a light showing from your bedroom window. I think if you closed the curtains a bit we wouldn't see it – perhaps.'

There being a certain amount of activity in the London theatre, it was decided to go to town and find a small furnished house. We accordingly took a three-bedroomed semi-detached house at 62 Upper Park Road in Belsize Park. With the vague idea of perhaps giving a few singing lessons or auditioning *Primrose Time*, the baby grand piano was taken out of storage from Whiteley's and placed in the downstairs back room. The buzz came round via Jack Davis, Mother's one-time agent (and the grandfather of John Howard Davis, who played Oliver in the David Lean film of *Oliver Twist*), that the well-known producer Jack Waller was planning to stage an American musical called *Let's Face It*. It was to star Fay Compton and they were looking for a young juvenile. Mother wrote a short scene for me as an embarrassed youth who was madly in love with a girl called, for some obscure reason or other, Myra, and she wove it round the song 'The Best Things in Life Are Free'. We rehearsed this for a week or so and then, accompanied by Mother's pianist Ronnie Linton, I went to the audition at the London Hippodrome. There seemed to be hundreds of people there, so I put my name down at the stage door and joined the queue. In the fullness of time I got into the wings and stood waiting and shaking. My name was called and I strode out on to the large stage and turned towards the vast but somehow friendly auditorium. Ronnie played the introduction and I was away. Some theatres, though dauntingly big, quickly give you the feeling that all is well and you are getting across. Drury Lane is one such and the London Hippodrome was certainly another.

The moment I finished, everyone in the wings and in the auditorium burst into spontaneous applause. I have never known anything like it to happen at an audition before or since. Dimly, over the footlights, I could see Jack Waller and Bill Mollison, his director, clapping and waving me down to the stalls. 'Come through the pass door,' shouted Jack, and the dazed Croft staggered unsteadily to the side because he wasn't wearing his glasses. Once I got there, Jack Waller shook my hand, saying, 'Your Mother did that, didn't she?' and offered me the part there and then. Jack Davis negotiated a salary of £10 per week for me, which was very good money, and I prepared myself to be a star. I took dancing lessons with Freddie Carpenter, where the fabulously beautiful, good-enough-to-eat Sally Gray avoided dancing with me in case I dropped her during one of the lifts. Mother gave me singing lessons, which she did very well, and when Freddie was called up I continued dancing with Buddy Bradley. All was going swimmingly for me when the Battle of Britain started up.

At first our reactions were for Mother to take no notice whatever, for Olive to take up permanent residence under the stairs and for me to go up on to Parliament Fields to see some spectacular dogfights. It is a matter of historical fact that Field Marshal Goering decided that the RAF was getting the best of this particular encounter, and as a result he switched to night bombing. A great deal of London thereupon took to the shelters and tube stations, anti-aircraft guns were moved to Parliament Fields and Hampstead Heath, and life became decidedly hairy. For us the culmination came at about three o'clock one autumn morning when, in the midst of a deafening gun barrage mingled with the tinkle of shrapnel on the roof tiles, there was an unusually adjacent scream of a bomb arriving, followed by a huge explosion. I was dozing on the sofa in the dining room downstairs and was lifted none too gently on to the floor. Mother was upstairs in bed under the covers, which were sprinkled with glass. Olive was safely under the stairs.

The bomb had dropped next door but one, demolishing a large

Victorian house that was fortunately unoccupied. The usual chaos followed, with wardens and rescue people rushing about and the police cordoning off the road. The neighbours got together and accused the poor Polish gentleman who lived next door to the bombed house of being a fifth columnist and shining a torch through his fanlight. 'Don't you be saying such damned lies,' he said. 'Do you think I am a fool that I shine the torch to the Germans so they will be dropping the bombs on my own head?' It was a pretty forceful argument — and a snatch of dialogue that I later used in an episode of *Dad's Army*. The bomb made a bit of a mess of our house, particularly at the back, where the French windows were blown in and broken across the grand piano. More seriously, it was deemed wise to shut the London theatres, and *Let's Face It* was postponed indefinitely. There was nothing for it but to put the piano back in storage and return to Bournemouth.

Many of the air raids aimed at the Midlands seemed to be routed over Bournemouth, with the result that the warning sirens started wailing just after dark and the drone of the planes was heard till just before dawn when the departing Dorniers and Heinkels usually dropped on us a few bombs they had saved up as a parting present. Considerable random damage was done to Bournemouth and Poole, and of course Southampton got a very heavy pasting, which could be seen nightly from Olive's attic room at the back of the cottage. Not that Olive was actually occupying the room. She was under the stairs wearing a saucepan. Grandma Drury was even further under the stairs because she was shorter. She had the pick of the saucepans for headgear because it was after all her house. She also clung to her handbag, which contained her pension book. Mrs Cole at the end of the road was by now an avid listener to 'That Lord 'Aw 'Aw' and would relay an enhanced version of his broadcasts to all the neighbours who were too patriotic to listen to the original version.

I was now seeing a lot of my cousin John Meldrum. We taught each other Morse Code, reaching a fair speed, but it was a talent that I never revealed when I joined the army because I knew full well that if I did I would be stuck listening to dots and dashes for the rest of the conflict or until it drove me round the bend – whichever was the sooner.

The Chocolate Soldier managed to keep playing round theatres in England and Scotland. We were grateful for the small addition to the £4 a week that Hugh was allowing Mother. One day a terse letter arrived from the Trading with the Enemy branch of the Home Office. We had been sending weekly royalty cheques to a Hans Bartsch in Budapest. He in turn had been handing on cheques to Oscar Strauss and Ralph Bernatsky in Berlin. Thus some of the money paid by the British public in, say, Liverpool was finding its way to Hitler. From then on the money stayed on deposit in the Midland Bank in Leicester Square. Mother now sensibly thought that her survival lay in giving lessons in singing and drama. After all, she had done it at the age of 13. We found a fine house called Knole Lea that had been built to a very good specification soon after the First World War in Ipswich Road, Westbourne. As this was near the part of the coast most likely to be invaded, rents were at rock bottom. Nobody wanted to be living in a seaside resort when the beaches were defended by mine-strewn steel scaffolding, 10-foot high barbed wire, concrete anti-tank blocks and pillboxes. The rent of this truly beautiful house was £200 a year. We moved in, the furniture returned to us and an advertisement in the *Bournemouth Echo* produced a viable number of pupils.

Food rationing began to bite very hard. Butter was down to 1½ oz per week. Rabbit was very highly prized because it helped to eke out the meat ration, which got down to about one shilling and sixpence and produced about a pound of stewing steak. Corned beef had to make up 2 oz of the ration – all good *Dad's Army* material. I continued my warden duties in a minute shed crammed up against Sir Robert Ropner, the shipping magnate, who was chief warden of the district.

Occasional visits to London were both exciting and frightening. The cinemas had discovered that if they placed ultraviolet light in front of specially painted bills, it would light up the print in a ghostly but striking fashion. Piccadilly Circus and Leicester Square were awash with people all bumping into each other.

My career had to all intents and purposes ceased when, out of the blue, Ronnie Waldman asked me to go to the BBC's variety hideout in Bangor to broadcast in a revue he was producing, written by Jimmy Dyrenforth and Leslie Julien Jones, to be called *Acid Drops*. A few days later my call-up papers arrived. I was to report to the Royal Artillery basic training camp at Blandford. I knew they were coming as I had already been summoned to Southampton for a surprisingly thorough medical. Luckily the call-up date was for a couple of weeks after the radio show, so I was free to trek up to North Wales.

The BBC Variety Department had just about taken over Bangor. Every church hall had been turned into a studio or a rehearsal room. The pubs were overflowing with inebriated actors, well-known radio personalities and musicians, and Horace Percival, Mother's former leading man, was there to welcome me. When I got the script I found that I had a lot to do, including a couple of duets with the legendary Dorothy Carless, who was one of the great wartime voices. I was fixed up in a small Welsh bed and breakfast while we rehearsed for a couple of days.

Billy Ternent conducted the full orchestra and I was in my element. Dorothy Carless sang a poignant little wartime ballad entitled 'We're Going to Build a Brave New World'. In one of our duets we were supposed to be a young couple wildly in love and the song was called 'Babes in the Kingsley Wood' – Kingsley Wood being the chancellor of the exchequer. The first line was 'I'd like to fill out a joint return with you'. It was a charming show and all devised, written, scored and played by the talent assembled in Bangor.

I came back to London by train with Ronnie Waldman and Dorothy Carless. Ronnie was due to go into the RAF in a few weeks and I had only a few days before joining the army. It was to be four and a half years before I would be a civilian again and able to pursue a show business career.

6

The Army and Butlins

It was with some trepidation that I went down the garden path of Knole Lea that May morning in 1942, leaving behind the tearful Olive and the stoical Mother. Not only was I uncertain of my own future but I had serious misgivings about Mother's survival. Brother Peter had joined the merchant navy as a wireless operator in 1940, so I had been the 'man about the house' for the last three years, handling all the business, correspondence and handyman functions. Sons were leaving their families all over the country, but it was going to be particularly hard on Mother in her none-too-good mental state. There was no getting out of the situation, however, so I took myself, railway warrant in hand, to Bournemouth West station and from there to Blandford. There I spotted an army lorry being boarded by a mixture of civilians like myself but decided that, being in no hurry to join the hoi polloi, I would start my army life by visiting the Railway Inn. I ordered half a pint of mild, which was a mistake because I found it pretty foul.

I took a bus to the camp, which was a pretty bleak affair, like most army camps. Near the entrance there was a low hut marked out with whitewashed stones and a white flagpole on which flew the Union Jack. I went up the steps of the veranda to be greeted by a surprisingly pleasant sergeant. He introduced himself as Sergeant Hoare, and I gave him my name, whereupon he said he was pleased to meet me as I was a potential NCO. I was naturally uplifted by this announcement, but I have to say that he never mentioned the matter again for the entire four weeks I was there. After I had signed in he directed me to my hut, which was one of about six forming a 'spider' group. Other 'spiders' were spread out to make a very large camp surrounding various lecture and administration huts and big asphalt parade grounds.

Inside the hut there were twenty or so beds and bunks drawn up neatly on either side, with a coke stove in the middle. I grabbed a bed that had three mattress 'biscuits' and a pillow lying on it and nothing else. Most of the lorry-load of recruits were hanging around rather fearfully waiting for something to happen. There was one enormous

61

bloke who claimed to be a former guardsman. He stood 6 foot 4, so nobody asked him what the hell he was doing joining a ragbag of Royal Artillery squaddies. Opposite me was a rather fat, jolly Dorset lad, and next to me was a slender bloke, older than the rest of us, who had been in a reserved occupation and seemed fairly civilised.

We were collected by an aggressive bombardier (the Artillery equivalent of a corporal) and marched untidily to be fed with a stew and watered with a fairly atrocious cup of tea. We were then marched off to be issued with three very rough blankets and marched back to the hut and told to make up our beds. Rather tactfully, nobody suggested that we make ourselves comfortable. Lights out was at ten o'clock. Anybody who has been to boarding school has nothing to fear from army life. True, there were no sheets, and pyjamas would have been regarded as garments for the most raging homosexuals, but otherwise I was in a fairly familiar situation. However, most of the young lads in the hut were spending their first night away from home. I distinctly heard some sniffles and maybe even a suppressed sob.

Next morning army life began in earnest. Amid the obligatory shouting from bombardiers and sergeants, we were marched hither and thither to collect a bewildering amount of kit, rifles, boots and webbing things. We were also given a sheet of brown paper and some string with which to send our civilian clothes home. This, I presume, was a precaution to prevent large numbers of civvy-clad soldiers from absconding across the countryside, having been shocked by the introduction to army life. A civilian barber, a mean-looking weedy man with a thin cruel mouth, ran electric clippers in a wholly heartless fashion right through my precious hair up to the very edge of my crown in a distinctly inartistic manner, leaving my head looking like a pink fuzzy rugger ball. As a further indignity, a couple of doctors shoved stethoscopes at my chest and thrust their fingers in the usual personal places with the usual not-too-polite requests that I should cough. This was the forerunner to an even more undignified army ceremony known as an FFI, which was short for 'free from infection'. For this we were lined up trouserless while an army doctor examined our 'wedding tackle', if necessary using his leather officer's cane to move intervening bits to the left or right, upwards and – infrequently – downwards, to give a better view.

Sergeant Hoare, his pleasant manner now discarded, reintroduced himself with the memorable sentence, 'My name's Sergeant Hoare, spelt H–O–A–R–E, and if anybody wants to have a laugh about it, he'd better step forward now.' There were no takers.

Square-bashing and rifle drill were no novelty to me. At Durlston Court we were taught rifle drill and the old 1914 foot drill where we were formed up into two ranks and were then commanded to 'Form fours'. There then ensued a complicated dance-like series of steps while shouting 'One – one two' and we would all bump into each other prior to finding ourselves in four ranks. Having sorted ourselves out, this would be followed by Pat Cox yelling, 'Form two deep' and, after shouting 'One – one two' again, we scrambled once more into two ranks. The War Department struggled for many years with this drill until somebody tumbled on the idea of forming up into three ranks and staying that way. This greatly reduced the chaos and revolutionised modern warfare. The simple act of marching in step proved too much for two or three members of our happy band, who insisted on sticking their left arms forward at the same time as their left legs, which produces a penguin-like gait and understandably sent Sergeant Hoare apoplectic.

Even more difficult to overcome were the intricacies of rifle drill. Three or four of our number were completely uncoordinated, but the not very patient Sergeant Hoare triumphed in the end. I had more sympathy for him many years later when trying to make Captain Mainwaring's platoon perform the same manoeuvres. The older members were ex-soldiers, but Pike and Walker and several younger members of the squad had to start from scratch.

The process of turning us into soldiers proceeded more or less uneventfully and, after a lot of shouting and kit layouts and marching up and down and shouldering arms, we were deemed to have done our preliminary training and were given weekend leave. In my case, this included a railway pass to Buxton in Derbyshire.

Mother and Olive seemed to have survived my short absence comparatively well. So having done a few running repairs, I proceeded to the Light Anti-Aircraft Training Unit at the Empire Hotel, Buxton. To my surprise, conditions here were markedly down on the spider huts of Blandford. The imposing Empire Hotel had embarked on the process of falling down and, there being no beds, we slept on the floor. In order to soften the impact of skin and bone against wood, we were issued with large cotton bags. We were then loosed a dozen at a time upon a room full of straw, where we jostled and scrambled to fill our bags to capacity. In a few minutes you couldn't see across the room for straw dust and we were all sneezing ourselves stupid. Inevitably, one or two timid souls ended up with practically empty bags and we then each duly contributed a few handfuls of our straw towards their comfort. This scene came in handy in an early episode of *Dad's Army* in which, of course, Private Godfrey was the one with the empty bag.

We were being trained to operate the Bofors 40-millimetre gun which was controlled by an unbelievably heavy predictor invented by an enterprising colonel named Kerrison. The predictor was a 3-foot metal cube thing that needed six men to lift it on to its stand. A couple of the crew then looked through little telescopes and tried to follow the enemy aeroplane. I was deputed to stand behind the thing wiggling a wheel that entered in my estimate of how far away the said plane was flying. The predictor was then supposed to work out how long the shell would take on its journey and aim the gun so that the missile collided with the plane. It was hoped that the enemy would then fall from the sky. I very much doubt whether this had any effect upon the fortunes of war, but hopefully it had some beneficial effect upon the fortunes of Colonel Kerrison. I hope he was on a percentage.

The Bofors was in fact a big machine-gun firing 60 exploding bullets, each weighing 2 lb or so, per minute. It was operated by a team of ten men whose task it was to unhook it from the truck that towed it and, in two minutes or less, put the damned thing together and use it to shoot down low-flying planes. The bright idea of the War Office Training Department at this stage was that we should all go about our different tasks simultaneously shouting out at the top of our voices what each of us was doing. This resulted in the loader yelling things like 'I am now placing the lever foot pedal "Held" to the position "Held" and reporting "Held",' following which the unfortunate lad would turn his head in the direction of the Sergeant Instructor and yell 'Held'. This was in fact the same as saying, 'I've put the safety catch on.' The Geordie who was deputed to put the hefty side girder into its socket was once heard to yell 'I'm putting this fookin heavy fookin iron thing in this fookin hole and trying to get this fookin retaining pin in this fookin little socket and it won't fookin go.' Ten men all shouting running commentaries on their activities produces a sound of complete chaos, the like of which I have never heard since.

left: Anne and Reggie (mother and father) in *Follies* at the London Hippodrome, 1920.

below: Reginald Sharland (father) trying to be Errol Flynn, Hollywood, 1931.

right: DC either laughing or crying – the arm belongs to Olive Rawdon.

above: Anne Croft as Nadina in her own production of *The Chocolate Soldier* at The Shaftesbury Theatre, 1935.

left: DC with brother Peter in Melbourne, Australia, 1927.

below right: Our Annie's Boys: DC aged 12 with Peter.

bottom: Mother (centre) DC, Peter and others, Sydney, Australia, 1927.

above: DC on Jack Barty's boat, 1935.

left: Ivy Rawdon – an irrepressible, fun-loving extrovert.

opposite top: The valiant pen-pushers of the 4th Independent Infantry Brigade, Group Headquarters. Brigadier J. S. McCully centre. Staff Captain DC 2nd row, extreme right. Singapore, 1945.

opposite bottom: First days in the Royal Artillary at Blandford, 1942. (DC back row, 4th from right.)

right: DC – note golden curly
hair – 1947.

below: Brother Peter and DC –
we ploughed the fields and
scattered – in Hampstead.

left: DC with Daphne de Witt – alias Mrs George Lacey.

below: DC (a very close friend of the Artful Dodger) in *Oliver Twist* at Wolverhampton Rep.

bottom: Wild Violets at the Stoll Theatre, 1949. The boys (from left to right) are Allen Christie, Ian Carmichael and DC.

My wife Ann.

Some four weeks into this training I was summoned from morning parade by the major. At the time I was carrying a rifle at the 'slope' and I realised that I was not supposed to salute with my free hand. I therefore 'presented arms', which was the right thing to do. A rather embarrassed major returned my salute, following which I 'sloped' again. Since this is no position from which to conduct a conversation, I then proceeded to 'order arms'. All this takes a lot of time, so I politely said, 'I hope this is right, sir,' to which the major replied, 'It looks very good to me but could you hurry it up a bit?' I finally got to a 'stand at ease' position, following which he said that he wondered if I would be interested in going to India to an Officers Training Unit to take a commission in the Indian Army. For some reason or other I didn't fancy this as my army career. At that stage I had no idea of the luxurious way of life of the Indian Army officer, so I declined. Had I known more about it, and also realised what the next couple of years held in store for me, I would have jumped at the chance. At the same time, by making that decision I probably saved myself from becoming involved in the Burma campaign and also probably saved my life.

From Buxton I was sent to a firing camp set on an idyllic site on the hills overlooking Penhale, near Newquay in Cornwall. The weather was outstanding and, under the command of an exceedingly intelligent and civilized sergeant, we bathed and lounged and sunbathed between sessions of shooting off the Bofors at cotton sleeve targets towed by brave pilots in biplanes. Except for the enormous bangs made by the gun, the war seemed far away, which was just as well because it wasn't going very smoothly. General Auchinleck was barely holding Rommel at El Alamein, Hitler was hammering at Stalingrad, and the British raid on Dieppe had been a fiasco.

My next posting was to 285 Battery of the 64th Light Anti-Aircraft Regiment in a very cramped camp in Birmingham. We were obviously being prepared for service overseas, but we were given no clue as to where. After a few weeks at this muddy but undistinguished group of corrugated iron Nissen huts, I decided it was time to make a serious effort to obtain a commission. Here I came up against the battery commander, a sinister Scottish major called Wilson, who possessed the sparkling sense of humour of a turtle. Although I was well recommended by the captain and lieutenant who were my troop officers, Major Wilson thought I was trying to evade our inevitable posting overseas. Not being the type to mince his words, he said that just because I had been to a public school I needn't think I was entitled to a commission, and furthermore he considered that I lacked the drive and initiative to become an officer. I told him I thought he was wrong, to which he replied that he didn't give a damn what I thought, and that was the end of the interview. There was no appeal from that sort of situation, so there was nothing for it but to settle down and await events.

We were a pretty mixed unit, mainly from Glasgow. Numbered among us were former members of Glasgow gangs such as the Dairy Boys, the Billy Boys and the Postle Boys. They were a great bunch but were not to be pushed around, as became evident a few weeks later when we went to firing camp at Butlins in Clacton-on-Sea. This was my first encounter with Butlins camps, which were to figure a great deal in my career in post-war years. However, Butlins in 1942 was a very different kettle of fish from the *Hi-de-Hi!* camps that I came to know later. The chalets had of course been stripped of beds and curtains, and the fuses had been taken out of the junction boxes in the chalet lines. The resulting lack of light was quickly remedied by inserting a paper clip or a hairpin, which would carry enough current to light Clacton. From somewhere or other my lads had found an electric fire, so in no time we were as snug as bugs in rugs – which were not, incidentally, present in our rugs up to that time.

On the day after we arrived there ensued a remarkable scene. The colonel of 64th Regiment, whom we had not clapped eyes on until that point, decided to address his troops. We were therefore – all 200 of us – assembled in a large hall, which in happier times had been furnished as one of Billy Butlin's boxing arenas. The ring was still standing, so the colonel arrived with his entourage and proceeded to climb through the ropes. For some reason this looked hilarious, and was thus received with barely suppressed laughter, which of course resulted in sergeant-majors and NCOs shouting 'Silence in the ranks!' and 'Quiet!' and 'Shut up!' in the usual army sergeant fashion. The colonel, instead of making a joke of the whole incident, was visibly put out, which added to the humour of the situation. Once order had been restored, he started on his speech. Regular army officers frequently speak in a dialect that is just as distinct as cockney, and it does not go down well with the troops – particularly troops from the Gorbals. I don't recall precisely what he said, but the general gist of his speech was that we were a load of conscripted raw material which he and his staff were going to turn into real disciplined soldiers come what may. The result was a low mutinous murmur from the ranks. Crowds in film scenes produce this sound by saying 'Rhubarb, rhubarb, rhubarb'. Our crowd produced it by saying 'Who the feckin feck does he think he's talking to?' in mainly Scottish accents. This resulted in frenzied shouting of 'Silence in the ranks!' from the sergeants. When order was restored the colonel summoned what dignity he could, drew himself up to his full height and said, 'If that's your attitude, I feel jolly sorry for you.' At this point he tried a dignified exit, which was difficult because he once more had to duck under the ropes like the frightened referee in a boxing match. More suppressed titters and more shouting from the sergeants followed, after which we were doubled from the boxing arena to the playing field, which did service as a parade ground.

There was much coming and going by senior officers from area HQ carrying clipboards. Nothing more was said to us by our battery and troop commanders, but from that point onward we were treated with great suspicion and made to double everywhere, which is the army's usual response to any breach of discipline. During the following fortnight, we banged off our guns at the usual sleeve targets with pretty disastrous results, inasmuch as we missed. I had a good crew. Joe Postlethwaite, a fierce-looking, red-headed Glaswegian bus conductor, was gun-layer on one side, and Peter Wyper, a tall, very strong and straight-laced paviour, was the other, while Frank Lock, who played full back for Charlton Athletic, was the loader. Our gun got the best results out of a pretty poor bag.

After shooting our guns and guarding unimportant things all night, we returned to the Birmingham area to Packington Park, a Georgian pile in Meriden. By now, winter was beginning to set in and our accommodation consisted of leaky First World War bell-tents. Packington Park was a picturesque enough site in fair weather, but in winter, with five or six hundred troops with their guns and trucks sprawling all over the place, it soon became a distinctly muddy area. We were roused every morning by a distant, damp bugler, following which the duty sergeant would come round shouting, 'Let's be 'aving you!' This was accompanied by a couple of bangs with his stick on the frail fabric of each tent, which sent a shower of condensation on to the ten men huddled in their damp blankets within.

At about this time I was given another stripe. This made me a full bombardier with a pay packet of just over £2 a week, which enabled me to send a few bob to Mother, who was still struggling on in Bournemouth on £4 a week. After a few wet weeks we were all sent once again to Clacton to bang away at more sleeves with marginally better results. Our gun again managed the top score, which proved to be a great advantage a short while later. This time we were returned to a village further outside Birmingham called Wishaw. This consisted of a single street with a few houses, a pub and a village hall. We slept on the floor of the hall, which was a marked improvement on the old threadbare tents of Packington Park. It has long been a favourite saying of mine that 'It takes no talent whatever to be uncomfortable' and, not wishing to partake in the traditional scramble to fill a cotton bag full of straw to sleep on, I bought for myself a heavy-gauge, rubber blow-up mattress. To the great amusement of all the gun crews, I would blow this up every night and deflate it every morning so that it could be concealed under the neatly folded blankets of my kit layout. I slept in comfort every night, punctuated by the late arrival of Joe Postlethwaite. On most nights, having had a skinful at the only pub in Wishaw, he would crawl on hands and knees through the blackness of the hall over our prone bodies to the snoring form of his mate 'Moose'. Having got there he would prod him saying, 'Moose, Moose. Did ye get yer hole?' The sleepy Moose would reply, 'Mind yer own fecking business you fecking uncivilised clint.'

Our future became a little clearer when we were called upon to draw tropical kit in the form of khaki drill shirts and shorts, and our old guns were exchanged for new grease-covered Bofors. There followed a fierce debate as to whether we should scrape the paint off the brass screws and polish them to a gleaming brightness, or leave them covered so that the bright brass would not shine in the sun, thus betraying our presence to the enemy. The 'dull' faction prevailed. To my great surprise I was issued with a tommy gun, as used by Chicago gangsters, plus a large quantity of bullets to go with it. On the two occasions I fired it I couldn't hit a door at 10 yards, but I was stuck with it, and it was damned heavy and awkward.

This was swiftly followed by embarkation leave, which fortunately coincided with Christmas. It is worthy of note that at this time, in order to get leave, we had to apply in writing, ending our letters with the words 'I beg to remain, Sir, your humble and obedient servant'. This was not popular with the Glasgow contingent, many of whom were card-carrying communists who frequently started to sing 'The Internationale' as a marching song. As a further exercise in stupidity we had to take all our gear home on leave, presumably in case we were called to the boat directly. I was therefore to be seen with very full kitbag, large and small packs, water bottle, tin hat, ammunition-laden pouches and tommy gun tottering on to a crowded train to London. I spent a few days there which included a bizarre dinner with my brother Peter and Colonel Jack Votion of the US Forces at the Ritz Hotel in Piccadilly. Jack was staying there in an amazing room on the corner overlooking Green Park. Dinner cost five shillings, which was the most any meal was permitted to cost during that stage of the war. There was, however, a 15 shilling cover charge.

After a reduced Christmas in Bournemouth, to which my Army Emergency Ration coupons were a welcome addition, I then lugged all my gear back to Birmingham on an even more crowded, darkened train in a distinctly Alfred Hitchcock atmosphere. A short time after reporting we were told that we would be off next morning, but nobody knew where to. Dawn duly came and the roll was called to reveal that one of our number, a mild-mannered, ginger-haired chap named Thornley, had sloped off during the night. I never heard what happened to him, but he would assuredly have been found sooner or later and would have received a pretty heavy sentence. The rest of us with all our gear mounted our vehicles in the dark and proceeded to a station that we soon identified as New Street. There was a heavy presence of Military Police to ensure that we got into the compartments, which were promptly locked. The train then puffed out to its unknown destination. On the few occasions when it stopped, the platform was lined with MPs in case anybody tried to scarper from the locked train through a window. Evidently our reputation had preceded us from the boxing arena at Butlins Holiday Camp in Clacton-on-Sea!

7

Troopship to North Africa

Shortly after consuming our sandwiches, which were smeared with a pink-coloured meat paste that had a barely discernible taste of nothing at all, we arrived at a large station that somebody recognised as Liverpool Docks. The platform was again lined with Military Police. We were urged, amid much shouting, to get off and to embark on a fair-sized boat of some 15,000 tons, which turned out to be the good ship *Empire Pride*. This was one of those boats welded together in great haste to carry troops at fair speed to wherever they were needed. We were to sleep in hammocks, which was a bit of a shock as far as I was concerned, but I soon learned to bless my luck. They were tied on to hooks at regular 2-foot intervals with us all overlapping each other after the fashion of sardines. We were issued with enormous kapok life jackets that were never to be removed during the voyage. The same rule applied to our boots, which could be loosened but not taken off.

It transpired that, owing to our prowess at firing camp at Butlins, my crew had been chosen to defend the ship by manning the port Bofors gun at the side of the bridge. This gave us a commanding view of all that went on during the trip to wherever we were going, which remained a deadly secret. As soon as we were stowed aboard, we cast off and made for the estuary. There was no cheering from the jetty, as there is in films, for the simple reason that there was nobody there to cheer. Once clear of the estuary and into the Irish Sea, the convoy began to get together and progress into the open water. A couple of small Navy corvettes buzzed around for our protection. They signalled in Morse on Aldis lamps, and I could read their signals, which impressed the gun crew enormously. The assembled convoy of some thirty or forty ships of sizes varying from 5,000 to 15,000 tons was the most awe-inspiring sight I have ever seen. There was a sense of enormous power as they steamed along in three columns spaced out at intervals of four or five hundred yards. Every ten minutes, at a signal from convoy commander, the whole mob would turn left or right about 20 degrees to make ourselves a less easy target for German U-boats, which were terribly active and successful at this stage of the war. Each ship was trying to produce as little smoke as possible so as not to give away our position.

I like everything to do with ships and the sea, but unfortunately I am an absolutely rotten sailor. Once we were out into the Atlantic, the ship started to heave and buck and lift and wallow, and from then on I was useless. I was not alone in this, as huge metal tubs were strewn about the place for the convenience of the troops, who were throwing up all over the ship. Those not on the gun crews – and there were only two guns on the ship – were obliged to be on deck from dawn until about 10.30 a.m. regardless of the weather, while the troop decks below were cleaned up. We manned the bridge gun for two hours and then tumbled into our hammocks for four hours throughout the day and night. The hammock was a blessed refuge for me because it cancelled out the motion in one direction and made the pitching bearable. When we were on duty the lads would tell me when any inspecting officer approached so that I could get on to my feet and look competent, even if green and emaciated. The remainder of the time I was prone in the ammunition locker. The storms during those early weeks of 1943 were some of the worst on record, but at least it kept the U-boats at bay. One black night the bridge itself took a wave aboard. We went westward into the Atlantic for days and then turned south, so rumours were rife that we were going to India, but after a day or two we turned east. One joker suggested we were going back home. After about ten days of this I was in a pretty bad state. I had not taken any food and precious little liquid, so I was dehydrated.

At long last we caught sight of land, which we calculated was probably Gibraltar, so it was decided that we were bound for North Africa. There seemed little point to all this secrecy about our destination because the chances of a German agent hiding aboard and being equipped with a miniature transmitter tuned in to Hitler seemed, to say the least, remote. As soon as we passed Gibraltar my whole world was transformed. Firstly I ceased to throw up all over the ship including, in one instance, over the irate captain. Secondly, the temperature lifted from perishingly cold to mild and, furthermore, a scented breeze was wafting its way from the African coast on a gentle southerly wind. In these days of air travel we never seem to experience the change in the scent of the air in quite the same way. The whole world seems to smell of diesel.

71

As we steamed through the falling light, the bow waves and the wake were lit up with a luminescence I had never seen before, and we hung over the rail and watched it for hours. But for the fact that we expected to be bombed and torpedoed as we progressed along the coast to Alexandria, all seemed right with the world. To our surprise, the captain took a sharp right turn and headed straight for the coast of Africa. A short time later we anchored in a beautiful bay that, having seen the movie with Charles Boyer, we identified as Algiers. We were all looking forward to exploring the kasbah when the captain had the anchor pulled up and we were off once again. We hugged the coast for a few more hours and then pulled into a small harbour and tied up against a long, low jetty with the assistance of some scruffy Arabs. The 'La-de-dah Gunner Grahame' in our party happened to have a crumpled atlas in his kit and he identified our destination as most probably being a place called Bône (now Annaba in Algeria). It was a small sprawl of Arabian-style houses with a French colonial main street and very little to recommend itself to a boatload of British gunners. We disembarked, leaving our kitbags in a pile on the quayside, and marched three or four miles eastward to a large, undulating area of open scrub near the sea. There we collected two-man tents and tried to work out how to put them up.

That night information came through that a German commando unit had landed up the coast towards Bizerta and something had to be done about it. Sergeant Regan's troop was to patrol up the coast in arrowhead formation. It was Sergeant Regan's perverse decision that yours truly should be at the very point of the leading arrow with my gun crew spread out behind me. I had no infantry training. It had been given to the unit in the weeks before I joined. Nevertheless, I was to be found walking stealthily up the beach through the black night with the pounding surf on my left, crouching low in the hope that I wouldn't be noticed whilst clutching my loaded tommy gun for comfort and looking out for German commandos. Sergeant Regan marched 50 yards to the rear. I couldn't see him, but I strongly suspect that he had a grin all over his chubby red Scots face. After about an hour word came through that it was a false alarm, so we thankfully turned about and headed for our two-man homes.

Next morning we all decided we were hungry. Fruit trees, including peaches, had been seen during our march to the scrub area. I seemed to be the only person, including the officers, who had a few words of French, so I hailed some nearby kids and gave them enough money to purchase 'Des pêches – dix des pêches'. They were gone some time. When they returned they were triumphantly clutching ten newspapers. The local rag was called *La Dépêche* (The Dispatch). My reputation as a linguist never recovered.

It was now officially admitted that we were in fact in Bône and were proud members of the First Army, although our guns only arrived about a week later. Each gun had its own gun-carrier, which bore most of the ammunition, and also a 3-ton truck, which carried our gear, more ammunition, the predictor, a generator to run it, and us. Our task was to defend the small RAF airfield east of Bône, from which flew a few Wellington and Sterling bombers.

We decided to reject the two-man tents, as they were impossible to sleep in with the complication of two mosquito nets and the frequent presence of scorpions. Instead we plumped for a wrecked house with four low walls and no roof. Here, with the aid of a few lengths of wood and the gun tarpaulin, we improvised a shelter into which we put beds made from three stout planks. These kept us off the floor, and we used our kitbags as pillows. We didn't have the advantage of bags of straw, and my blow-up mattress had sprung a puncture. There was not a lot of spring in three 1-inch planks, but a couple of blankets folded under us at least prevented us from getting bedsores. Food was entirely tinned. A stew made by someone called McConichie was good but hardly the grub for the tropics.

We manned the gun at dawn and sunset, and one of us would be in the gun-pit by the telephone day and night. The area was pretty heavily infested with mosquitoes, so after twilight we were obliged to wear net covers over our tin helmets, which made us all look like bee-keepers. We also had to take a pill called Mepocrin, which gave us all the yellowish appearance of jaundice sufferers. Every ten days or so we each had a day off – alone – and could go into the town to see what was going on. Nothing was going on. There was the periodic alert when we would all 'stand to' but, apart from that, a few months went by without incident. It was then decided that, since nothing was happening in Bône, we would be better employed defending Philipville, a small port sixty or so miles to the west. It was a pretty little township and our gun-site was on a hill with a commanding view of the port. The main street, with its French colonial buildings, was wide and tree-lined with the odd café. Only Algerian red wine was on offer. I was not a wine drinker at this stage but I thought it pretty rough stuff. The lads were used to drinking by the pint, which caused a few problems at first, but we managed to hide most of the drunks until they realised that a subtler approach was necessary. From our gun-site we could see the comings and goings of the town and the port. Royal Navy corvettes driven with great panache would arrive in impressive style. They would approach the entrance to the port very fast, conduct a couple of wiggles to get inside and then slam on the brakes, producing a froth of white water, before tying up in no time at all. I think naval officers are quite different from army officers. An army officer can lead his troops into the valley of death, lose half or them and emerge with a medal. If a naval officer bashes into a jetty rather vigorously, he is likely to lose his job.

Enemy activity increased considerably. For night raids an anti-aircraft barrage was devised, which didn't do much good, but the tracer shells were very spectacular. In daylight the enemy raids were rather more exciting because we could see and identify the planes that on rare occasions shot back at us. A few months later our role was taken over by the Americans, who arrived with a bulldozer to dig the gun-pit deeper. They also sported large tents, bags of boiled sweets and tins of turkey. We went back to the same gun-pit in Bône, but this time with a great sergeant by the name of Bob Barber, a distinct improvement on his ignorant predecessor who sucked his teeth incessantly. Bob had served in the International Brigade during the Spanish Civil War but could not be persuaded to talk about it. He had the cool confidence of a born leader and was one of the most impressive men I ever met in the army.

My health had begun to deteriorate, probably owing to the vitamin deficiency in our diet. It started with a bad bout of impetigo. It was the custom to treat this with an ointment known as gentian violet. As the name implies, this was a concoction of an almost luminous violet colour which, on top of a freckled red face heavily tinged with Mepocrin yellow, made me look like some bizarre jungle growth. My twenty-first birthday approached when – surprise, surprise – my brother Peter showed up aboard a Norwegian whaling factory ship called the *Uniwhaleco*. On putting into Bône he had promptly gone to see the town major to find out if my unit was in the district, only to be told that I was barely 4 miles away. He was a not a little alarmed at the sight of me and my living conditions, and promptly secured a bottle of ship's lime juice, which had been introduced in the nineteenth century to prevent sailors getting scurvy. This he hoped would do something about my impetigo and stop me looking like a jungle weed. I was awarded one whole day off for my twenty-first birthday, and Peter persuaded his captain and officers to give me a birthday lunch. They spoke not a word of English between them, but the food made a very nice change, although it was not enhanced by the pervading scent of dead whale.

In the next week my health went downhill rapidly. I suspected that I was suffering from arthritis, which had hit my father very badly in Hollywood. It soon got to the stage where two of my mates had to take an arm each to help me to stagger to the gun-pit. The regimental medical officer, who was not the most sensitive member of his profession, finally came to the conclusion that the matter was worthy of further investigation, so I was sent a few miles up the line to the military hospital.

It was no surprise to me that they kept me in. I was overjoyed to be there. Although the hospital was tented, there was every comfort I could wish for. There were beds with mattresses, sheets and pillows. The nurses were members of Queen Alexandra's Nursing Yeomanry, all very highly trained and most of them very attractive. My doctor was an American who swiftly cured my impetigo with sulphanilamide and from my symptoms diagnosed rheumatic fever. I was placed with my legs in a sort of tent, with a metal frame covering my swollen knees and electric light-bulbs to give them warmth. I was given large doses of soda salycil to bring down my blood sedimentation rate. Peter meanwhile detected that the American doctor was woefully short of Scotch whisky, which the Norwegian ship had in abundance, and one way or another it was swiftly arranged that I would be transferred to a hospital in Algiers. I duly found myself on an ambulance train heading westward, while Peter sailed for the landing at Anzio. The train was an odd experience. We were stowed on racks one above the other and three deep, as if in some nightmare grill, which was distinctly claustrophobic. The rolling stock was an adapted cattle train with very little in the way of springing. I was glad that the journey only lasted that one night.

Once in Algiers, we were transferred to a temporary hospital that had been improvised in the university building. I was placed in a large ward on the second floor with high-shuttered windows and twenty or so beds. Here British doctors came and peered at me and my growing pile of medical records. In the next bed was a gloomy young man who spent his days designing tombstones. Opposite lay a mildly spoken man with a voice like Larry the Lamb, who had entered the hospital with an infected leg and while there had managed to acquire malaria, then dysentery, which turned into peritonitis, following which he died. I am not a believer in spooky occurrences, but the moment he fell off his perch, the shutters flew open with a pronounced 'Whoosh'. It was a completely still, windless night.

By chance a French youth came round the wards selling oranges. I fell upon these with great gusto and remarkably quickly started to make a recovery, so much so that in about three weeks I thought I would be returning to 285 Battery. Then, to my intense delight, I discovered that I had been marked down for return to the UK – perhaps by the American doctor. For two or three weeks I was on tenterhooks in case the doctors changed their minds. By now I was allowed out of bed and was roaming round the wards. On the day scheduled for my departure I was at the foot of the wide stone staircase when one of my mates leant over the banisters and yelled, 'David – they're here for you.' I leapt up to the second floor two stairs at a time. At the top were two Italian prisoners of war with a stretcher. I was down on the records as a stretcher case, but I knew better than to argue. With a polite 'Scusi' I lay myself on the stretcher and said, 'Andante con moto', which was all the Italian I knew from my music lessons at Rugby. The bewildered POWs carried me to a waiting ambulance that took me to the very business-like hospital ship *Southampton*. Once aboard, I was put to bed by yet another attractive member of Queen Alexandra's Nursing Yeomanry and lay comfortably back on my pillow in the knowledge that I was soon to head for home. We set off within an hour or two, with light blazing from the portholes and the Red Cross on our side brightly floodlit.

The Mediterranean is a small sea when you look at it on the map, but it stood the *Southampton* on end before we got to Gibraltar. Safely in my comfortable bunk and with the assistance of a pill or two I managed not to be seasick, although I said no to most of the food. After a few days we sailed up the Irish Sea to dock once more in Liverpool. As I was being carried on a stretcher down the gangway a small posse of cleaning ladies waved and raised a half-hearted cheer. The hero was home!

8

Hospitals and Home

Ambulances swiftly conveyed us to Clatterbridge Hospital, near Liverpool, where we were housed in cosy wooden-hut wards. It was now very near to Christmas so, as I was fit to travel, I was swiftly discharged and sent home on leave with instructions to report myself to a hospital in Bournemouth ten days after the holiday. Expecting a discharge on medical grounds, I made a flying visit to London to see Haddon Mason, who had been the stage director of *Tulip Time* and was now a leading figure in an agency called Filmrights. He was delighted to see me because male actors under 55 were thin on the ground, and he told me that as soon as I was released he would gladly go to work on my show business career.

I duly reported to the Bournemouth hospital ward, hoping to be out of the army in a matter of weeks. The sister in charge was a portly Irish lady who didn't like me very much. During the day, for the good of my health, I was placed on the open balcony attached to the ward which, it being January, was exceedingly cold. Reading could only be carried out for a few minutes at a time, otherwise the hand that turned the page was in danger of frostbite. After three weeks or so the Irish sister, whom I had not managed to enchant with my personality, said boldly to the consultant who was tending me, 'We can't find anything wrong with this patient.' The wodge of documentation accompanying me bore witness that there certainly had been something wrong with me, even if there was, miraculously, little remaining evidence. I was discharged from that hospital and sent to a beautiful Edwardian mansion near Wareham that had been requisitioned and turned into a convalescent hospital. Here, for three or four weeks during the early spring of 1944, clad in the army's hospital blue, I played endless games of Monopoly, completed jigsaw puzzles and took quiet country walks.

After that I was declared fit enough to be sent to the convalescent depot in Taunton, Somerset, for the next stage of recovery. This was an altogether more rigorous affair that started with 5-mile walks and finished up with 25-mile route marches. The physical training also included that fiendish exercise where eight of you chuck a telegraph pole from shoulder to shoulder and run about with it as if it were made of balsa wood. It made a very funny sequence for Jones and Godfrey in *Dad's Army*. To my great alarm, after completing the course at Taunton, I was finally thought to be fit and was sent to the Royal Artillery depot at Woolwich.

To sum up the whole history of my army medical trauma, I think it is fair to say that once I had reached the field hospital in Bône, Algeria I was very well looked after by conscientious nurses and doctors until I was again in good health. When in a unit on active service the whole process of 'going sick' is severely discouraged. To see a doctor you are required to parade in a pathetic-looking bunch, separated from the main body of troops, while the rest of the mob is duly inspected and counted. This happens come rain or shine. You are supposed to have with you your so-called 'small kit', which includes soap, towel, razor, tooth brush, etc. Before seeing the doctor you are supposed to hand in all your worldly goods, including uniforms and guns, to the Quartermaster's Stores. If he is bloody-minded he won't accept your possessions tied up in your kitbag but will require them to be individually handed in, registered and signed for. You then see the doctor who will prescribe M and D, which means 'medicine and duty', or 'light duties', or, if you happen to be at death's door, hospital. At best, the process takes half a day and is designed to be not worth the candle.

Woolwich Artillery Depot is a place to be avoided. Although picturesque, it is primitive from the ordinary soldier's point of view. I was employed mainly at the Woolwich Arsenal, breaking down various small pieces of equipment into their component parts for the purpose of salvaging the more valuable metal bits. I also escorted the odd deserter back to Woolwich from various London police stations. For this duty I would be handcuffed to the failed runaway and accompanied by a sergeant. I hoped that the two stripes on my arm would distinguish me from the prisoner, but I would always put my folded overcoat over the manacles and grab his hand so that we appeared to be two rather over-friendly soldiers.

By this time I was well acquainted with *King's Regulations* and other various army enactments, including *The Manual of Military Law*. I had both volumes in my kitbag. I knew that I was entitled to get a medical consultant's opinion about the state of my heart, and that I was also supposed to have a full-blown medical board after being in hospital for six months. I accordingly took myself to the heart hospital in Harley Street to see if the rheumatic fever had left me with any permanent defect. It hadn't. I appeared before the medical board to see if I had any inherent arthritis. I explained my concern to the aged colonel who was president of the board. 'Let's see your fingers then,' he said in an avuncular voice. I showed him my hands, of which the right one had a barely discernible swelling round the third finger. He then produced his own gnarled mitts, the fingers of which had almost Disney-like lumps and swellings. 'I don't think you'll have too much trouble with those,' he said, and passed me A1. My chance of resuming my acting career having slipped down the plughole without as much as a gurgle, there was nothing for it but to resume military life.

Since being back in England I had discovered that I had one unique advantage. I had a medal – the Africa Star. The Eighth Army was riding very high at the time, having pushed Hitler's Afrika Korps out of Africa. The fact that I had the First Army clasp was neither here nor there. The general public recognised the Africa Star for the simple reason that it was the only medal that had been issued. As soon as I appeared in a pub, pints were offered. I was the nearest thing to a hero that many people had seen up to that point. The Eighth Army was still fighting in Italy. I found a sympathetic officer whom I persuaded to recommend me for a commission. I am almost certain that he was impressed by the medal. To become an officer at this point in the war it was necessary to attend a War Office Selection Board. The one I went to was based in a large Lutyens house in Platts Lane, near Hampstead Heath. The board lasted for three days and was the most intensive experience I have ever had. One felt oneself to be under 24-hour scrutiny. There seemed to be endless sessions of intelligence tests consisting of complicated diagrams and mathematical problems. Nothing similar to these tests had previously been published, and they had not been used in schools, so they were completely unfamiliar. There were further tests in which we were shown something like an ink smudge and were invited to write a story based on it. These tests were interspersed with initiative tests in which, for example, we were given a few planks and lengths of rope and asked to cross a crocodile-infested ravine. To place one foot in the imaginary water on the grounds that the croc couldn't move fast enough to give you a nip was to fail.

One such exercise was carried out on the top of Hampstead Heath near the children's boating pond in full view of the public. We were strolling along in an informal group when the officer in charge shouted, 'Get down. There's a lunatic in that pit over there – he's got a hand grenade. What are you going to do about it?' Answers such as, 'Walk on and pretend he isn't there' and 'Send for the police' were not encouraged. Even during meals we felt we were under close scrutiny to check that we performed such manoeuvres as spreading our toast with marmalade instead of putting it on a dab at a time. I am a 'marmalade spreader' to this day. Also, we all felt a compulsion to stand out and show our brilliance from time to time, which can be a bit tedious from the social point of view. Finally there was a board of three officers chaired by a colonel who asked such questions as, 'Why do you want to be an officer?' The truthful answer to this is 'Because it's a damn sight better than being in the ranks and much more comfortable most of the time', but as far as I know this particular response has never been used by a successful candidate. The most important fact about this interview was the complete absence of medals on the three chests of the members of the board. A week later, back at Woolwich Artillery Depot, I was notified that I had passed the Selection Board and was to report to Sandhurst for training as an officer in the infantry.

I was eagerly looking forward to being a Sandhurst cadet. I had seen newsreel pictures of the passing-out parade, in which the best cadet received the sword of honour in front of serried ranks of immaculate fellow students, while the adventurous adjutant rode up the marble steps astride a gleaming white charger. I arrived at Sandhurst on the back of a 15-cwt truck to learn that I would be there for only a few short days while I was assessed for my infantry knowledge. My living quarters consisted of a leaky tent near the tradesman's entrance in a field somewhere round the back. This tent I shared with half a dozen fellow cadets, including Johnny Spittal, who was a burly, down-to-earth builder from Birmingham. Later on the first day another 15-cwt came on the scene, loaded to the top with kitbags and every sort of army gear. In the front was a short, exceedingly smart Czechoslovakian with a trim moustache wearing a neat beret carefully pulled down over the right ear. His name was, surprisingly, Barry Stewart-Fisher, but he had adopted this because his real Czech name was something unpronounceable. Before Hitler had annexed his country, Barry had been a solicitor in Prague. He proceeded to use his negotiating skills to persuade us to allot him enough space in the tent to accommodate his pile of kitbags containing illicitly acquired uniforms. The unlikely trio of Johnny, Barry and I became firm friends in the course of our very tough training.

During our first day of documentation, Barry caused something of a sensation when the formidable sergeant-major asked him what his religion was. 'Agnostic,' he replied. 'What the hell's that?' said the sergeant-major. 'I have no religion,' said Barry in his clipped, precise accent. 'In that case you're Church of England like the rest of us,' said the sergeant-major. Having put brilliant white bands on our hats to denote that we were training to be officers, we were then required to show how much we knew about being infantry soldiers. In my case this was precisely nothing, in spite of my leading the patrol against the German commandos along the African coast – an adventure I thought it best not to mention. Barry and Johnny also failed to pass, both being from non-infantry units. We were therefore all sent to a Pre-Officer Cadet Training Unit, which was situated on the top of the escarpment at Wrotham, Kent. This escarpment is probably only 300 feet in height, but every other training period took place either at the top or the bottom of it and, being young, fit and eager, we were expected to run both ways. By way of diversion we were able to watch the Spitfires shoot down the doodle-bugs that were on their way to London. After a month of this we were all very fit, a bit less eager and a lot less ignorant of the way to survive as infantrymen. From Wrotham we were sent to the 164th Officer Cadet Training Unit in Barmouth, North Wales.

We lived in the principal hotel in a first-floor room that looked out on the dark grey sea. Other cadets were housed in requisitioned boarding houses with names like Tal y Bont and Cors y Geddal. The parade ground was ruled by an enormous and frightening regimental sergeant-major from the Grenadier Guards named Copp, whose favourite threat to the fearful cadets was 'I'll give you all a wet shirt' – a threat that he frequently carried out by the simple means of doubling us up and down with rifles at the slope. His other favourite threat was 'I'll have you on the 7.18', which was the morning train to London. It was quite beyond his power to do this, but nobody had the nerve to say so.

We were, of course, under constant observation to assess our suitability for the role of infantry officer. Father, with whom for many years now I had had a close postal relationship, found it hard to understand to what extent times had changed since his day, when a couple of good recommendations from senior officers resulted in a subaltern's pip on the shoulder a few weeks later. Now we were trained to virtually commando standard and monitored all the way. We were lucky to have as our commander the craggy-faced Captain Jack Edwards, who was a brilliant leader, the embarrassed possessor of the George Medal, and a cultured and proud Welshman. During our training marches he loved to show us treasured beauty spots and remote lakes and valleys that were accessible only after long expeditions on foot. Our training was exceedingly hard and, as the winter closed in, conditions on the wet and windy Welsh mountains grew distinctly uncomfortable.

On one memorable occasion during a long bash against a biting wind full of freezing sleet, one of our number finally reached the end of his tether and chucked his rifle to the frozen ground, saying, 'Right – that's it. I've had it. I give in.' You will understand that these were not his precise words but represent the gist of what he wished to convey amid a stream of what is politely known as invective. The scene that followed is sometimes seen when a rugby player accidentally loses his trousers. Immediately ten cadets completely surrounded him. His rifle was picked up and thrust back in his hands. His back was patted, while phrases such as 'Don't give up, mate', 'We're nearly there', 'Bash on for God's sake' and the like flew through the air. He staggered on, and Jack Edwards kindly looked the other way. The man completed the course with the rest of us.

Sadly, about this time I received a telegram from Peter telling me that Father had died. He had suffered from rheumatoid arthritis for much of his time in Hollywood. He had stayed in the desert for weeks and even moved to Mexico in the hope that the drier climate would give some relief, but nothing seemed to work. He had married a beautiful young Swedish girl named Herta, who looked after him with great devotion, and we received a letter from her telling of Dad's final days. He was buried at Forrest Lawn and his friend the film star Herbert Marshall delivered an oration. It was sad that I came so near to seeing him just before the outbreak of the war, and even more sad to learn that he had been keen to get back to England, where he wanted to spend the last years of his life. Jack Edwards arranged that I should get a weekend leave, so I spent a couple of days with Peter in London.

On the evening before the passing-out parade I staged a sort of concert-cum-revue with the platoon. I wrote a couple of songs with the aid of a talented chap called Stan Pearsall, who played the piano exceedingly well by ear in D flat, which means employing all the black notes. Some of the lads were quite talented. We had a very good-looking former Coldstream Guards sergeant-major called Cunliffe, who sang with an excellent baritone voice. He gave us 'These Foolish Things'. Another chap had a beautiful bass voice but flatly refused to appear in front of the public. I solved this by having a group of us singing in close harmony round a camp fire with the stage in complete darkness.

I managed to rustle up some stage make-up but forgot to get any remover. The result was that the passing-out parade took place in front of a bewildered general and an apoplectic regimental sergeant-major, who were confronted with a lot of cadets wearing strong blue eye shadow and very red lips. Cunliffe got the sword as the best cadet. So what other memories remain of 164th OCTU? Making a lot of wild bayonet charges at straw-filled sacks while screaming bloodcurdling yells and trying to be fierce; trying to stay awake at afternoon lectures under threat of instant dismissal; running along the sea front at the end of the day to a tiny café and consuming ten pancakes every evening – Barry consumed 15; and running up and down those damned mountains. Finally, one dark December morning, we were all to be found on the 7.18 to London clutching suitcases containing our smart new service dress uniforms and wearing one new pip on our epaulettes. On arrival at Paddington Station I received my first salute from a stray soldier. I was an officer.

9
Learning to be a Lieutenant,
a Captain and a Major

A few weeks before we were passed out of 164 OCTU, we were all asked to say which regiment we would like to join. I plumped for the Warwicks because I had been attached to that regiment while in the Cadet Corps at Rugby. Johnny Spittal was born and bred in Birmingham, so for him it was a natural choice. Barry Stewart-Fisher also selected the Warwicks, hoping that we might be able to stay together for the rest of our service. In the event, I was sent to the Dorsets, Johnny ended up in the West African Rifles, and Barry, the Czech, was posted to the Warwicks. We all received a week's leave. I spent a few days in London, which was now a much more cheerful place because the war was going well in Europe. I then had to get myself to Norwich Castle to join the Dorsets.

By now it was Christmas and, being the most newly arrived and junior officer, I was of course made duty officer. There is a tradition that the officers serve the other ranks their Christmas dinner, so I duly waited on a few tables of bewildered squaddies who had never seen me before and were delighted to be cheeky to a new and inexperienced young officer.

My next adventure was 'battle school'. This was centred on Attleborough in Norfolk, but most of it took place on the Stanford Battle Area near Thetford, where I was later to film most of the outdoor activity of *Dad's Army*. The novelty of this particular battle school was that, instead of using blanks, the exercises were conducted using live ammunition. This at least taught you to keep your head down. I was given command of the company night attack – an exceedingly frightening affair that I conducted rather well. As a result, I got a B plus, which was a high mark in the world of battle schools.

Before long I was selected for service in India and, as was the custom in the army, I was given seven days' embarkation leave. *The Chocolate Soldier* was still trickling round on tour, but unfortunately George Bernard Shaw had got wind of it. The libretto blatantly plagiarized his play *Arms and the Man*, chunks of which had been stolen verbatim. The old gentleman had always been angered by this, not least because *The Chocolate Soldier* always made money and *Arms and the Man* was inclined to empty theatres wherever it appeared. Shaw, not for the first time, threatened an injunction for the breach of copyright. Mother phoned Miss Patch, his secretary, and was given an appointment to see him at his home at Ayot St Lawrence in Hertfordshire. She hired a chauffeur-driven car from the nearest station and, with a typical theatrical gesture, took me along as the young officer in full uniform complete with medal and well-polished Sam Browne belt. We arrived at about three in the afternoon and were shown into the hall with its hatstand full of eccentric hats and knobbly walking sticks, and from there into the Shaw drawing room, which was a homely and comfortable affair loaded with Victoriana. After a few minutes the great man himself appeared, greeted Mother warmly, and ordered tea.

There followed the usual polite enquiries as to how we had got from the station to the house and polite comments from Mother on the peaceful atmosphere of the house and what a joy it must be for such a busy man to be able to escape 'far from the maddening crowd', as she put it. Shaw let this one pass. Conversation then turned to *The Chocolate Soldier*. Mother said he could hardly blame anybody for wanting to set his wonderful play to music. This provoked an immediate reaction from GBS. 'I have already set it to music,' he said 'the music of the English language – the most beautiful language in the world.' The interview could not be said to be going great guns at this point, but fortunately tea arrived so GBS was distracted by having to be 'mother', pouring and enquiring who took milk and sugar. He then returned to his theme. Why didn't we produce some of the works of Offenbach? He then started to sing some of his favourite extracts in a high falsetto voice. 'Voici ma sabre!' is one phrase that stays in my memory. Mother pointed out that she would dearly like to produce all Offenbach's works one after the other but unfortunately production costs for musicals in wartime were particularly high and there was no way she could raise the dough for a new show since *The Chocolate Soldier* was barely breaking even. GBS got the message – he ultimately withdrew his injunction and the show continued.

Upon returning to my unit I found myself with another bunch of young soldiers I had never seen before, loaded with tropical kit and boarding the *Empire Deed* bound for Bombay. The *Empire Deed* was another hastily constructed troop carrier a little smaller than the *Empire Pride*, but this time I was a junior officer sharing a cabin with 12 other junior officers, with a comfortable bunk to sleep in instead of a hammock. Since the war in Europe was drawing to a close, we sailed happily through the Mediterranean and, once through Suez, we were no longer blacked out. My only duty during this voyage was to visit my platoon at mealtimes and say, 'Any complaints?' One of the troops had done a runner to escape the draft a couple of times, and so had been brought aboard in handcuffs, which were not removed until we were well out to sea. His reply to my query was, 'Well, it's pretty awful grub, sir, but let's face it, there's not much you can do about it, is there, sir?' The man was right.

So, in comparative idleness, we ploughed on to Bombay. No alcohol was available on the ship throughout the voyage, so we lolled about on deck, cautiously ogling the few girls from ENSA (the forces entertainment service) and the few women officers. We attended classes in Urdu and pored over the language books in a fruitless endeavour to master the rudiments of that tongue. We bathed on the decks in the warm sunlight and we played poker. From time to time we heard news of the war in Europe, which was very near its end, but we were not over-concerned. The Japanese in Burma were slowly being pushed back at last, but we were under no illusion about their willingness to fight fanatically for every foxhole all the way down the Malay peninsula and finally in Japan itself. The climax came as we steamed into Bombay harbour, when it was announced that the war in Europe was at an end, and we all looked forward to celebrating ashore. However, it was decided that a further boatload of British troops let loose in Bombay would only add to the chaos, so instead four of us managed to secure a bottle of South African brandy and did our best to celebrate over further games of poker. I won £4.

After a further day or two sweltering on the *Empire Deed* I reported to Kalyan Transit Camp. This dusty, fly-blown settlement in the desert lay about 25 miles east of Bombay and was my model for the set in *It Ain't Half Hot Mum*. It was unbelievably hot. The water in the cold shower was too hot to stand under for the simple reason that the tanks supplying it were placed on the roof in the full glare of the sun. This particular camp contained a sort of main street with tailors' shops, barbers, leather merchants, a laundry, souvenirs, etc. However, the best feature of Kalyan was the proximity of Bombay, where a good steak with the luxury of an egg on top was a unique treat after the fare available in wartime England.

The journey to Bombay entailed a trip by train. This was the inspiration for one of the best scenes ever staged in a BBC sitcom, where we endeavoured to reproduce the chaos of an Indian station with the teeming masses of people trying to board an already crowded train. The climax comes when the guard blows his whistle and waves his flag, whereupon all those without seats or, for that matter, without tickets, climb on to the roof or cling to the sides. In television we couldn't afford a couple of hundred extras to make up the crowds, but we made a pretty good stab at it considering that it was staged in a studio and the episode was shot in 90 minutes in front of an audience of 350.

After a couple of weeks in Kalyan I received orders to join the Essex Regiment at a place called Ranchi. I borrowed an atlas and discovered that this was a town about 150 miles west of Calcutta. Getting there involved a three-day train journey right across India. A first-class compartment had been reserved for me. The carriages were, needless to say, the non-corridor variety, so it was as well not to have 'Delhi belly' or any other dreadful Indian affliction during the passage. The reserved first-class compartment consisted of two wooden benches with luggage racks above. I found that my camp-bed fitted neatly between the benches, so sleep was possible, if not actually comfortable.

As the days passed, I would gaze at the endless Indian plains. The train stopped for breakfast, lunch and dinner to enable the passengers – mostly British officers – to decant themselves into some sort of station eating place and eat whatever was on offer. At the end of the meal we would tell the waiting railway official that we were ready and we would all re-embark, he would blow his whistle and wave his flag and we would be on our way. In the event of our not being ready, the poor chap would be told to go away while we continued with our meal.

If the train slowed up near any small town or village, hordes of vendors would leap on to the side of the train and try to sell their goods. The welcome ones were the char wallahs who all peddled excellent tea, sweet and very hot. The unwelcome ones would be those trying to sell things like gold rings, which they dangled on string into pots of liquid that they alleged was acid while they cried, 'Real gold, sahib – real gold – very cheap.' They also carried 'real gold watches and real gold bangles'. Others offered haircuts, chiropody and manicures, not to mention fortune-telling and soothsaying. Night-time posed a bit of a problem because thieves known as 'loose wallahs' would prey on the trains, so it paid to keep the windows closed, which made the journey excessively hot.

I finally joined the Second Battalion of the Essex Regiment and settled down to jungle training. The regiment was part of the 29th Independent Brigade Group, which in turn was part of 36 Division, which had recently been in Burma.

The colonel commanding the battalion thought it would be a wizard idea if I, as a newly arrived officer, could go on a route march at the head of my men wearing a beret instead of a topi or bush hat to show the troops that the impact of the sun on the head was being grossly exaggerated. With the obligatory show of eagerness I started on the march but two hours and some 7 miles later I began to feel that another half-hour would see me completing the journey by stretcher or ambulance. By some miracle, a dispatch rider tore up on a motorcycle with orders for us to return to base forthwith. He was mercifully followed by a couple of trucks to speed us back, so my humiliation was avoided. The reason for this sudden change of plan was an order to take the battalion to Poona straight away.

Being the most newly arrived officer I was deputed to take the unit's 13 trucks right across India on the Grand Trunk Road to Poona, which is 100 miles or so south-east of Bombay, while the rest of the mob went by train. Map in hand, I sallied forth at the head of my little convoy. Having, as usual, had a good look at the regulations relating to the conduct of trucks on the move in India, I discovered that we were entitled to one day's rest in three, so I planned a leisurely trip taking in any worthwhile attractions and lasting, in all, 13 days.

The Grand Trunk Road was not as grand as its title suggested. It was barely better than a B-class road, never, as far as I remember, breaking out into three lanes. The traffic consisted of every known wheeled vehicle, with a liberal sprinkling of lolloping bullock carts, rickshaws and handcarts, as well as pedestrians carrying everything, including the kitchen sink, balanced on their heads. Hurtling down the road from time to time would come convoys of 20 or 30 Indian Army lorries driven by laughing Indian drivers, most of whom had set their throttles at about 25 miles per hour and were steering their trucks through the window while standing on the running-board.

Along the way I dropped in at some fabulously luxurious officers' clubs in places such as Allahabad and Jhansi. They were staffed by immaculate, turban-clad waiters and servants – all resplendent with gleaming brass buttons. All the clubs had marbled swimming pools and lofty rooms cooled by slowly turning ceiling fans. On the other side of the coin I also bedded down in some exceedingly hot and dusty transit camps where offices were kept cool by the picturesque 'kuss kuss tatti'. This device consists of a rush mat covering the entrance door, over which a bearer throws a bucket of water every few minutes – another scene for *It Ain't Half Hot Mum*.

Most impressive of all was the city of Benares on the banks of the Ganges. Our visit coincided with a religious festival, so I hired an Indian guide to take us round the town and to prevent us offending anyone by stepping into the wrong temple. The guide's choice of monuments consisted mainly of illustrations of various acrobatic sexual positions which the Indians are wont to depict in stone. He would then proudly point out his various favourites and say, 'This, sahib, is very good way to enjoy.' Since my young charges, and for that matter myself, had not 'enjoyed' in the simplest missionary fashion up to that point, he was confronted by a couple of dozen very bewildered young men.

Poona is almost classed as a hill station and, truth to tell, is a bit less stifling than towns situated on the plains. We were placed at Uruli camp, which is on a hillside 5 miles or so from Poona. I had a tent known as an EPIP, which I think stood for European Personnel Indian Personnel. These tents were about 12 feet square, so were quite generous for one person. I slept on my camp-bed under a mosquito net, and at night I had a paraffin pressure light, known as a Tilley lamp, which hissed like a python but was a distinct improvement on candles. The camp was approached through Uruli village, which was rife with plague, beriberi and yellow fever, so I was immediately injected for all three. Shortly after our arrival the unit was renamed 4th Independent Brigade and the division was renamed 2nd British Division and I was made liaison officer to the battalion. I was given a motorcycle and told to become good at riding it as soon as possible, so I swanned around the countryside riding it on all available surfaces and falling off it a couple of times.

After I had been hanging around Brigade Headquarters for a month or so it was realised that I was pretty quick on the uptake, so I was made station staff officer, brigade entertainments officer and brigade intelligence officer, and promoted to captain. I had only been commissioned just over seven months, and the brigadier – a regular officer – pointed out that he had been a lieutenant for 17 years.

As entertainments officer I tried to get ENSA shows and any other attractions that were available in the district to come to Uruli camp. I secured one indifferent show of the concert party type that proved a disaster in more ways than one. By this time I was firmly left wing and wildly enthusiastic about the Beveridge Report, the prospect of the National Health Service and the welfare state, and the abolition of poverty. Nowadays I am slightly right wing but I am still of the opinion that we voted the best way in 1945 after the war in Europe was over. Anyway, it always seemed to me that the custom of placing all the officers in the front row of the theatre was a bit unfair, so I decided that for this ENSA offering we, the officers, would all occupy the third row. As a further egalitarian gesture, the cast would be entertained in the Sergeants' Mess afterwards, instead of the routine party with the officers.

Accordingly, I gave instructions to the sergeant in charge of the theatre to put my revolutionary seating plan into effect, and bemused troops were placed in the front row, leaving the third row vacant for the officers. Unfortunately I left the theatre to escort the colonel to the show, and while I was gone a sergeant-major, seeing the front row occupied by the rude soldiery, ordered them all out. In the meantime the third row had been quickly filled by opportunist squaddies who saw their chance to grab better seats. As a result, the boys who had been lording it in the front row found themselves standing at the back. By the time I returned with the colonel, something little short of a riot was in full swing. When the officers arrived and took up places in the front row it could only be described as an ugly scene. The colonel was incandescent. Sergeants and sergeant-majors stormed up and down, shouting until order was restored, whereupon the pianist played like mad and the entertainment proceeded with a very lively and not very sympathetic audience.

The next debacle occurred when the members of the ENSA cast discovered that they were being entertained in the Sergeants' Mess instead of being able to hobnob with the officers. Apparently they felt insulted. Perhaps the girls had hoped to entrap some rich chinless wonder. There were one or two chinless wonders numbered among us, but I don't think they were rich.

I discovered there was an organisation in Poona called Combined Services Entertainment, which was a services-based outfit. Rumour had it that they had under their wing a play called *While the Sun Shines*, which I vowed to get for my camp theatre, so off I went to Poona. The company was managed by a gangling 19-year-old youth called Robin Nash. I saw no reason why this young man shouldn't be in the army like the rest of us, so I invited him aboard my motorcycle and rode him to Uruli via every rut and pothole I could find. He proceeded single-handedly to construct the set for the show and, since the leading man and the understudy were laid low with 'Delhi belly', he took over the principal part. To say he wasn't a very good actor is perhaps an understatement, but he 'kept the curtain up', as we say in the profession. I played the part in repertory at Wolverhampton some years later and I wasn't very good either. I later found out that he had a rare bone disease which kept him out of the services, and through the years we became firm friends. He was a brilliant stage manager in *Wild Violets*, in which he also played my son, and we were fellow producers at the BBC, where he later became an incorruptible head of variety. He fought many battles for me when he was head of comedy and he paid a very touching and very moving tribute to me on *This Is Your Life*.

One of my duties as staff captain was to meet Jack Lawson, the new Labour government's war minister, who was arriving for an official visit. The poor man staggered off the train in a crumpled linen suit as if he'd spent the night in a washing machine. He was a Geordie and engagingly confided in us: 'They give me a mule to mind in the last war. This time they give me the lot.' He was a nice enough man but gave the impression that he was totally out of his depth as war minister and a poor successor to Anthony Eden.

We went diligently about our training for the invasion of Malaya, which was an operation that no one in their right mind was looking forward to. The Japs were expected to fight like demons every foot of the way down the peninsula, and then fight even harder in Japan. We did a certain amount of land training in which, as brigade intelligence officer, I stuck a lot of flags on to maps and made chinagraph lines where I thought the troops were dug in. The seaborne training was to come later. Unexpectedly, but to my intense delight, we heard on the radio that the atom bomb had been dropped at Hiroshima. Let there be no mistake about our attitude to this event. We were facing another couple of years of most intense fighting. The Japs were a cruel and ruthless enemy whose war record was atrocious. The bombs made us wild with delight and immense relief. Now there was every chance that we would all survive this long war.

My immediate superior was sent to Singapore to prepare for our arrival. The brigade major started to make out the order to move the brigade to Bombay, where we were all to board the aircraft carrier HMS *Colossus*. He soon became bogged down with starting lines and timings, the independent brigade being a pretty complex unit. Apart from three infantry battalions, we had a company of Royal Army Service Corps (RASC) trucks, a field bakery, a field ambulance and a battery of 25-pounders. He finally said, 'Oh, you do the damned thing, David,' so I moved the brigade to Bombay. I went with the brigadier in a luxurious staff car, arriving at the quayside in time to see a very long queue. This was caused by a 'jobsworth' military police sergeant who insisted on writing down the name and number of every soldier who went up the gangway. The captain of the *Colossus*, spotting this from the bridge, went on to the quayside. 'What are you doing?' he said to the sergeant. 'I'm taking the name and number of all the troops boarding the boat.' 'Whatever for?' asked the captain. 'In case the ship sinks,' replied the sergeant. 'Then I'll try to arrange that it doesn't sink – go away.' The sergeant put his clipboard under his arm and slunk away.

My immediate boss having been sent home to England on LIAP (Leave in Addition to Python) and being most unlikely to return, I was now acting brigade major, so I was given a cabin to myself which had belonged to the commander flying and was therefore, in naval terms, luxurious. In fact it was a windowless cupboard no bigger than a small loo, but it was all mine and I felt very important. We didn't carry any planes, so all our vehicles were parked on the flight deck, which cleared the decks below for all the troops. The captain insisted that his naval officers should be in charge of the whole operation, so we had absolutely nothing to do except lounge about and drink the navy's gin. I lay sleeping in the shade of our trucks for one afternoon and as a result became crippled with sunburn, which was a bit of a surprise. I was confined to bed in my cabin and my batman brought all my meals.

We arrived in Singapore and I could barely stagger down the gangway to meet the major who had commanded the advance party. 'You've got to take charge of 90,000 Japanese prisoners of war,' he told me. 'Do I have to count 'em?' I asked. We took up quarters across the causeway in Jahore Baru, housed in pleasant colonial villas. Japanese prisoners of war abounded as sweepers and servants. Every morning a venerable Japanese army officer named Colonel Naito, together with a colonel of the air force and a captain of the navy, paraded humbly before my desk to receive the day's orders. I was assisted by a brilliant Asian interpreter. The only time I found him at a loss was when I asked him to tell the Japs to 'take their bloody fingers out', which I understand did not readily translate into Japanese. My task was to evacuate about 400 Japs per day to an island called Rempang off the south coast of Singapore. To do this I had under my command a company of RASC trucks, a train and a ship. The Japs from the Southern Malayan Army under General Kinoshita were gathered 80 miles up country, where we had a couple of dozen Japanese-speaking British intelligence officers who interrogated them all individually to weed out any suspected of war crimes. Those considered doubtful were retained in the 'Black Camp' for further investigation and, if necessary, trial.

I also had charge of half a dozen arms dumps where captured rifles, machine-guns, automatics and samurai swords were stored under the guard of Jap soldiers because we didn't have enough troops to do the job. I quickly acquired for myself a wicked-looking Beretta automatic and a large Colt 45 just for the pleasure of possessing them. Singapore was struggling to get back to normal and goods were mysteriously appearing in the shops. The bar of the Raffles Hotel was open but the main hotel had been requisitioned by Earl Mountbatten, supreme allied commander in South-east Asia, as his headquarters.

We continued to evacuate four or five hundred Japs per day to the island, although the Chinese couldn't understand why we were carrying them in trucks along the same roads where they had forced the Australians to crawl on their hands and knees. Our leisure was spent reading and drinking a concoction called BMA (British Military Authority) Gin. This was a preparation hastily brewed up by the army to replace a lot of illegal liquor that had been mixed in the bath out of wood alcohol and aircraft cooling fluid which put a lot of unwary officers in hospital. I wouldn't be surprised if the illegal stuff tasted better.

Brigade Headquarters was then moved to Singapore, where we had a really luxurious house that used to belong to the wealthy Werne brothers, who were said to be the owners of an airline. I had a large air-conditioned suite consisting of a double bedroom, bathroom, dressing room and large balcony, and my batman lived the life of Riley because he was able to contract out his duties to four Jap prisoners for a packet of ten cigarettes.

To cap it all, my boss, Major Demetriade, was sent home to be demobbed, so I became Deputy Assistant Adjutant and Quartermaster General to 4th British Independent Brigade Group, with the rank of major at the ripe old age of 23. While on Singapore Island we managed to acquire four horses that had been used as pack animals for the previous four years. With much patience, we persuaded them to let us ride side by side. I mostly rode the brigadier's horse, which was quite a handsome beast when we got him back into condition. We fed the animals on unhusked rice, which they did quite well on as long as we didn't overwork them.

Mountbatten and Lord Kilearn, who was the cabinet special envoy and adviser to the forces out east, visited us in the mess and stayed to dinner, which was quite brave of them considering the standard of our cooking. The most remarkable thing about them both was a very camp, loose handshake, which I was told was adopted by all war heroes and politicians to prevent the occurrence of something akin to tennis elbow when they were being congratulated on their wartime achievements.

My duties consisted of processing a lot of brigade paperwork, such as confirming court martial proceedings. This I found rather easy, being a bit of a barrack-room lawyer when in the ranks. A minor crisis occurred when I had to tell the brigadier that, having evacuated about 70,000 Japs out of the believed total of 90,000, the other 20,000 seemed to be missing. The brig was remarkably calm about the whole affair and simply said, 'I shouldn't worry too much about it, David.'

It was discovered that General Kinoshita had not surrendered his sword, and he seemed inexplicably anxious to do so. In his position I would have kept quiet about the whole thing and carried my sword back to Japan, but he seemed to want a full ceremony. In league with the brigadier, I decided to thwart his ambition. It was my view that the Japanese had behaved quite appallingly throughout the war, and the idea of some honourable hand-over being staged was simply unacceptable. I arranged that he should surrender the sword to the brig in my office in the presence of myself, my staff captain and my chief clerk. He duly arrived with the interpreter and, somewhat put out by the poor attendance, proceeded with an elaborate explanation as to how the sword was fashioned and its antiquity. At the end of all this he handed the damned thing to the brigadier, who said, 'Thank you very much,' and we sent him back to his camp.

By this time evidently the brigadier was strangely impressed with my administrative abilities because he sent for me one day to tell me that there was a vacancy at Division HQ for the post of DAAG (deputy assistant adjutant-general) which carried the rank of lieutenant-colonel or, if I didn't fancy that, a post on the War Crimes Commission in Kuala Lumpur which carried the same promotion. I thought that with my limited experience I was hardly up to either of these posts. Besides, I wanted out of the army as quickly as possible and I thought that, if I were to take either of these posts, I would be bound to stay in at least another year. But by this time events took a different turn.

I had been receiving letters from Mother that caused me some concern. They were sprinkled with capital letters and heavily underlined, which is frequently a sign of schizophrenia. They were mainly concerned with the various methods by which Hugh Gough had purloined her (non-existent) fortune and was having her followed all over London by secret agents. I wrote to Peter about this and he persuaded her to see a psychiatrist. Together they said my presence was urgently needed to attend to matters and, if necessary, get her into a home. An order arrived from the War Office that I should be returned to the UK by air. A few days later I boarded an Imperial Airways flying boat on a four and a half-day journey to Poole, Dorset, with a ticket priced at £195.

10
Back on the Home Front

I was roused well before sunrise to rendezvous at Singapore docks, where a launch took us to the Imperial Airways Sunderland flying boat. An air vice marshal who was to be my companion on the flight informed me that we had to take off at the crack of dawn because the air was thicker at that time and gave better lift to the four noisy engines that propelled us across the choppy waters of the harbour. The seating arrangements were quite different from present-day air travel and much more luxurious. The 16 of us sat at tables for four, as in a first-class railway dining-car. I had the air vice marshal next to me who, when I felt sick, obligingly provided me with a travel pill – something few people had heard of at that time. Opposite sat a couple of senior officers, and on the other side of the gangway sat four more. Unfortunately alcohol and refreshments were not served on the flight, and conversation above the noise of the four propeller engines was only possible at shouting level. After about six hours, when we were all getting a bit peckish and thirsty, Penang appeared below us, and with a spectacular display of spray we landed for lunch. Having consumed a light and gentlemanly meal, we took off again for the next leg of the flight, after which, as night fell, we landed at Rangoon. Here we were met by launch and decrepit bus, which lumbered us to an ancient hotel where we were fed, watered and bedded for the night. The second day of the journey saw us taking off with a packed sandwich lunch on an all-day flight over India to Karachi, where we spent another night in a similar hotel.

After a deafening pre-dawn dash through the spray we were in the air again the next day and on our leisurely way to lunch in oven-hot Bahrain in the Persian Gulf. We then flew at a painfully slow speed over the Arabian Desert, which seemed to me to be a risky business for a flying boat without landing gear, but we were rewarded with a beautiful view of the Pyramids and the Sphinx as we landed on the Nile just as a blood-red sun was setting. We were treated to a very good dinner on a barge, but after a decent interval we took off again for a night flight to Sicily. To my surprise, shortly after we were airborne a steward tapped me on the shoulder and said, 'Major – your bunk is ready.' I was conducted up a staircase to a bunk-bed, whereupon I put on my pyjamas and slept soundly until I was roused – without morning tea I should add – for our landing at Brindisi followed by breakfast. The last leg of our journey took us to Poole Harbour, where I was able to spot the bungalow that I was born in before the pilot made a sedate landing. This seemed a fitting round off to the eventful first 23 years of my life, although I still had the best part of a year to spend in the army before I came up for demob.

Following a benign meeting with a very friendly customs officer, who treated me as a returning hero, I hopped on a train at Bournemouth Central. By evening I was safely lodged in a comfortable house at the Vale of Health in Hampstead with my brother Peter, his wife Sally and his son Michael, and attended once more by Olive, the old and faithful family nanny and friend.

I went to Harley Street to visit the psychiatrist who had attended Mother. He explained her condition as well as he could and said there would be no difficulty in certifying her and getting her into a home of some sort. I then went to see Mother, who was living in a tiny flat in Albany Street. She was surrounded by her possessions, which were piled ceiling high, but on the whole seemed sane enough to me, apart from being convinced that Hugh Gough was arranging agents to follow her night and day. I pointed out that this sort of surveillance would cost about £100,000 per year, to which her reply was: 'I know, and where's the money coming from?' Apart from the fact that she was now adding Olive and me to the list of those misappropriating her fortune, she seemed pretty harmless. In her more normal moments she was amusing, good company as usual and a long way from being certifiable, so I refused to take any further action.

After a short leave I received orders to report to the Dorset Regiment's depot in Dorchester. Knowing about army depots from my stay at Woolwich, I was keen to avoid this posting to a place where life was guaranteed to be – in army terms – 'regimental'. I remembered seeing a general order that returning staff officers should report themselves to the adjutant-general's department at the War Office in London, so I dropped them a line telling them that I was back. I got a reply telling me to report for an interview with Lieutenant-Colonel Nangle at MO12 at the War Office in Whitehall. This sounded a bit like MI5 and distinctly exciting, so I duly toddled along. Nangle had a small, old-fashioned and rather dusty office on the first floor. He was an academic-looking officer of considerable intelligence, but not unfriendly. I explained to him that my experience was limited to the adjutant and quartermaster branches, but I added that I was quick to learn and didn't have to be told anything a second time. He seemed to accept this and took me on there and then.

I accordingly reported for duty at the War Office and was shown into an equally dusty room that contained four very large tables covered to the point of invisibility by files, round which sat about five officers, including a Major Metcalfe and a Captain Macnabb. We were jointly responsible for all operations east of Suez, including Burma, Malaya and Indo-China. Having just returned from Malaya I was regarded as something of an expert, which was barely the case, but at least I had a bit of local knowledge. Opposite me sat a worried young captain who dealt with India, including a plan for the hurried evacuation of all British troops in the event of serious trouble. This was contained in a secret document, of which he was the sole custodian, called – appropriately – 'Operation Madhouse'. We were never allowed to see Operation Madhouse, but it is worth noting that the hand-over and partition of India were not plans of which we were aware at the time.

I proceeded to lead the life of a civil servant, although still in uniform. I lived at home in Hampstead, and travelled to the War Office by tube every morning. I took lunch at a local pub and returned home every evening – usually to one of the famous Hampstead Widows' pubs. These five pubs were run by the fearsome widows of the original licensees, who had mostly departed this life owing to overindulgence in their produce. Beer wasn't rationed but was in very short supply. The procedure was that you had to be a regular and it was the custom to knock on the door of the chosen pub, which would be opened an inch or two. If you were recognised, the proprietor would look to see if anybody else was about; if it was 'all clear' you would be beckoned inside.

The War Office was distinctly civilised. Our main activity was to brief the director of military operations and the chief of the general staff (General Alanbrooke) for chiefs of staff and cabinet meetings. This meant that we had to see minutes of the relevant meetings. In between times my colleagues did *The Times* crossword – my contribution was minimal, I'm afraid – and when they got stuck they would ring up the Joint Intelligence Committee. 'Have you got 18 across?' they would ask.

'We'll ring you back,' was the usual reply, and five minutes later they would phone with the answer. I once inadvertently went to the wrong lavatory to spend a penny. To my alarm I was joined at the next Thomas Crapper piece of porcelain by Alanbrooke. Having fulfilled the purpose for which he came, he did up his flies and said, 'Cor! That's better' – and that concluded my encounter with a great and legendary chief of staff. He was later replaced by Field Marshal Montgomery, but sadly I never spent a penny with him.

The most exciting thing about working at the War Office was from time to time being the overnight duty officer. Serious-faced messengers would arrive at all hours of the night with the traditional red boxes that I, having the keys, would open. They usually contained one quite unimportant signal, which I would place in someone's in-tray. I also had access to all the files and whiled away many a midnight hour browsing through fascinating items on germ warfare and new lethal gases and the like.

Being in London, I was able to set about readying myself for entry into show business. I started to take singing lessons with Gwynne Davies, who was still pushing pianos about with his stomach. He was married to a red-headed lady who was something of a model for Mrs Mainwaring because, although she was of normal size, she remained permanently upstairs in her room and I don't believe I saw her more than a couple of times in two years. I took private dancing lessons with Max Rivers. Max was the choreographer for Mother and Father in 1926. He had developed into a rather seedy-looking character who owned Max's Rehearsal Rooms in Windmill Street. He never removed either his battered trilby hat from his head or his half-smoked roll-up cigarette from his lips, but he could tap-dance like fury and he was exceedingly cheap.

Another major character in my training was a semi-inebriated journalist called Eric Barker. Eric had a column in *The Evening News* under the pseudonym of 'The Stroller' and was noted for having the front of his suit jacket covered in cigar ash and liberally spread with the gravy from several previous meals. He had been a slavish admirer of Mother in her earlier years but had developed into a very boring if kindly regarded joke who was liable to turn up every week at our house in Hampstead for Sunday lunch. His great plus as far as I was concerned was the fact that he was given two excellent seats at every first night in the West End. Provided I escorted him drunk and burbling (usually) or sober and burbling (seldom), I was able to be present at the premieres of one of the most glittering seasons in theatre history, for which reason I shall always be grateful to him. I saw the first night of *Oklahoma!* when Howard Keel with his huge physique and great baritone voice leapt over that picket fence and, had I realised it at the time, rang the death knell of my musical comedy career. I saw the first night of *Annie Get Your Gun* and was present when Emile Littler hung a star on the dressing-room door of Dolores Gray in accordance with the lyric of 'There's No Business Like Show Business'. I saw Ralph Richardson and Alec Guinness in *An Inspector Calls*, and later played the Guinness part in the same play at the Grand Theatre, Wolverhampton, and was incredibly bad in it. I saw Richardson and Laurence Olivier in *The Alchemist*, Richard Burton and John Gielgud in *The Lady's Not for Burning*, Richardson and Margaret Leighton in *Cyrano de Bergerac* and the great Harcourt Williams in *You Never Can Tell*. Night after night I was present at great premieres. I was very lucky and I knew it.

London night life prospered through institutions called bottle clubs. I visited one called the Orchid Room, which was a basement room of Stygian darkness where all the waiters carried pencil torches. You bought a bottle of Scotch for £5 and when you had drunk your fill it was marked on the side and saved for your next visit. I presume the place was frequented by ladies of the night, but you certainly couldn't see them.

Peter and I spent our weekends cultivating the garden of a house belonging to the Guinness family right at the top of Hampstead Heath by The Spaniard's Inn. We grew a very large amount of vegetables, including 1½ tons of tomatoes. Our friends used to arrive on Sunday morning and pick their own veg for knock-down prices.

As end of my service approached, I went to see Felix de Wolfe, who had been my agent four and a half years previously. He sent me to see his new partner, Colonel Richard Stone, who had an office in Eaton Square and, in an abrupt manner, took me on, probably because I was in uniform. I never left him. He became a lifelong friend and I am with his office to this day.

I went to see Brinkman's, who had been my father's tailors, and ordered a very dark blue overcoat and two suits, anticipating that I would need some prosperous-looking new clothes to attend auditions.

I found that the War Office was a first-class place to view the Lord Mayor's Show, but apart from that my service drew peacefully to a close. On 17 January 1947, having taken a train to a nearby depot to receive my demob suit, mackintosh, hat and shoes, I was duly discharged with a letter from the adjutant-general's department thanking me for my invaluable services during the emergency. So much for four and a half years of my life! To be fair, however, and taking a longer view, nobody has profited more from their wartime service, except possibly the Krupp family, who owned munitions factories. Those years gave me *Dad's Army*, *It Ain't Half Hot Mum* and *'Allo 'Allo*, so I mustn't be ungrateful.

I have long held the theory that in this life one thing leads to another, and this very profound philosophy kicked into action in an unexpected way to speed me on my journey into show business. I was by now taking singing lessons with Gwynne Davies three times a week. The Government, God bless 'em, were paying the fees and I was getting a small maintenance grant. Gwynne persuaded me to team up with a sweet girl pupil of his to do a sketch and a song for a concert at the London Welsh Association one Sunday night. I wrote a five-minute 'thing' that we rehearsed and duly performed. It was received politely and one could almost say with some enthusiasm. In the audience for no known reason was Winifred Shotter, who had been the Ingénue in countless Aldwych farces with Ralph Lynn and Tom Walls in the 1930s. It so happened that she had been asked to appear in the try-out of a comedy by Lawrence O'Madden at the 'Q' Theatre in Hammersmith called *The Reluctant Bachelor*. There was a good comedy part going as a young lieutenant and, on her recommendation, I got it. The 'Q' Theatre was a great post-war institution. It was run by Herbert and Beaty de Leon – mostly by Beaty – and the policy was weekly rep with a liberal sprinkling of new plays because it was near enough to London for all the West End theatre managements to be persuaded to come along.

Herbert de Leon was a well-known theatrical agent with a surprisingly good stable of clients including, for instance, Greer Garson. The resident director was a tall, charming, helpful – and quietly gay – character named Geoffrey Wardwell, who was also a good friend of my brother Peter. I got all the laughs going in *The Reluctant Bachelor* and as a result Geoffrey cast me in an Ivor Novello play called *We Proudly Present*, which was based on the early career of Tony Forward, who became Dirk Bogarde's lifelong companion. It traced his early years in management, when Tony and his then partner took over a derelict theatre.

Beaty always attended the Monday afternoon dress rehearsal. She would sit at the side of the stalls in the third row and consume several ice creams. Provided everyone knew their parts she considered they were earning their £10 salary, so she rarely made any comment.

The part of Tony Forward was played by a young Rank starlet whose name escapes me and, since he later escaped from show business altogether, he can remain anonymous. It was my earnest hope that the Rank Organisation would come to see their young artist and would then be struck by my great talent. They came – and they weren't. Also in the company was a luscious young girl whose first name was Lalage. She insisted that the correct pronunciation of this was 'Lalagay'. I asked her if she kept her car in the 'garagay' and she wouldn't speak to me for the rest of the week.

However, Geoffrey Wardwell must have had some confidence in my ability because he cast me as Mortimer in *Arsenic and Old Lace*, which was the part played by Cary Grant in the film. It is a major role and I was scared stiff. On the first rehearsal I tried really hard to be funny, only to hear Geoffrey's voice from the darkened stalls saying, 'David – don't cod it – be real.' Just that one phrase was a lesson in comedy playing that should last a lifetime, and if I didn't learn it then, I certainly learnt it later. The one thing fatal to any comedy scene is for an actor to try to be funny or even to think he is being funny. Years later I used to make a speech to actors just before the first performance of a TV comedy: 'Don't try to help the comedy. Stay right inside your character. If the laughs don't come, it is our [the writers'] fault.'

I heard that a new musical was being planned for the Saville Theatre – now the ABC Cinema – Shaftesbury Avenue. It was to be called *Belinda Fair,* with book and elegant lyrics by Eric Maschwitz, who wrote 'These Foolish Things', and with tuneful but unmemorable music by Jack Strachey. It was financed by a rich and very ancient gentleman from Bolton named John Buckley, who was a dead ringer for Young Mr Grace in *Are You Being Served?* It starred Adele Dixon, a very glamorous star of many musicals, whose face wore a permanent glassy smile because she couldn't see more that a couple of feet in front of her and didn't wish to be thought unfriendly by people she knew but couldn't recognise.

The 'character comic' was the delightful but unfunny Jerry Verno. I auditioned and got the very small, one-grunt part of a half-wit gaoler

– and the task of understudying Jerry. I knew that Jerry would never be off, even if he had to play the part prone on a stretcher, so there was absolutely no hope of ever appearing for him, but it was work and in the West End, so I was glad to be part of the production.

The show was directed by Charles Goldner, who was an excellent actor with some experience as a director. Being under-employed in the show, I glued myself to Charles, carrying his case and script, taking notes for him and generally trying to make myself indispensable. He was a talented director, but he made the mistake of demonstrating to the actors how to play every part. This he did with enormous skill and humour but I saw the whole cast lose all confidence in themselves because they thought they could never play their part as well as Charles. He was very firmly of the opinion that the personality and emotion of an actor was almost entirely to be seen in the eyes, and I think this is particularly true in television and film. I hate close-ups where only one eye is seen, as an actor cannot register his feelings in profile. These were lessons well learnt.

I also hovered around Eric Maschwitz, for whom I had enormous admiration. He had for many years been the head of variety at the BBC, as well as the author of a whole bunch of musicals, and was a great figure and achiever in the world of the musical. If there was anything to be learnt from these two experts, I was going to learn it.

Buried in the cast was Stella Moray, who had a gorgeous, warm singing voice. She was going around with Clive Dunn, whom I met for the first time. He was a leading figure at the Player's Theatre under the arches of Charing Cross Station. His tour de force there was a number called 'The Ghost of Benjamin Binns'. For this he wore a large white ghost sheet, under which he concealed extending arms that got longer and longer with each gesture, until each one measured six feet. It was always a riot.

I relished every moment of rehearsals, technical run-throughs and band calls. The show was beautifully dressed, regardless of expense, but unfortunately *Oklahoma!* had happened and the critics gave our effort a good panning. We teetered on for a few weeks at the Saville, and when our figures dropped below the 'break' figure we transferred to the Strand Theatre, but it was to no avail. In the closing days it was attended mainly by nurses from the surrounding hospitals. When the curtain went up, pronounced scents of operating theatre disinfectant came wafting across the footlights.

However, all was not lost as far as I was concerned. A tour was planned, with Leo Franklyn playing the Jerry Verno part. Leo had a lot of clout with the management and refused to play the part as written. I knew the show backwards and seized the opportunity to write some pretty outrageous comedy scenes that Leo forced into the show. To my surprise, Eric Maschwitz gallantly allotted me half of 1 per cent on the gross box-office takings from his share of the royalties, which was a very kind gesture to a presumptuous beginner who had frankly driven a truck through the integrity of his piece. The tour ran for several months and proved a nice little earner.

Early in 1948 a production of *She Stoops to Conquer* was planned for the Library Theatre, Manchester, and I landed the part of Tony Lumpkin. It was an excellent production and the part suited me well. We were attended by a number of schools that season, the play being on the School Certificate curriculum. At one point there was an unavoidable break in the action to accommodate a scene change. I volunteered to fill the space with a three-minute bit of business with a snuff box. It was a joy to see a whole row of schoolgirls turning the pages of their textbooks trying to find my interventions in the original.

Not much was happening for Peter either in films or the theatre, so he took himself, plus wife Sally and son Michael, up to Wolverhampton Rep for a season. There was a vacancy for a 'character juvenile', so it was suggested that I join as well. The rep was housed in the Grand Theatre, which has a beautiful Victorian auditorium seating nine hundred or so and is decorated like a piece of blue Wedgwood china. It was doing very good business and was run by Derek Salberg and his cousin Basil Thomas. They also had a company at the Alexandra Theatre, Birmingham, which had a policy of two-weekly rep. The standard at both these theatres was of the very highest.

Wolverhampton Rep was quite a social organisation, but the key to it all was cricket. The whole company was expected to turn out at weekends for the current match. Derek fancied himself as a batsman, as did Basil. Other stars of the company and the cricket field were Peter Vaughan, who later had a most distinguished career acting in television, Anthony Sager, who was an excellent jobbing actor whom I used in many television shows at the BBC, and, of course, my brother Peter, who earned his salt both as a leading man and an opening bat. After a few short practices at the nets and a disastrous appearance on the pitch itself, when I scored a duck and dropped several catches off balls bowled by Derek, I was consigned to the pavilion, where I could keep the score, being as usual unable to add to it.

It was my first encounter with repertory, and I found it a marvellous and frightening experience and exceedingly hard work. Learning the lines was always a slow process as far as I was concerned. Actors employ all sort of devices to help them to get away with certain scenes in which they are not too sure of the text. In *An Inspector Calls*, in which I was truly terrible in the Alec Guiness part, the actor playing the father thought he had arranged a wonderful wheeze. The piece opens with the prosperous family seated round a beautifully set dinner table. This actor had most of the talking to do, so he had copied his part on to menu cards which were propped up against various candlesticks, pepper pots, napkins and salt cellars. Unfortunately someone had left the large scene dock doors open, so as soon as the curtain went up on Act One a huge draft was created and his menu cards fluttered prettily towards the first three rows of the stalls. The only line he remembered was 'I'm speaking as a hard-headed man of business'. Thereafter he ad libbed various lines that J.B. Priestley would neither have recognised nor appreciated, liberally sprinkled with desperate insertions of 'I'm speaking as a hard-headed man of business'.

The next week I played a young and eager sailor in *No Medals* and this time I was the one who was not too sure of the text. I remember sitting on the sofa in the first act opposite the gorgeous leading lady who, regrettably, was enamoured of Peter Vaughan. Going completely blank, I hissed to her, 'What do I say next?' Understandably she hissed back, 'How the hell do I know?'

I next played in *Thark* and in this I got a lot of laughs. I used a trick I saw employed by Sidney Howard in *Dear Love*. He would brace his thighs and feet in a manner that enabled him to lean sideways at about a ten-degree angle, which looks ridiculous and seemed to be appropriate for the eccentric character that I was playing.

After that, there were no more parts for me for a number of weeks, so I was packed off to Hereford to the County Theatre, which was run by Derek's brother Reggie.

11
Sex, Musicals and Ann

Those of you who have been paying attention may well have remarked on the general lack of 'girls of the opposite sex', as I was wont to put it in *'Allo 'Allo*. The reasons for this omission are twofold or, to be more accurate, one and a half fold. In the first place I was most painfully shy of women, and for this I suppose it would be convenient to blame a public school education of the monastic variety. I don't personally blame that system. I think I was just painfully shy. The half reason is perhaps that because I was in North Africa, India and Malaya for some of my formative years there was a lack of girls and therefore a lack of opportunity, but that is a bit of a half-baked excuse.

When I got into rep in Wolverhampton I thought it was high time I sorted the matter out. I joined Peter in his digs in a row of dull, early Victorian terraced houses in a dreary alley called Drummond Street. I had a small back room and we shared a sitting room with a cosy coal fire. One of the assistant stage managers in the company was a girl I will call Doreen. She was about 19, dark-haired, bright and sexy. We hit it off from day one. During intense canoodling in front of the fire one night, while ostensibly hearing me rehearse my lines, she made it clear that she too was in a state of serious virginity and didn't wish to remain that way a day longer than was necessary. I therefore set about preparations to sort us both out. Firstly, I moved into her digs, which were situated in a large Victorian villa and shared with one or two other members of the company and a few itinerant civilians who were not in show business. Secondly, I set about securing some sort of contraceptive device.

Only two methods were available as far as I knew. The first was known as a foaming pessary. The recommended method of using this was to dip the tablet into a glass of water and to insert it without delay just before the magic moment. This seemed to me unromantic to say the least, and the prospect of the whole operation being accompanied by a welter of fizzing foam attracted me not a bit.

The second method was the time-honoured use of what was in those days known as a 'French letter'. These were not available at Boots, Timothy White's or any respectable chemist. To obtain them you had to visit an establishment known as a 'surgical store', similar to the place where I had been fitted for a truss all those years ago. These were usually located in some back street and the shop window would be decorated with trusses of various types, support belts and numerous red rubber tubes with bulbs and phallic-shaped things, the use of which was not even hinted at. Having passed by two or three times to see that the coast was clear, I turned up the collar of my demob mac and slid inside. The door had an unusually loud bell which resulted in a thin man in a grey factory overall coat appearing from a back room – presumably where he fitted the trusses.

'Durex,' I mumbled. 'I beg your pardon?' he replied. 'Durex,' I repeated more loudly. 'Of course, sir – how many?' After a quick think I tentatively said, 'Three.' 'Three, sir,' he said, diving under the counter. 'No,' I said. 'Make it six.' I didn't want to have to come back and go through all this palaver again. He retrieved his two packets and started to wrap busily. 'Will you be requiring any lubricant, Mr Croft?' So much for my anonymity. The man was a regular rep theatre-goer and, to my discomfort, he proceeded to discuss the recent productions. He was a particular fan of my brother's.

That evening I found a note from Doreen under my pillow that simply said, 'Ce soir?' With my usual linguistic expertise I left a note under her pillow which said 'Oui!' When the house was asleep she padded up to my attic and crept into my bed, and she was warm and clinging and cuddly, and the deed was deliciously done. This is probably why I didn't know my part too well in *No Medals*.

Hereford, in contrast to Wolverhampton, was a noble little township with its spectacular cathedral and the beautiful River Wye. The scene designer used to anchor his scenery flats to the river bed, leaving them for the rushing water to clean away the old paint. The County Theatre was a simple old place, built for I know not what purpose – maybe it was an early cinema – and seating about four hundred and fifty. It had a small stage, one dressing room for the boys and another for the girls. There was no scene dock, so the flats had to be designed and painted on their side in the low space under the stage. It had a loyal audience who would half fill it most of the week and just about fill it on Saturday.

Arthur Lowe was in the company just after the war because his wife Joan was at that time a bit of a local star and had used her influence to get him a job. Even in those days he had the extraordinary ability to dry up the other actors by means of a wicked glint in his eyes, which the audience couldn't see, but which reduced anyone playing a scene with him to helpless giggles. It was a talent he retained right through the *Dad's Army* days. He lived in the same digs that I took a year later. They were run by a Mrs Alekejar, who acquired that unusual name by marrying an African gentleman, which was a bold step to take in the late 1940s when living in a cathedral town. He had left her some years previously, so neither Arthur nor I ever met him. Mrs Alekejar's place was situated in a large Georgian terraced house close to the river and five minutes' walk from the theatre. She was a fair cook, which was important because it was the custom to live 'all in', for which she charged about £3. 10s. per week. However, once again I had the attic, which wasn't too convenient because Mrs A frowned on female company and, after a week or two, I was having a fling with a girl whom I will call Lorraine. She was on the theatre staff and was loving and great fun, but she wasn't notably small and as a result made the stairs creek.

The company was directed by a cadaverous 65-year-old actor of the old school called Vernon Fortescue. He knew his trade and was quick to set the moves of the plays. He was tolerant of the experienced actors and helpful to the younger ones such as me. The routine was to set the whole play on Tuesday, rehearse Act One on Wednesday, Act Two on Thursday, Act Three on Friday, run the whole play on Saturday and have a dress rehearsal on Monday before the opening that evening. There was no time to hang about. A big part in a four-hander entailed a mountain of learning.

I reckon that when I first started I was giving a passable performance by Thursday, and after a few weeks I got to be tolerable by about Tuesday. We did the usual rep plays by Agatha Christie and J.B. Priestley, emptied the theatre with Shaw's *Arms and the Man*, and filled it again with Aldwych farces. We also performed one of the earliest stagings of *The Reluctant Heroes* by Colin Morris, which became the play that pioneered Brian Rix's long stay at the Whitehall.

Being fed up with climbing attic stairs, I deserted Mrs Alekejar and settled myself in a pub called The Seven Stars, where I had a first-floor room and a nice little sitting-room all for the same £3. 10s. Since I was getting £9 per week I could send a pound or two to Mother, beer being only 3d a half-pint.

The pub was owned by a delightful homely couple, and I was looked after by a simple middle-aged lady who absolutely refused to go to bed until she had given me a delicious hot supper. The ability to have a pint after hours upon returning to the pub was a particular joy. To make my life complete, the new young assistant stage manager in the person of Monica Grey came to occupy the front bedroom. She was 19, wildly enthusiastic and enormous fun. In no time at all we fell in love and became lovers, and the whole world felt very good. Our joy was short-lived, however, because her formidable mother came to see how her daughter was making out and, on realising that she was sharing digs and probably a lot of other things in a pub with a penniless young actor, moved her into the posh Green Dragon Hotel, where she thought she would be safe. Mother was right. Between the night porter, the day manager and the ever-alert staff, the furtherance of our romance had to be confined to the seldom dry banks of the River Wye.

A few weeks before Christmas the season in Hereford came to an end. Wolverhampton Rep always staged a successful pantomime season, employing mostly the rep company, which ran for a couple of months. During the run, Peter landed a screen test, so I deputised for him in the panto for a couple of performances so he could go to London to do the test. I played the part of a jocular Friar Tuck, a jolly 'Ho, ho, hoing' Father Christmas and also the handsome and serious King Richard, who returned from the wars to oust the wicked Sheriff of Nottingham. Peter was a fair three to four inches taller than I was. This was unimportant in the cases of jocular Friar Tuck and jolly Father Christmas, but it was catastrophic in the case of the serious King Richard. The chain mail, which in the interests of economy had been fashioned out of silver-painted floorcloths, could not be hitched up sufficiently to clear the floor, so King Richard glided on as if on wheels, without visible feet and with chain mail sleeves that reached well past his hands. This resulted in the Sheriff of Nottingham being consigned to life imprisonment in the castle dungeon while convulsed with mirth, and Robin Hood and his merry men – not surprisingly without Friar Tuck – collapsing with ill-suppressed giggles. Nevertheless, Maid Marion married her Robin Hood overseen by the benign King Richard who, on descending the castle stairs, was forced to gather up his chain mail skirt like some shy debutante making her entrance at Queen Charlotte's Ball.

109

The best part of a year in rep was fabulous experience and gave me the confidence of knowing that I could play any part I was suitable for. However, I was keen to return to my first love, which was the musical. I auditioned for the juvenile lead in a television musical version of *Derby Day*, which was to be directed by Desmond Davies. He gave me the part, but the show was never actually produced. Desmond Davies was a brilliant pioneer of TV production and wrote the definitive book on the craft. Years later I won his award for Outstanding Creative Contribution to Television, which was presented to me by Arthur Lowe at the London Hippodrome, where I had spent the first weeks of my life in Mother's dressing room.

Prince Littler was planning a revival of *Wild Violets* with music by Robert Stoltz. Richard Stone sent me along to Drury Lane to audition for Frank Marshall, who was Littler's general manager and had been entrusted with directing and staging the production. The audition worked and I got the job. The salary was £15 per week, which wasn't bad at that time. All Littler's resources and a lot of money were thrown into the show, which was aimed towards filling the Stoll Theatre in Kingsway – a bit of a white elephant built as an opera house by Oscar Hammerstein II.

We rehearsed in the huge rehearsal room at Drury Lane and we were a mostly young cast assembled by Frank Marshall. There were parts for three boys. For one of them he cast Ian Carmichael, who was at the outset of his very successful career and was also a favourite client of Richard Stone's. I was cast as Eric, and the other part – the lead – was played by Allen Christie. There was a large chorus of singers and dancers. Most of the girl dancers were lovely, talented and from South Africa, and most of the male chorus were, as was usual, gay.

We opened at the Hippodrome, Bristol. Because of the size of the production we normally opened on Tuesday and played for two weeks. Robin Nash, my one-time pillion passenger at Poona, was the stage manager and, with that strange laconic efficiency for which he later became notable, got the enormous show to work. It arrived loaded into 15 large lorries and included a 30-foot revolving stage. One enormous truck contained the two-storey front of the Swiss finishing school for girls, which had a long balcony that trundled forward and then went round on the revolve to reveal the girls' dormitories. Other bits and pieces came in and out and up and down to make the whole thing fit together. The dress rehearsal went on until four in the morning and continued next day until the curtain went up at 7.30.

Bristol was followed by two weeks in Newcastle at the Theatre Royal. By this time Ian Carmichael and I had established a firm friendship, so we decided to share digs. In fact we shared a room in a chillingly cold house in the Jesmond Road. Our sitting room was warmed by a not very efficient gas fire. We were forbidden to turn this up beyond the point where four burners were lit. As soon as the landlady left the room I turned up the other four burners, and Ian and I crouched over the heat and endeavoured to read our books. A few hours later a furious landlady burst into the room. 'I thought so!' she said. 'Who turned on the other burners?' 'I did,' I confessed. 'Well, you've ruined my Christmas puddings!' The landlady's half of this dialogue was conducted in the broad Geordie accent that I find impossible to impersonate, let alone write down. She later confided in Ian: 'That Mr Croft is a sour-faced gentleman – as soon as I clapped eyes on him I knew I should never have had him in the place.'

We were then booked in for a five-week season at the delightful old Lyceum in Edinburgh. All the theatrical digs were full and I was lucky to be able to throw in my lot with Ian, his wife Pym, their enchanting three-year-old daughter Lee and their new baby Sally. Stella Moray made up the party and we all stayed and had a magnificent Christmas with Mrs Carruthers, who was one of the great theatrical landladies.

Wild Violets finally transferred to the Stoll Theatre, Kingsway. It was a beautiful auditorium with the customary row of boxes round the dress circle level and a huge stage. On the first day, just before we started rehearsal, Ian Carmichael encountered Stella Moray standing quietly at the side of the stage. 'What are you up to?' he said. 'Waiting for a number two bus to take me out to the middle,' was the answer.

The show went well enough on the first night, but the critics, having tasted some really great Broadway musicals, were very tepid about a 1930s' British/Continental revival. One of the notices said: 'The dances could not have been more pedestrian had they been taken directly from the Highway Code.' We struggled on for 16 weeks but eventually, with the scent of formaldehyde growing ever stronger as each curtain rose, our London run drew peacefully to a close.

So too did my affair with Monica. By this time she was in repertory with Brian Rix in Bridlington. I journeyed up there on a couple of

Sundays during the Stoll run, and struggled back to London on the Monday in time for the show, but the difficulties of meeting coupled with the firm opposition of her family proved too much for us. Our affair petered out, but we saw each other and remained friends until, sadly, she recently died.

A further tour of *Wild Violets* was planned, but not until later in the year. I was about to be out of work but Richard Stone offered me a job helping Ian Carmichael to stage a concert party consisting of two shows on Clacton Pier. This was to be my first introduction to a form of entertainment that continued to be part of my life at various levels, from the end-of-the-pier-type shows to reviews at the London Palladium, and that kept me busy until several years after I became a producer at the BBC. This time I was grandly called 'The Production Manager', but it is worth noting that my budget for props for the two shows was £6. Richard Stone didn't throw his money about.

In sunny Clacton-on-Sea Ian and I once again shared a room, and this was to be the start of a show business learning curve from which I benefited for the rest of my career. (I don't quite know why learning is curved, but I suppose it is something to do with Einstein's law of relativity – time/space is alleged to be curved, so why not learning too?)

There were two shows on Clacton Pier. The big one starred Tony Hancock in an all-dancing, all-singing extravaganza produced by Frank Adey at 'this' end of the pier. The other was a very small one produced by Richard Stone and was to star a complete beginner of a comic in a tiny nine-handed concert party at 'that' end – the far end – of the pier. The said beginner was Terry Scott. He had his 'horrid schoolboy' act and virtually no other material, but he was a funny man who could get laughs in even the feeblest of sketches. He was so new to the business that he asked if he could have a couple of seats for his landlady 'at cost'.

This was my first introduction to the 'cross-over' routines that followed the opening chorus and featured the comic, his feed and anyone else who wasn't occupied in getting ready to be in the next item on the programme. They consisted of quick ten-second gags based on such gems as 'Two farmers meeting in the street', in which the comic and feed would greet each other with bucolic noises such as 'Ooh-aah' and then 'milk' hands by using each other's fingers as udders. The next couple would follow on after the announcement 'Two turnstile attendants meeting in the street', whereupon they would link arms and turn a couple of circles. Next would be 'Winston Churchill meeting Mr Attlee in the street', and the comic sporting a cigar would meet the feed who was wearing an Attlee moustache and would hold up two fingers and blow a loud raspberry. These and a whole bevy of similar wheezes would get the laughs going and warm the show up.

I used these and similar gags in countless summer shows at seaside resorts and Butlins camps, and even had the temerity to include them in a West End revue at the St Martin's Theatre under the guise of a number called 'Corn Is Coming Back'. It closed the first half and was a resounding success.

After we returned to London I landed my first role in a television show. TV was a fairly 'Heath Robinson' affair and was very much the poor relation of radio and films. The productions were staged in the BBC's first TV studios at Alexandra Palace. 'Ally Pally' had two studios, both of which were small while at the same time being long and rather narrow. Each was equipped with three black and white cameras. Only one of these could be moved while operating. The other two were mounted on crude wooden tripods with tiny wheels stuck on the ends of the legs. The movable camera was screwed perilously on to a tricycle affair consisting of three pram wheels and strewn with bits of bicycle chain, which could be shoved in or out or even moved sideways by one of the careful white-coated operators. Each camera had only one lens, and the viewfinders were added on to the side as an afterthought. They showed an upside-down image on a piece of ground glass, like the old quarter-plate cameras used by early stills photographers who would hide under a black shroud. If the camera panned left, the upside-down image also moved to the left, and if tilted upwards, the picture also went upwards instead of downwards, which was very confusing. With only one lens, if the director wanted a close-up, the operator had to track in and, following that, had to track out again to resume normal shooting.

The floor manager held a bell push at the end of a long wire. If an actor 'dried', he was expected to press the button, which blanked out the sound. This would allow him to give a prompt, whereupon he would release the button so that normal transmission could resume. Actors – very experienced actors – dried on me during two of the first three shows I ever performed in. All actors had experience of forgetting their lines during a performance, but for some reason doing it on television was quite different. A look of stark panic spread over the actor's face and you could see that he was silently saying, 'God – please let the studio floor open and swallow me up.' I suppose that a maximum of 100,000 viewers could be watching at that time, but somehow the effect on the performer was total paralysis.

Richard Stone had fixed the principal comic for this performance and, with great presence of mind, fixed for me to write the script. This, considering that I had never even seen television, let alone been in a studio where it was produced, was quite an achievement. I was completely fascinated by the whole process and, happily, it all went well.

It was at about this time that Stella Moray and Ian Carmichael introduced me to Cyril Ornadel, my first writing partner and my lifelong friend. Cyril was conducting the orchestra at the Adelphi Theatre for Jack Hylton in a review starring Tony Hancock. He was two years younger than me, a great accompanying conductor and a positive musical dynamo. He was living with his parents in a large and luxurious flat in Berkley Court in Baker Street, and we straight away commandeered his father's baby grand piano and started writing a musical for television called *Cora*.

I heard that James Shirvell was about to put out a tour of *The Belle of New York*. Knowing both James and the production, and needing to earn a living, I auditioned for the juvenile lead – the part of Harry Bronson. In the musical he was the son of millionaire Ichabod Bronson, who was to be played by the star comedian George Lacey, a legendary pantomime dame. My audition was well rehearsed and planned, so I landed the job at £15 per week. The show was to open at the King's Theatre, Southsea, and then go on tour. Rehearsals were to be in a room over a pub in Great Windmill Street, so at ten o'clock on the appropriate date I turned up wearing my best Brinkman-tailored suit. A few of the cast were assembled when I got there, but, being of a retiring nature, I sat myself at the far end of the room. Opposite me were most of the members of the chorus. Among them sat a young lady with blonde hair, wearing a well-tailored grey flannel suit with a remarkably small waist. She gave me an encouraging smile and promptly came across to invite me to join the rest of the singers.

The young lady was Ann, who was to become my wife, the mother of our seven children and the architect of my life and happiness.

12
The Belle of New York, Butlins and Marriage

Early in the rehearsals for *The Belle* it became clear to me that an opportunity to put in a new song had presented itself. The last scene of the musical included a cabaret spot that had been left open so the performers could do their party pieces. George Lacey was to perform his well-known routine and dance, which was quite brilliant. Although in his late sixties he was amazingly agile and could pirouette round the stage like a ballet dancer. Hannah Watt, a gorgeously flamboyant actress who was taking the part of Cora Angelique, was scratching around for an Edwardian type of number and was going to be open to suggestions as to what it should be. I quickly wrote a song called 'Mother, Mother, Mother – Let Me Go on the Stage!' which had a period feel about it. I hurried round to Cyril's with a lyric and a top line for the first 32 bars, and we quickly devised something that would fill the spot perfectly. Hannah was delighted and, being one of the stars of the show, insisted that it should go in. Cyril came in like a whirlwind and rehearsed the chorus as they had never been rehearsed before, and he produced band parts for the orchestra and conducted them for the band-call. The song was an instant success, and I stood proudly in the wings every night to hear Hannah put it over.

We opened at the King's Theatre, Southsea, which was a strange coincidence because Mother opened *The Belle* at the same theatre in 1939 at the outbreak of the war. I knew James Shirvell from 1940 when he had put out a tour of *The Chocolate Soldier*, but I had not realised how tatty his productions were. The scenery, made from canvas-covered wooden frames as was the custom in those days, was patched like a tramp's trousers, with the slack canvas flapping in the breeze like the sails of a Thames barge. The standard method for preventing the flapping of the canvas was to paint it all over with size. These flats had received the treatment so often that they were shedding size like dandruff. I kept well out of the way during Monday fit-ups to avoid the disparaging remarks of the stage-hands.

The costumes, under the supervision of a disastrous wardrobe mistress called Lillie Vere, were well worn and ill fitting. The knickers that Ann had to wear for a number whose opening line was 'We're the Ornamental Purity Brigade' ripped from hem to crotch on the first fitting and were anything but pure. My millionaire's Edwardian evening tail suit had probably long been discarded by an Edwardian waiter. In desperation I visited a second-hand clothes merchant called Harry from Hackney, who ran his business in a fine wreck of a Victorian house. He had a room full of Edwardian tail suits which covered his floor to a depth of 4 feet. 'Medium size,' he said, having measured me with a practised eye, and straight away plunged his arms into the appropriate corner of the room. In no time at all he had unearthed four possibles, and for £3 I left with a passable costume.

My character, apart from ultimately marrying the Belle of New York, was heavily involved with little Fifi, a French girl who had the hots for me for reasons I can't recall – possibly because of my millionaire father. This part was played by George Lacey's wife Daphne, a delightful if frail slip of a girl with a son who was, if anything, even frailer. We had a couple of duets – one of which entailed her singing, 'When we are married,' to which I replied, 'Why, what will you do?' I was proud of the fact that we sang this for 16 weeks without getting a guffaw from the audience.

The second duet was 'Teach me how to kiss, dear, teach me how to squeeze. Teach me how to sit upon your sympathetic knees.' This included a dance during which little Fifi leapt into my arms and I whirled her round a couple of times. This was fine until Daphne fell ill. Her understudy was the director's wife, known to the company as 'Jillykins'. Although not exactly a big girl, Jillykins could scarcely be described as frail. She launched herself at me at a height of about 6 inches from a range of 6 feet. Stepping swiftly aside to avoid a foul ankle-crippling tackle, I caught her at this very low level and attempted to hoist her into the double whirl position. By the end of the manoeuvre a roller-skate could scarcely have been inserted under her not inconsiderable bum, but at least I didn't crash on to my sympathetic knees before she scrambled to her feet.

By the second week of the tour – in Peterborough to be precise – Ann and I fell in love and got together, which is a state we have been in ever since. At this point in history 'getting together' was not the straightforward activity it has since become. Landladies were very careful to preserve their good name, so anything that approached 'hanky-panky' was frowned upon and, as a consequence, made rather difficult. Various subterfuges were employed. On one occasion we both shared digs with Ronnie Marsh, who played Blinky Bill in the show. It so happened that he had booked the only double room, which he obligingly vacated at 11.30 every evening, swapping with Ann so that we could spend the night together in comfort. At eight the following morning they would swap back again so that all reputations remained unblemished. Ronnie later became a BBC producer, and we would occasionally pass in the corridor and give each other a knowing wink.

I continued to spend my spare time writing the television musical. When possible, on Sundays I would return to London to work on the latest scenes with Cyril. Two other things stand out in my memories of this period. The first was a visit from Ann's mother and father when we were playing Bournemouth. I had very good digs that week, and one sunny afternoon Ann thought it would be a good idea for them all to visit me – unannounced. They all steamed into my bedroom where, as was my habit, I was having an afternoon nap. I greeted them from the bed with what dignity I could muster and they swiftly departed. On leaving, Ann's mother remarked that I was probably the rudest young man she had ever met because I didn't even get out of bed to shake hands. There was a very good reason for this lapse of good manners. I wasn't wearing any trousers.

The second thing I recall is George Lacey's habit of calling a full meeting of the cast of the show whenever Philip Purser – the director and husband of Jillikins – paid us a visit. When we were all assembled George would produce his 'Diary of Disaster' and read from it every incident when the stage management had failed to give him his spotlight or cue or music, or any scene delay or accident, all of which were recorded with time and date.

When we played the Wood Green Empire, George and I shared a dressing room. We got on like a house on fire, but when his friends or relations came round to see him he steadfastly refused to bring them into the room, and interviewed them at the stage door instead. He was also at pains to disguise from me the fact that he wore false teeth. Every subterfuge was employed to prevent me from seeing the offending dentures, but nevertheless the wash basin was always coated a quarter of an inch thick in fixative glue.

By the end of the tour Cyril and I had finished the television musical, so Ian Carmichael brought along Michael Mills to hear it. This was my first meeting with the bearded Michael, who was a wonderful enthusiast, a pioneer of television production and a senior BBC producer. He saw the possibilities of the musical and swiftly arranged for Ronnie Waldman to hear it. Ronnie was by now the head of television variety at the BBC. He was a man of many talents, among which was the ability to play the piano with considerable skill and also to read a musical score. He liked the show, told us we needn't have played it to him because he could easily have read it, including the music, and said it contained some of the best comedy scenes he had ever heard. In the event he did precisely nothing about it. However, our contact with Michael bore fruit for many years to come.

I was keen not to go back into *The Belle* for another tour, so I signed on to play Cousin George in Bernard Delfont's tour of *Bless the Bride* and to understudy my brother Peter, who was playing Thomas Trout. We opened at Cheltenham and, after a few dates, finished up at Barrow-in-Furness, St Helens, Brighton and finally the Essoldo Cinema at Clacton-on-Sea during the week after Christmas. I think it was as I lay shivering in bed in my digs at Barrow, while the landlady vainly tried to light one lump of coal in the minute fireplace in the corner of the minute bedroom, that I decided that perhaps a better future lay ahead for me in writing.

Clacton-on-Sea during the week after Christmas was the absolute pits. One of the stage-hands said to me, 'If it goes here, it'll go anywhere,' to which I replied, 'If it comes here, it's already been everywhere.' On the first performance the conductor had to start the overture twice because the orchestra became hopelessly lost and ground to an undignified halt.

After Christmas, Ann went to join the rep company in Kendal, Westmorland (now Cumbria), for the early part of the season before our wedding, which was set for 2 June. Kendal was a charming town with a lovely little theatre, but the rep, run by C. Mostel Willie and his wife, was a bit chaotic to put it mildly. C. Mostel Willie had but a sketchy idea of most of the plays, so was inclined to make up the dialogue according to his own interpretation of the text. However, there were several good actors, including Stratford Johns, who later achieved fame in *Z Cars* and became one of our leading character actors.

Following the end of the tour of *Bless the Bride*, I started to become involved in Richard Stone's productions for Butlins Holiday Camps.

I was nominally his production manager and producer, but this involved every kind of activity known to the theatre. I scoured Hampstead to find rehearsal rooms. These consisted mostly of church halls, which were frequently shared with local primary schools and where the unforgettable odour of school dinners filled the air. I obtained bits of scenery by answering advertisements in the *Stage* and supervised the construction of other bits in various workshops. I loaded the same scenery on to trucks at most of the London railway stations. The railway companies would provide a scenery truck if you bought six tickets. The worrying aspect of this operation was the fact that the six tickets only entitled you to a 30-foot truck. Each one of our companies had 32- or 35-foot cloths, which were attached to wooden battens. The railways were reputed to own only two 30-foot trucks, so we gambled that we would always get a 45-foot truck and all would be well. The nightmare scenario was that we would arrive at the station with the 35-foot scenery and get only the 30-foot truck we were entitled to. Luckily, the nightmare never came to pass.

Over the years I put shows into Butlins camps at Pwllheli, Clacton, Filey, Brighton and Margate. I don't think I ever put a show of which I was not deeply ashamed into any of the camps. All the Butlins theatres were large and made of concrete, with no surfaces that would absorb sound, so they echoed like vast caves. They all had crude amplifying systems that were controlled from a central point at each camp known as 'Radio Butlin'. If you got 'amplifier howl' going round in any of the theatres, you had to send a runner to Radio Butlin with a request for them to please turn the sound down. Each show consisted of four programmes, none of which could be allowed to run more than 60 minutes because to run longer would prevent the campers from drinking in the bars. We did what we could with lighting to make the shows look acceptable, but Billy Butlin personally decreed that the house lights should always be kept on during the show in case the campers wanted to read the newspaper – and they did! Camps were run by a camp controller, who in most cases was an ex-army major. Each camp had an entertainment manager who had usually been a sergeant. They were backed up by devoted male and female Red Coats who spent every waking moment trying to help the campers have a good time. Kids were organised into fun clubs to take them entirely off the hands of the parents. All the fairground-type activities were

119

entirely free. The ballrooms were decorated with things such as Dutch windmills and little bridges over streams, or else kitted out like the Hawaiian Ballroom in *Hi-de-Hi!* Every moment of the day was taken up with functions such as the Beauty Competition, the Glamorous Grandmother Competition, the Knobbly Knees Competition and the Campers' Talent Competition. From breakfast onwards the camp comedian would appear in various guises and disguises. He would contrive to wring laughs out of campers of all ages. Everybody would assemble and march to meals, which were served at table by waitresses and the Red Coats. The campers were given a couple of choices for the main course and the last meal of the day at about 5.30 was a sort of high tea. This meant that if you got hungry in the evening, you had to buy sandwiches or fish and chips, which were quite pricey and were a great source of income to Billy B.

I always thought that Billy Butlin richly deserved his knighthood. The Continental holiday, with its good weather guarantee and surprising cheapness, had not happened. The holiday alternative was a couple of weeks at the seaside in digs where the landlady didn't want to see you between breakfast and lunchtime, and where every activity meant putting your hand in your pocket and forking out hard-earned cash. Billy had a direct if unusual approach to problems. If he wanted to know whether the campers were enjoying the food, he didn't do an officer's round asking, 'Any complaints?' He looked in the cookhouse dustbins. When severe east coast floods covered his Skegness camp to a depth of 4 feet, the mattresses were dried out and sent to the Pwllheli camp. New ones were sent to Skegness. No one in Pwllheli looked to see if the beds were damp. My first show was staged at Clacton, which was the very camp that I had twice visited during the war. It hadn't changed much.

Each show was accompanied by an orchestra of 14. Richard Stone didn't think it necessary to have band parts or orchestrations, so I was required to purchase 15 copies of every song, which were placed on the musicians' stands, and they all picked the notes that they thought would sound best – transposing if necessary. After a season or two I persuaded him that this was scarcely adequate, and I conned various arrangers into producing musical scores without charging too much.

Filey camp was a bleak, windswept place. It had its own railway station actually on the site so campers, who came mostly by train, could be brought right to the centre of the camp. From time to time it used to suffer from what the locals called the 'fret'. This was a cross between cold sea mist and small drops of rain which seemed to remain suspended in the air. I also had to stage the show in a sweet little theatre in Filey town for the benefit of the non-Butlins population.

Pwllheli was a much more picturesque camp, with lovely mountain views and beautiful gardens. Hugh Lloyd was the comic. To be honest, Hugh didn't have an act worth mentioning, but he performed with such disarming charm that no one seemed to notice. He used to start and finish with a song that I believe he composed himself and that started with the line 'I've fallen in love with someone' and finished with the unforgettable tag 'So I feel so toodle-oodle-oo'. This he solemnly sang wearing a battered top hat and, furthermore, he then persuaded the audience to join in the chorus, following which he wandered off to tumultuous applause. Later in the show he sang a Sinatra song, stepping over the prone girls as they swooned at his feet, while never changing the bored expression on his face. I found him hilarious.

Summer shows and concert parties loomed large in my repertoire for the next ten years or so. I staged shows at Yarmouth and Weston-super-Mare with Terry Scott and Hugh Lloyd, at Worthing with Teddy Johnson and Pearl Carr, at Margate with Donald Pears, at Bridlington with Ronnie Hilton and at Scarborough with Alma Cogan. The last of these was staged at the Floral Hall, a large, airy auditorium surrounded by a solid wall of lightly curtained windows. It was impossible to black it out, which was unfortunate, because on the bill was a brilliant Hungarian ultraviolet act that required complete darkness. For the first house in the early summer evening you could clearly see black-clad figures holding aloft various specially painted wooden figures representing fish, sea horses, lobsters and crabs. It got better laughs than the comic, and later I had to deal with an understandably livid Hungarian who said I had single-handedly destroyed a reputation it had taken him a lifetime to build up.

After all these experiences I can truthfully say that I knew a lot about the summer-show business and I definitely didn't need a technical adviser when it came to doing *Hi-de-Hi!* But I am getting ahead of myself.

Amid all this chaos, with the assistance of a very helpful young man at a house agent called Batty & Stevens and with a mortgage nobly guaranteed by Cyril, I contrived to buy part possession of a house in

Finchley. Built at the turn of the century, it was semi-detached with five bedrooms. On the ground floor were two further rooms and a kitchen containing a bath covered with a wooden plank. On the floors above were two flats with two lady tenants. The ground floor was to be ours, and the sum involved was £1,750 freehold. Ann saw it and managed to be unbelievably enthusiastic within about five minutes, agreeing that it made good financial sense to buy a dilapidated two-roomed thing with a bath in the kitchen rather than taking a rented flat.

My stag party before the wedding was a bit of a disaster. Proceeding down Albany Street as the police would phrase it – and they did – and crossing over the Marylebone Road, we encountered a taxi proceeding in the opposite direction. Said taxi decided to make a right turn. Cyril was driving, which was not one of his prime skills. Ian Carmichael was next to him. I was in the back on the right-hand side. My brother Peter – the best man – was on my left. Never let it be said that Cyril was drunk. On the other hand, I am not saying he was completely sober. The taxi caught us amidships and it was a considerable blow. We were all decanted from the car by helpful bystanders and spread out on the pavement. We were then approached by a mysterious person who said he had a message from the other side. Assuming that this was some intermediary of the taxi driver fraternity, we listened to him carefully, but it transpired that he wished to convey a message from the hereafter – from people who had already crossed the Styx. We got rid of him. Somehow we all managed to get to Cyril's Weymouth Street flat, but Cyril didn't conduct anything for a week, and Ian was out of his West End review for ten days. The groom and best man managed to limp to the wedding.

Ann and I were duly married in a large church in Finsbury Park by a vicar who didn't trust theatricals and therefore wanted payment in advance and in cash. He seemed unaccountably nervous about the whole proceedings and asked me if I would take this woman to be my lawful wedded husband, to which I refused to reply. Ann's aunt Mahala, a frightening and outspoken headmistress, staged the reception at her large house in Digby Crescent, and we finally escaped to the *Bournemouth Belle* which left from Waterloo. I had decided that I could afford just one night at the Palace Court Hotel with dinner, after which we would decamp to the same digs where I had first met Ann's parents.

On the first and only night in the luxury hotel, our romantic and expensive dinner was interrupted by the surprise presence of Harry from

Hackney, the second-hand clothes dealer. He greeted us long and loudly, with ribald remarks to the waiters to hurry up and serve us because, being newly wed, we had more interesting and exciting things to do than sit eating veal escalope and profiteroles. I carelessly allowed my feet to get sunburned within a couple of days, which was probably why my eldest son was born ten months after the wedding instead of nine.

On our return from honeymoon we were immediately involved in producing a summer show in Lyme Regis. On arrival we discovered that no advance publicity for the show had appeared at all, so Ann and Richard Stone set about painting posters proclaiming our presence. The other way we let the people of Lyme Regis know of our presence was by employing the town crier, who went round the town ringing his bell and declaring that *Lymelight Rendezvous* was to be seen that very night. This service cost three shillings and sixpence. It seemed to work because business was quite good. We staged a rather attractive show starring Harold Berens and Anthea Askey – Arthur Askey's daughter. Bill Dickey, a fine operatic tenor, partnered Peggy Thompson, who was a very good soprano. Peter Greenway, who later accompanied Noël Coward, was the pianist. I think this was the first summer show I had staged that I was pleased about. It was a sweet little theatre, the only disadvantage being that the high spring tides caused a small flood in the ladies' dressing room, which resulted in the girls' shoes sloshing away down the drain. Harold Berens generously gave a party for Ann's twenty-first birthday, and it was a thoroughly enjoyable engagement.

On our return we were greeted by two letters. The first was from the War Office and commanded me to report to the Dorset Regiment on Salisbury Plain for two weeks' training on Z Reserve. The second was from the manager of the Hampstead branch of the NatWest bank informing me that I had an overdraft of 17 shillings and fourpence. We were seriously broke. In a fit of wild extravagance, Ann bought a front doormat for 16 shillings. Since we had no capital available, she arranged to pay for it at the rate of two shillings a week. She laid out our furniture, which consisted of a bed, a wooden armchair and a basket chair, as best she could, but we also had a rather nice low, glass-fronted Minton bookcase, a beige wooden table lamp and a silver-topped sherry decanter. These she arranged separately against the wall near the bay window with a small vase of flowers, and they looked

123

marvellous. 'One day,' she said, 'our whole house will look like that.' A few years later, it did.

My brief return to the army was brought about by the Suez crisis. I found myself once again sleeping in a bell-tent, which was a way of life I thought was well behind me. It was also a little dangerous. We took part in the usual sort of army exercise, which involved waiting in trenches while the 25-pounders fired live ammunition over our heads. Unfortunately it was a very foggy morning and the artillery spotters could not see where the shells were landing. The trench 50 yards to my right received a direct hit that killed one of the soldiers.

On my return to London, Michael Westmore came to my rescue. Michael was a BBC producer of considerable talent and sensitivity who was concerned mainly with children's programmes. He received a brief to stage a show to appeal to the youth of the country, who until then had been entirely neglected. I suppose it was the first of the 'yoof' programmes. He devised a magazine show called *Teleclub* which tried to appeal to young viewers. We had the musical director Steve Race with a bunch of good musicians and a lot of pretty girls. I featured in a weekly sketch in which I played a character called Will Try. My task was to – unsuccessfully – try a new job every week. We did a bit of outside filming to make the thing look authentic. One scene involved me wandering aimlessly along a canal path kicking an empty beer can. Michael shouted 'Action' and I did my wandering and beer-can kicking. As he shouted 'Cut,' I became aware that the author – a Canadian – was convulsed with laughter. 'Great, David,' he said. 'That walk is hysterical – really funny.' Which was worrying, as I had just been doing my normal walk. I came to the conclusion that they don't do much walking in Canada.

Michael gave me another job later in the year. He produced a major version of *1066 and All That* starring Tony Britton and I played several parts including Sir Francis Drake, which entailed wearing a beard. I rather fancied myself in that. There was no means of recording television at that time so, as they needed a repeat performance, we did it all again two days later with a different camera crew. The show was shot at the new studios in Lime Grove, and by now the cameras had four lenses and small television screen viewfinders. Television was still the poor relation of radio, but things were coming along.

13
The Actor Becomes the Writer

In the meantime, in order to make ends meet, Ann worked at anything that presented itself, including serving at the Ideal Home Exhibition and in department stores and modelling. I was also looking for more work. Cyril, in his capacity as one of Jack Hylton's musical directors, had some very good contacts. One such was Anna Lett, who was Bill Lyon-Shaw's secretary. Bill was one of the best and most prolific producers at the BBC, who really knew what he was doing. He was planning a TV series to be called *Don't Spare the Horses* starring the great comedian Jimmy James. Anna persuaded Bill to give us a chance to write some production numbers. This was the start of a long and happy association with Bill that led to a lot of work. The show was staged as an outside broadcast at the Granville Theatre, Walham Green, in Fulham. One of the great disadvantages of working with the outside broadcast department was the sound technicians. They made a good job of recording the cheers and boos of a football crowd, but balancing an orchestra, singing group and solo artistes was totally beyond them.

The association with Bill had an important side-effect for me personally. Bill and several other producers thought that the George Mitchell Singers, of *Black & White Minstrel Show* fame, were getting more work than was justified, so he decided to form a singing group called the Tunesmiths. Cyril, Bill and I auditioned singers for the combination and, being short of a second tenor and in need of the work, I roped myself in as one of them. This was a good move because the lead baritone was a brilliant musician named Wilfred Johns. Wilfred was one of the very few singers I ever knew who had perfect pitch. If you asked him to sing an A, he would sing the note spot on. Wilfred was impressed with my confidence and score-reading ability – little knowing that I had written the songs and therefore knew them backwards. He knew Cliff Adams who, along with BBC sound producer Johnny Stewart, was also disenchanted with the George Mitchell Singers. Johnny was forming the BBC Show Band with Cyril Stapleton as conductor. This was to include the Show Band Singers, which Cliff Adams was putting together with Wilfred. Naturally enough, he asked me to join, not knowing that I was a faker. I needed the work, so I eagerly agreed. I had a good ear and could read music up to a point, inasmuch as I knew whether the music was going up or down. However, I was in deep shock at the first rehearsal when the second tenor parts were slung at me and I was expected to sing my part straight away without separate rehearsal.

Also in the show band was Cliff Adams's brilliant group the Stargazers. They formed part of the 12 Show Band Singers. I found myself singing into the right ear of Freddie Datchelor of the Stargazers, another fine musician, but if I sang a wrong note he never let on, so I survived.

The Show Band was a wonderful outfit, with such stars as Bill McGuffie on the piano. Although short of the third finger on his right hand, Bill could play like a dream. He could also detect a wrong note anywhere in the orchestra and used to draw attention to it by calling to Cyril Stapleton in a loud Scottish stage whisper, 'Cyril, Cyril! The third trombone is playing an A natural. It's supposed to be A flat.' Jock Cummings was the ace drummer, and the brass line-up included Kenny Baker and Tommy McQuater on trumpets and Laddy Busby, Don Lusher and George Chisholm on trombones. Bert Weedon was on guitar. They were all leading session players who went from sound sessions to television sessions to recording studios as fast as their taxis could carry them, and they all became legends in the music world. I am very proud to have worked with them. Their ability and professionalism were awe-inspiring. They would be sitting ready, with their instruments tuned, at the appointed time. They read immediately and accurately any part placed before them, however complicated, and they demanded and received payment for an extra hour 30 seconds after the three-hour session ended. The discipline in the brass section, however, was of the naughty schoolboy variety. On one notable occasion Cyril Stapleton announced: 'Would the gentlemen of the trombone section kindly not remove their slides and shoot the leader of the orchestra with paper pellets during the actual transmission.' George Chisholm, let it be said, was the principal pellet puffer.

Most of the great American singers sang with us. Frank Sinatra was almost worshipped by the band. His career was at a low point when he came to us. He was accompanied by half a dozen sinister-looking men who all kept their hats on during the rehearsals. He ended his act with 'Old Man River' and received such a storming reception that he was reduced to tears. Nat King Cole was another of the greats. He brought his own drummer, who made the show band rock in a most remarkable way with his style. Jock Cummings looked on in speechless admiration. Among the less admired were Johnny Ray and Guy Mitchell, but they were all great entertainers.

The resident British singers were Julie Dawn, who was a super vocalist, and Dick James, who sang the signature tune to the TV series *Robin Hood*. The memorable lyrics in that particular entertainment were 'Robin Hood, Robin Hood – riding through the glen'. He later founded Northern Songs and published all the Beatles' songs and deservedly became extremely rich. Carol Carr, sister of the great Dorothy Carless, sang with us from time to time. Jimmy Young made frequent visits to sing his famous 'Unchained Melody'. Always with him was his then wife, who followed his every note on the score and made copious notes on his performance, which he would go through with her bar by bar after each rehearsal. All this took place at the Paris Cinema, a wonderfully warm, responsive studio that had started life as a small cinema in Lower Regent Street near Piccadilly Circus. Unfortunately it was sold during John Birt's disastrous era as director-general of the BBC, when the importance of such locations was simply not understood.

For all these broadcasts I needed a dinner jacket, so the ever-helpful Cyril sold me one of his old ones for £3. Thus, the Show Band and many recording and film sessions paid the rent and enabled me to remain in London while making the transition from actor to writer. It was during a rehearsal for *The Show Band Show* that I got news that Ann had actually given birth to Nicholas, our first son. She was at Queen Mary's, a comfortable maternity hospital in Hampstead, and she had gone through a very long labour. Cliff Adams quickly said, 'Forget about rehearsals – get there as quick as you can and be back in time for the transmission.' I gratefully dashed off and saw Ann looking proud, tired and radiantly happy with a large and healthy baby at her side. The date was 26 March 1953.

Don't Spare the Horses with Jimmy James was a great joy. The sight of him and his two stooges struggling to learn the dance routine will always be a treasured memory, and he was wondrously funny in the corniest of sketches. In one such he played the captain of a trawler battling through a storm and crying, 'Oh, will this cruel north-east wind never cease?' while a stage-hand threw handfuls of artificial snow at his left cheek. Suddenly another stage-hand threw snow at his right cheek, at which he cried, 'Oh, will this cruel south-west wind never cease?' Anyway, I thought it was funny. The show was not an entire success, largely because Jimmy was being required to work to particular cameras, and his type of comedy should never have been lumbered with considerations of that sort. His was a unique talent, honed and fine-tuned by years of variety theatre performances, and he should have been allowed the freedom he was used to. Cameras and camera angles are a director's problem and should never bother an actor.

Michael Mills started to commission us to write special songs for his programmes. One of the first was for a show called *Well, You've Asked for It*, consisting of viewers' requests. It was a bad title and we succeeded in writing a bad song for it.

Freddie Carpenter, the dance director of Mother's *Tulip Time* in Hull, created another turning point in my career. He was regularly producing pantomimes for Howard and Wyndham, who were major theatre owners in Scotland and the north. They owned the King's, Edinburgh, the King's, Glasgow, the Theatre Royal, Newcastle, and the Royal Court, Liverpool. He was planning a brand new *Aladdin* for Edinburgh. All his life, Freddie had wanted to produce big musicals for the London theatre. Unfortunately, nobody ever asked him to do this, so he therefore made his pantomimes like big musicals and he loved them dearly. In the early days of television at Alexandra Palace he had done some spectacular work with Michael Mills and Ian Carmichael under the most primitive conditions, and I think they mentioned that I was writing for them, so he asked me to write the script of *Aladdin*. Richard Stone negotiated the princely sum of £50 for my fee, which was not a lot even in those days, and I began writing the first of a long line of pantomimes, which ultimately became a major occupation.

I learnt a hell of a lot about pantomime from Freddie Carpenter. He borrowed freely from pantos going back to the Edwardian era, and he in turn had learnt a lot from the likes of George Lacey. I did detailed research on the subjects and even read the original story of Ala Adin in *The Arabian Nights*. It was interesting, but what that boy got up to with Princess Badrubledor was far too rude to be included in a family entertainment at Christmas, particularly in Edinburgh. Freddie had a large flat off Haverstock Hill, paid for largely by the proceeds of the Sid Fields film *London Town*, which he choreographed for J. Arthur Rank

previous page: AC and DC with wedding cake – note hired suit and wholly owned pickled onions.

top: AC and DC with first son (Nicholas), first daughter (Penelope) and bucket.

left: A rare picture of Olive, with my son-in-law John Sims.

right: My daughter Rebecca with husband Simon Cadell – Sir Donald Sinden nearly in the picture.

opposite: Ann and David Croft, 1956.

above: DC with Fiat Samantha.

left: DC going grey – *Hugh and I,* 1964.

opposite: With Jimmy Perry and a couple of OBEs.

right: The wife, 1974.

below: Ann with daughters (left to right) Jane, Becky and Penny at Plage Garoupe, Cap d'Antibes.

above: The Croft family at our Golden Wedding party, summer 2001.

left: David Croft, 2004.

for a large sum of money. Writing for Freddie had its own special hazard in the form of his much-loved poodle, which spent most of its time trying to copulate with my right leg. I tried to discourage it with sly kicks from my left leg, but these had to be delivered without the knowledge of the ever-alert Freddie. Nevertheless, extremely good shows got devised and written around about this time and for many years to come.

They included four beautiful pantos for Howard and Wyndham, all specially designed and choreographed, several for Derek Salburg for Birmingham and Wolverhampton, and I have lost count of the number for the London Palladium for Robert Nesbit, Val Parnell and Leslie Grade. I once wrote a pantomime for George Formby. This entailed visiting George in his suite in the Grosvenor House Hotel, which he shared with his wife, the dreaded Beryl. George was reputed to have a roving eye for the girls, so, to ensure that no other part of his anatomy got a chance to do any roving, Beryl never left his side, or even the side of the stage when he was performing. Talking about Freddie one day he said, 'This chap Freddie Carpenter – he seems to have all his chairs at home.' Being well acquainted with Freddie's home and indeed his chairs, I readily agreed. I found out later that it was a northern expression for being 'on the ball'.

I wrote *Goldilocks and the Three Bears* for Tommy Steele. Freddie had seen him at the very start of his career and persuaded him that in order to succeed in show business he would have to control the audience and stop them yelling and screaming while he was actually trying to put a song across. He also told him, 'By the way, you'll have to get rid of that dreadful mop of hair on top of your head.' Tommy got rid of it.

For Robert Nesbit and Val Parnell I wrote a more elaborate *Aladdin* starring Norman Wisdom for the London Palladium. This was an exhausting business because, just when I thought I had won an argument with Norman about a particular scene and I was saying goodbye on his doorstep, he would say, 'I still think I'm right about that scene,' and we would start arguing all over again. He had an appetite like a truck driver and would have his cook produce great mounds of stew and vegetables, but he was also one of the slowest eaters I ever knew – largely because he never stopped talking. He was always absolutely charming and totally exasperating. To get him to cut anything required an act of parliament.

Humpty Dumpty for Bob Nesbit with Harry Secombe, Bruce Forsyth, Charlie Drake and Roy Castle was quite the loveliest panto I ever wrote for the Palladium. It was very elaborate scenically, with Harry as Father Christmas driving a sleigh about 15 feet above the stage. Bob really loved his pantomimes, and that particular love is an essential element in any show business endeavour. Without it you get the kind of soulless rubbish that distinguishes most of our pantomimes today, and television is suffering the same fate. Bob was not especially interested in comedy, so he often became unaccountably absent when it came to the funny scenes, which usually fell to me to lay out.

Bob was a great person to work for. Apart from being one of our greatest experts at lighting he knew exactly how to hang all the cloths and lamps in the grid and how to pack the loads of scenery on to the not very spacious Palladium stage. He also knew a lot about music. On one occasion, not being satisfied with the drum effects for a comic's 'prat fall' from a rather sophisticated drummer, he leapt into the orchestra pit and demonstrated what he needed on side drum and cymbals followed by a loud 'boom' from his left foot on the drum. I have given the same demonstration to several pop drummers since. He also taught us how to sell a song. 'Don't stop playing after one chorus. Play it again and again and again.' From then on we did as he advised and it worked. He was a great bon viveur and he gave one other piece of advice that I shall always remember, even if I don't follow it. 'You need a small car, David, so that you can park it, and you need not one but two chauffeurs because the other one is always off duty.' However, patience was not one of his virtues. At one technical rehearsal a poor lighting assistant fell 20 feet off a ladder and landed with a sickening thud on the stage. He was duly stretchered off, whereupon Bob called out in a bored voice, 'Can we get on please?'

For Leslie Grade I wrote yet another *Aladdin* and later *Cinderella* starring Cliff Richard and the Shadows. Cliff was marvellous in the parts and the complete professional, but the show was scenically cheap and, what's more, I couldn't persuade them to let me write the songs, which resulted in some illiterate lyrics being allowed to creep in. One that sticks in my mind was on the occasion when the wicked Abanazar shuts the unfortunate Aladdin in the cave saying, 'Stay in the cave for ever.' This was followed, if my memory serves me right, by Cliff singing, 'Here I am shut like a rat in a hole. What have I done? Not a thing have I stole.'

I wrote *Babes in the Wood* for Engelbert Humperdinck. On this occasion I tried very hard to get a percentage on the gross takings instead of an outright fee. Leslie Macdonell, the boss of the Palladium, said to Richard Stone in his broad Canadian accent, 'If I pay your client what he demands, that puts him in the Hemingway class.' These shows for Leslie Grade were written to budget and were poor efforts when compared to the great Nesbit days. Many of the Freddie Carpenter and Nesbit shows included songs and, in several cases, full musical scores specially written by Cyril and me. The Scottish ones were written in English and were then translated, for the benefit of the Scottish audience, into something I didn't recognise, but which tickled the Scots to everyone's satisfaction. One of these productions featured the great Stanley Baxter, who was a wonderful, beautifully dressed dame with the broadest Glasgow Gorbals accent you could imagine. One of his routines featured a 'speug' and a 'bogey', and I am still uncertain what it all meant. Pantomime writing for the Palladium continued right up to my joining the BBC, when I had a special clause put into my contract to permit this outside work. But I am again getting ahead of myself.

The first panto – *Aladdin* at Edinburgh – stands out in my memory. Freddie persuaded Stewart Cruikshank, the boss of Howard and Wyndham, to pay for Ann and me to stay at the luxurious Caledonian Hotel so that we could see the first night at Edinburgh. Being flat broke at the time we didn't want to waste money on the train fare so we decided to go up on the overnight bus. All went well, the journey was excruciatingly uncomfortable but the first night was sensationally successful. Stewart Cruikshank's mother took a terrific shine to Ann, which was hardly surprising because she was beautiful, outgoing and a lot of fun. Mrs C insisted on seeing us off on our train next morning and it was only with great difficulty that we persuaded her not to do this but simply to see us into our taxi. In a loud voice I told the driver to take us to the station and, once he had taken us a hundred yards, I added, 'The bus station.'

Some time before this it became evident, as these things do, that Ann was pregnant again. Needing more room in our house we enquired of the two elderly ladies inhabiting the flats in our part-possession house whether their future plans entailed moving out. We were told rather firmly that they had no such intention. One of them reinforced this point by leaning over the banisters of our staircase and saying in a loud and none-too-friendly voice, 'If you two intend breeding like rabbits, it is entirely your affair. Don't expect us to make room.' Ann at once started to look for another house and, with the assistance of the same young man from Batty & Stevens, found us a five-bedroomed house about 20 minutes' walk away – and at that time we had to walk – in Wickliffe Avenue. The price was £3,000, and with the cooperation of the Eastern Counties Building Society we bought it and what is more, although it was against the rules, Ann persuaded them to allow us to keep the part-possession house.

We couldn't afford a moving van, so Ann shifted our few possessions on a large carriage pram – usually with young Nicholas sleeping contentedly underneath. These included our 9-inch television set, acquired so that Ann could see the coronation, our precious radio and a couple of chairs from the three-piece utility suite lately bought on the never-never system from Waring & Gillow. The settee was pushed on a fruit barrow by Ann's helpful cousin Malcolm Callender, who was on leave from the merchant navy. Incidentally, all the campers at every Butlin's were assured that they would be able to view the coronation in comfort on specially installed large-screen televisions. I was at Pwllheli and gave the cast the day off. We sat down to view the great event, as did many campers, to be greeted by a large black screen with white dots and a sound-track like 3 lb of onions being fried in a very hot pan. After an hour, during which we saw not even a vague shadow of a coronation, we decided to resume rehearsal.

Michael Mills and Bill Lyon-Shaw used Cyril and me for more and more television shows, as did Kenneth Carter who did all the early Benny Hill shows. We were commissioned to write special songs and openings for visiting stars, boat race day and bank holidays. I have a large filing cabinet drawer full of songs specially written for such events, all of them performed. We wrote for the *Jewell and Warris* series, *The Pat Kirkwood Show*, *The Petula Clark Show*, *Variety Parade* and for many more one-off productions.

Thanks almost entirely to the efforts of Ann, we moved into Wickliffe Avenue in time for Penny to be born. This happened at home, which was quite usual at that time if no complications were anticipated, and as a result was a much more relaxed event.

Television production had become very complicated by this time, mainly owing to the ambitions of the producers. One very alarming incident occurred during the Daily Mail Award Show. This was a live transmission from the Scala Theatre and was the early version of what became the BAFTA Show. We wrote several numbers, including an opening called 'Window on the World', which was a good title for television as conceived at that time, and a scene for Prudence Kitten, Muffin the Mule and Mr Turnip. Heavily featured was *What's My Line* which was likely to receive an award. For this I copped the task of impersonating Gilbert Harding. I was awarded this role for the simple reason that I worked extremely cheaply. I was as much like Gilbert Harding, who was an irascible, middle-aged ex-schoolmaster, as Charlie Drake was like Hitler. The Scala Theatre was delightful, Victorian and very small. There was simply no room for the large orchestra except by halving the audience. Michael Mills therefore decreed that the orchestra should play in the upper circle bar and the sound should be relayed to the artistes (me) by two loudspeakers in the footlights. Unfortunately, when the time came for my introductory music, the outside broadcast sound engineer, true to form, failed to turn on the knob that operated the two speakers. The introduction from the orchestra locked away in the upper circle bar was inaudible. I launched myself into the verse. Not trusting myself to pitch the right note, I spoke it – *parlando*, as I believe Italian opera singers call it – trusting that Eric Robinson, the conductor, would join me at some juncture. The result was of course chaos.

Another not dissimilar event occurred during *The Pat Kirkwood Show*. Patricia, as her husband insisted on calling her, was appearing in Blackpool, so logically enough the show was staged in Blackpool. However, it was decided that the Blackpool musicians were not good enough to play the London BBC orchestrations. The orchestra was therefore booked in London and played from a London studio. It was further decreed that Pat would record her song with only a faint piano background. She would mime to this track, which would be played back to her in Blackpool and also to Eric Robinson on earphones in London, who would endeavour to synchronise the orchestra. Predictably, chaos again ensued.

Travelling on the top of a number two bus a little later, Ann and I discussed these and similar debacles. Ann suggested that perhaps the only way to prevent my hard work being totally screwed by technical imperfections was to become a producer and director myself. My naive theory about television up to this point had been that I would do the writing and loads of brilliant people would direct, design, choreograph and orchestrate it to improve it and thus achieve perfection. Nothing could be further from the truth. Unless each one of those roles is fulfilled to perfection, they all conspire unwittingly to screw the work into the ground.

Again through the good offices of Michael Mills, I applied for the post of trainee television producer. It is worth noting at this point that in light entertainment the term 'producer' meant 'producer and director'. There were no directors at that time. Producers did both jobs. A few weeks later I got a BBC board and was interviewed by Ronnie Waldman and several anonymous bodies from the personnel department. It was a very formal affair. I was asked what ideas I had for programmes. I did my best to make something up. Ronnie asked me if I had seen the Jimmy Wheeler show the previous night and what I thought of it. I replied that I thought Jimmy was trying out a lot of new material that wasn't going at all well, so he switched to his well-tried and familiar act. Significant looks from Ronnie and another member of the board led me to believe this was true. A few weeks later I was informed that the position was mine. Jimmy Wheeler had unknowingly got me the job.

I was over the moon about this until I got a letter telling me about the deal that was on offer. Producers started on a salary of £1,200 a year. I was offered a six-month provisional contract at half salary, which amounted to £300 for six months' work. I would, of course, have to forgo any writing and other activities. How could I survive? I owned two houses, but the bank manager said he simply didn't like property as an investment. I went to see Richard Stone and presented him with my problem. '£300 for six months?' he said. 'Ridiculous!' Commercial television was starting up in about four months time. He picked up the telephone to speak to a mate of his at Associated Rediffusion and explained to them that they needed somebody to take care of light entertainment scripts and that, with my experience of writing for television and all those pantomimes, I was just the bloke for the job. The mate agreed and straight away I was offered a year's contract at £1,500 a year. I took the job. There were no boards or interviews. I was to start the following week. I could cease to be a show band singer. I could pay the mortgages. I could buy a car. I was in 'commercial television'.

14
Let Us Not Be Baffled

Associated Rediffusion was a subsidiary of the British Electric Traction Company, a huge conglomerate that started business running trams. They went into show business with all the finesse of a tram company. At the top of their boardroom structure were former naval officers. Among the senior ones was Captain Brownrig. On being appointed to run one of the only two commercial television stations in the United Kingdom, he is reputed to have ordered an enormous quantity of rope because he was sure it would come in handy sooner or later.

The station acquired Adastral House in Kingsway, which in the war had housed the RAF. It was a large building with, I think, four storeys, and had fallen into disrepair. On arrival I was met by clouds of cement dust and a deafening clatter of pneumatic drills. For a few weeks I shared an office with Peter Willes, who had the title of 'talent manager'. He was a tall and very good-looking man in his mid-forties with a wicked sense of humour, a razor-like wit and a ruthless ambition. He was completely at sea in popular light entertainment. His idea of a show the British public would go for was anything starring Hermione Baddeley and Hermione Gingold. He later did most distinguished work in drama, where he encouraged and nurtured new writers and achieved a well-deserved reputation as an innovator. Initially we had no office furniture. Peter sat on a defunct central heating radiator under a window on one side of the office. I had a similar perch under a window opposite. We had a telephone each that we frequently used to talk to each other, this being the only way of being heard above the din made by the builders.

It was a farcical situation and led to hysterical laughter most of the time. The two of us were in fact the light entertainment department, and we set about trying to get some sort of organisation around ourselves. An early task was to recommend a candidate to be head. Ken Carter was an early recruit, but he didn't want to assume the responsibility. He was made senior producer and did become, in effect, the head of light entertainment because nobody was put above him. We took on various people as producers, including my brother Peter, who at least knew how to put a show together.

After a while I got a pleasant office overlooking the central courtyard and a delightful young secretary in the person of Sally Slatterly, who was the daughter of the vice chief of air staff. I started to put together programme ideas and to read the dozens of scripts sent in by writers who rightly believed that Associated Rediffusion would ultimately have to shove something out over the air.

Wembley Studios were acquired and adapted to give us several stages, including two large studios that could be converted into a single enormous one by sliding aside the great 25-foot-high folding doors. I gained possession of an expense account and was able to take selected writers to Simpsons in the Strand or Rules in Covent Garden for most excellent lunches. To the chagrin of Peter Willes and me, Jack Hylton got together with one or two senior figures of the company by promising to deliver shows containing the Crazy Gang and Arthur Askey. We realised that this would be a very heavy threat to our future with the company, and we fought against it like hell. We told everybody that Jack couldn't deliver any of these artistes, mostly because they were unavailable. We were right, and our opposition was so effective that Jack threatened legal action against the pair of us, so we had to back off.

I was very concerned that the company appeared to be planning to open the station on the first night 'cold', with no dummy runs or any practice at running the station, with all its programmes and commercials. This seems to be almost impossible to believe, but assuredly nothing was ever mentioned in the way of a practice week until Peter Willes and I badgered the management to reveal what the plan was going to be. In the event a whole week of practice programmes, which the public wouldn't see, was scheduled. As the opening date approached, excitement mounted until it assumed D-Day-like proportions.

The company would never have got on the air had it not been for the unofficial cooperation of the BBC. Everyone taking part was a former BBC employee, and they called upon their old mates to help them out. Vital components that had been ordered but not delivered to the Rediffusion studios were borrowed. The entire BBC sound effects library was spirited away a dozen records at a time, copied and returned.

Also vital to this operation was a guy named Lloyd Williams. Lloyd had joined Rediffusion from the BBC, where he was a lowly floor manager. Like Ko Ko in *The Mikado*, he was 'wafted by a favouring gale' and swiftly became a very important executive. Fortunately for the company, he knew a hell of a lot about the practical aspects of mounting a television show and was thus a critical factor in successfully getting us on the air.

A day or two before the opening, very late at night, a programme was actually transmitted to ensure that the system was working. It was a revue produced by my brother Peter starring Nicolette Roeg. It went out without a hitch, but it was a secret and received no publicity. On the day of the opening we all received an 'Order of the Day' from Captain Brownrig which read: 'Let us not be baffled.' Next morning, despite numerous mishaps, everybody received another one that read: 'We were not baffled.'

Rediffusion was initially responsible for Monday to Friday television, while ATV covered the weekends. Lew Grade and ATV occupied the floor above Rediffusion at Adastral House, and to mount that one storey was to move into a different world with quite a different atmosphere. There resided the people who knew what they were doing and who revolutionised British television. With Prince Littler (who had taken over the Stoll Theatre Group) and Val Parnell, they had long been running the popular entertainment world and they simply had a very good idea of what the British public wanted. They recruited the best of the BBC's producers and I found it a sheer delight just to walk along the corridors and breathe the confident atmosphere.

Down below at Rediffusion we muddled along, but it was difficult to get decisions when it came to planning programmes. Dick Lester walked into my office one day like a breath of fresh air, played the piano and sang the score for a production called *Curtains for Harry*. We ultimately succeeded in getting the show staged, with Bobby Howes starring and Philip Saville directing, but we failed to get a permit for Dick – an American – to direct it. Jack Hylton succeeded in bringing Tony Hancock to do a short series. Ken Carter produced it, but without Ray Galton and Alan Simpson, Hancock's writers, it died a death.

When we finally succeeded in gathering Dick Lester into the fold, he produced the first of the alternative comedy series in *The Idiot Weekly, Priced Tuppence*, which starred Peter Sellars and Spike Milligan. Spike wrote 'The Ying Tong Song' by way of a signature tune and the show was a great critical success.

Rumour had it that Lew Grade was wooing Frank Muir and Dennis Norden and offering them an exclusive contract to write only for ATV. I therefore took myself up to see Dennis and Frank and, entirely off my own bat, said that Rediffusion would match any offer Lew made. They assured me that they had no intention of signing any exclusive contract, and if such an offer were to be made, they would demand a sum that would stop Lew from talking for at least 30 seconds. I was reassured.

By now, ugly but well-founded stories were circulating that Rediffusion was in serious financial trouble and was within ten days of being wound up. The company had been spending money like water and, in all honesty, television production is a vastly expensive business and they were entirely without experience in that sort of field. An American called John Macmillan came on the scene and set about putting the whole operation on a firmer financial footing. Contracts were not renewed, expense accounts (including mine) were stopped, and redundancies rained down like confetti. It was painful but he undoubtedly saved the company.

My agent Richard Stone had by this time built up a very good relationship with Bernard Delfont. Largely as a result of this, Cyril and I were commissioned to write the score of a new musical written by Ian Stuart Black entitled *Starmaker*, which was to star Jack Hulbert, Cicely Courteneige and Jerry Wayne. The story concerned a disc jockey (Jerry Wayne) who, as a joke, played a 1920s' record that became a huge hit. This triggers a search for the vocalist, and it turns out to be Cicely, who is now a farmer. Jack Hulbert was to direct. Jack and Cis had been huge stars since just before the First World War. Jack had been the leading light of Gaumont British Pictures during the 1930s, starring in and directing many successful films. For me there were also strong family connections. Mother had taken over from Cis in *The Pearl Girl*, and Father had understudied Jack. Cis and Jack lived in a gorgeous house in South Audley Street, where Cyril and I used to meet them for briefings about the songs required and to play them our latest efforts. We met them mainly on Sunday evenings, when Cis provided 'cold cuts', and pretended to pay little attention to Jack and ourselves, while in fact keeping an eagle eye and acute ear on the proceedings.

This part of the operation was a joyful affair and we all went up to Glasgow with high hopes for the show's opening at the King's Theatre. The first night was pretty successful. Cis was on great form. Her first entrance got a huge reception. Jack sang and danced 'Friends', which we had written specially for him. He went down a storm, but it was Una Stubbs who stopped the show with the sheer energy of her dancing and her young, up-beat personality when she did 'Rock around the Clock'. Cyril and I had fought tooth and nail against the inclusion of this number, which was an established American hit, but Bernie insisted that it should be left in. Cis had to follow this spot and was absolutely livid. After the show she made herself clear to us all: 'I think the girl is very clever and she'll probably be a very big star, but NOT IN MY SHOW.' These capital letters were emphasised by thumps on her dressing-room table with her clenched fist. Una's number was moved forwards and backwards to every possible position in the running order, but no matter where it was put, she still stopped the show.

From the first night onwards Jack proceeded to tear the show apart, as had been his custom when directing shows in the past. We weren't too worried to begin with, but after a while it became evident that he no longer had the golden touch: having destroyed the show, he was failing to put it together again. He would call the cast together at ten o'clock every morning and would promptly go to sleep in the stalls. By the third week the cast complained to Equity, the actors' union.

For no obvious reason Jack and Cis would lose confidence in a song and we would be sent for to write a replacement. This we would do and either take the express train or a plane to wherever the show was being staged to play them the new one. We would return to London a couple of hours later so as not to get involved in the general destruction that was taking place. Ian Stuart Black, the author, was on the verge of a nervous breakdown, and one or two other members of the production team hit the bottle heavily. The ultimate experience for me came at Coventry in a matinee. During the actual performance Jack abandoned his role in the show, came down to the footlights, turned his back on the audience, folded his arms and watched the show like a member of the public, wandering back from time to time when it was his turn to deliver a line.

Word of the disaster had got back to London, and Bernard Delfont sent for Cyril and me. We went to meet him in his rather simple office over the tube station at Piccadilly Circus. The building was part of the original London Transport architecture, and the office was quite small with a strange half-moon-shaped window. Many years later when Ann was starting up on her own as a theatrical agent she had the very same office. During the meeting Bernie asked us to tell him frankly what we thought should be done. Cyril said he thought Bernie should abandon the production, and I very reluctantly agreed.

Cis was devastated because such a thing had never happened to her before. At the same time she remained completely loyal to Jack. I never heard her utter a word against him, although she knew exactly what was going on. Looking back, I think maybe it was the right decision, but oh, what a shame! So much of the show was right and it was a great idea. We had worked hard to get the music away. We persuaded Chappells to publish the score. Old Bill Cotton was approached to record 'Friends'. This he agreed to do, but he asked for 50 per cent of our royalties as part of the deal. I said I thought this particular demand was a bit steep. 'Listen, sonny,' he said. 'I sell records. It's better to have 50 per cent of something than 100 per cent of sod all.' The phrase he used was stronger than 'sod all', but I am sure you will get the message. I did, and I think it was one of the most valuable pieces of advice I ever received. For a number of years after, I used to meet the unfortunate gentleman who backed the show. He would place both hands over his wallet and say, 'David! Every time I see you I get an awful pain just here.'

Networking was in the offing at Rediffusion, and it was clear that before much longer they would not have any need for a light entertainment script editor. However, my contract had some time to run and we were still trying to produce television shows. I went down to Paignton to see a new comic called Bruce Forsyth, who was appearing in summer season. I reported that he danced, played the piano and sang well, but lacked charm. Ken Carter took him on with several other comics in an attempt to create our own Crazy Gang, but it didn't work.

About this time Ann took herself into rep at Folkestone, which was being run by Arthur Brough, whom I later cast as Mr Granger in *Are You Being Served?* He was a good boss and had a lovely stage personality, but even in those days he was a little unsteady with his lines. Peter Whitbread, a young actor in the company, said that he fancied turning *The Maker of Heavenly Trousers* into a musical. This was a 1930s' best seller by Daniel Varee set in the diplomatic quarter of Shanghai in the late 1920s. It was a sweet story and he was keen to write the book, so I secured a year's rights from Varee's widow. Many months later, after Cyril and I had worked on it and had written a great score, we played it to George Sanders, who was in England for a short holiday. It so happened that he was a good singer and, to our great joy, he agreed in principle to appear in it. I persuaded a BBC designer to do preliminary sketches of the sort of sets that would be suitable and, thinking I had a saleable package, we went along to see Bernard Delfont with the proposition. Bernie listened with interest but said, 'I don't like the idea of George Sanders. I know he's a big Hollywood film star but he has a cynical sort of personality and I don't think the public will go for him.' We were a bit shattered by this; we thought we had a cast-iron proposition and we couldn't think of any comparable star. End of *The Maker of Heavenly Trousers*.

Back at the factory I directed the odd 15-minute television show, but this was stopped because regular producers were being made redundant. Thus, in 1957, my stint with the chaotic Rediffusion came to an end. The writing career, however, was going pretty well. Cyril and I wrote songs for George and Alf Black to put into their shows at the Winter Garden and the Opera House, Blackpool. Each of the shows at the Opera House had a very spectacular ending to the first half, such as an oilfield fire, a liner sinking, or 'The Mighty Waters of Pitz Pallu' tumbling all over the place. We wrote musical *scenas* for all such eventualities. I did the usual summer shows for Harry Secombe and Norman Wisdom at the Palladium, and pantomimes for Birmingham and Wolverhampton were being staged for very long seasons. Ann went into *Anniversary Waltz*, an American play by Jerry Choderov, starring the great Bernard Braden and Barbara Kelly. She was covering Barbara, and at the Grand Theatre, Leeds, she played the part for a week opposite Bernard when Barbara had to have an operation. The play came to London but failed because all the comedy was about the commercials in television and that form of entertainment had not been running long enough.

Robert Nesbit was planning to open the Talk of the Town at the old London Hippodrome, where I had spent the first few weeks of my life sleeping in a laundry basket in the number one dressing room. I now spent long sessions at his office, where he had an enormous working model demonstrating all the functions of this project with its sliding stages and fountains. Cyril and I wrote a lot of material for the opening show. Bernard Delfont had huge enthusiasm for the whole proposition and even excitedly showed me samples of the carpets he was planning to lay over the whole vast auditorium. Ann and I were invited to the opening. We were distinctly short of funds at the time, and I decided that we definitely couldn't afford to face a large bill for food and champagne at the Talk of the Town, so I reluctantly said we had another engagement. The next day I discovered that Bernie was picking up the tab. It had been a free night!

Ann, who by now was taking all the important decisions in our lives, decided that we should move to the country. We had both spent a lot of our spare time papering and painting our Finchley house from top to bottom, so by this time it was a good proposition for letting. Being an avid reader of advertisements, she read in *The Times* about a beautiful property known as Kent's Farm House in Clymping, near Littlehampton, that belonged to the Guinness estate. We went along to be interviewed by Lord Normanby. This was a bit like applying for a commission in the army but, against considerable competition, we secured the lease. In due course we moved down there with Nicky, Penny and Olive, plus our newly acquired second-hand 1954 drop-head 2½-litre Lagonda.

It was a glorious house – mainly Queen Anne – with an impressive Victorian studio room. We both fell in love with it and spent all our spare time and money redecorating it and fixing the garden. The only problem with it was that we couldn't afford to live in it. It had a central heating boiler that was large enough to power a steamer and took a dustbinful of coke twice a day to keep it going. It also needed a cook, a maid, a daily cleaner and a gardener to staff it. All these we acquired. It was a feature of life at the time that if your telephone number was a 'toll' number people didn't bother to ring you because you lived too far away. As a result work began imperceptibly to dry up.

I now dreamt up an idea for a musical that I thought I could sell to Melville Gillam, who was running the Connaught Theatre, Worthing. It was to be called *The Pied Piper* and was based on a character who picked up a pipe that turned out to have belonged to the Pied Piper of Hamelin. Every time he played it, strange things began to happen. I committed the idea to a page and a half of foolscap and succeeded in selling it for production the following Christmas.

142

Cyril and I wrote the score, and I wrote the book. As soon as it was finished, Melville staged a reading in my studio with members of his rep company, including Susannah York, and all seemed well. When it came to casting, we went for Anthony Newley for the leading part, but he suddenly became unavailable for a few months and we were committed for Christmas. Gary Miller was engaged, and he played and sang the part wonderfully well. Melville hired a girl who was six months pregnant to play the leading female part. I think he felt sorry for her.

I had visualised that the story would be set in a quaint but decrepit German village, but Melville and his rather ineffectual director had the designer create a garish pantomime set. From then on they tried to make the show more and more like a pantomime, and this culminated in the booking of Duncan's Collies to do their doggy act towards the end of the first half, with Duncan officiating whilst dressed as a sort of tatty Robin Hood.

The show opened just before Christmas. Some of it was very good indeed, but the audience were at a loss to decide whether they had come to see a pantomime – which it definitely was not – or a musical – which it was from time to time. Business was less than brisk, but there was nothing I could do. I was just the writer and as such I had no power. Coupled with this, we were very seriously broke. Concentrating on the musical, I had neglected to find other work. Meanwhile, George and Alf Black were about to open up Tyne Tees Television, based in Newcastle. My very good friend Bill Lyon-Shaw was controller of programmes and they all wanted me to join them as a producer. The show still had a couple of weeks to run but, since there was nothing more that I could do, one cold morning early in January I took a train to Newcastle.

15
Have You Tried
This New Glue, Ned?

Arriving in Newcastle was a pronounced cultural shock. In contrast to my luxurious country house, my digs were in a large Victorian pile in the dreaded Jesmond Road. I had been given a small, dark attic at the very top of the cold house. The reason it was dark was because the only illumination was supposed to come from a skylight in the roof, and this was covered by 4 inches of snow.

The studios and the working atmosphere, however, were great. Tyne Tees under George and Alf Black was a professional outfit bursting with enthusiasm. I was introduced to my office, which was adequate, and to Jane Darling, my secretary. Jane was the daughter of Claude Darling, who was the vice-chairman of the company. I was less than happy about this. Sally Slatterly, my secretary at Rediffusion, was the daughter of the vice-chief of air staff, and at the beginning of operations knew precisely nothing about television, although she worked out extremely well. I was not keen to train another beginner – especially if she was placed with me just because she was the vice-chairman's daughter. As it turned out, Jane took approximately 30 seconds to master all aspects of the business and proved to be a wonderful asset. She fought battle after battle on my behalf and became a lifelong friend. She was a loyal powerhouse.

My first task was to find somewhere to live for Ann and the family, who were due to arrive in about a week. Helped by Jane, I rented a modern bungalow at a place called Ponteland, which I later found out meant 'the village in the bog'. It was aptly named because every time you stepped outside the back door your feet gave you the impression that you were stepping on a soft, interior-sprung mattress. The illusion was rather spoilt by the water that lapped around the ankles.

Ann then skidded her way up the A1 in appalling weather in the sports Lagonda with Olive, two kids, Hoover the Labrador and her 12 puppies, Mambo the mongrel and the Siamese cat, plus all the luggage and a few electric fires. The bungalow had a large reception room that was so cold we never entered it until the spring. The place had a lot of mirrors that, despite the presence of our electric heaters, were always cloudy. Between the kitchen and the dining room was a spectacular aquarium with a wealth of exotic tropical fish. Every breakfast time started with the funeral of one of these rare and delicate creatures that had floated lifeless to the surface.

Tyne Tees went on the air very soon after I arrived in Newcastle. My first task was to direct an advertising magazine, known in the business as an 'admag'. This was a strange form of entertainment that went under the guise of a 15-minute magazine programme but featured various products that the artists or presenters could idly discuss. The one I copped was called *Ned's Shed* and was designed to cater for do-it-yourself products such as glue, fertiliser and garden tools – in fact, all the bits and pieces that would only fit uneasily into a regular admag. It was presented by Lisle Willis and Dan Douglas, who were two genuine Geordies. In fact they not only presented it but wrote it, and they also wrote many of the other programmes that Tyne Tees did. It all took place in a garden shed where Ned and his mate chatted about Ned's wife, 'Wor our Bella,' and went on to breathtaking lines such as, 'Have you tried this new glue, Ned? It sticks glass and cardboard and mends tears in your trousers and it's only one and six a tube.'

After a short time we started to run out of do-it-yourself items so, with great ingenuity, we introduced a gas ring that allowed us to advertise things that had to be heated, such as fish glue and 'Marmade'. The latter consisted of a tin of orange peel, to which Ned added water, sugar and one or two other things to produce – you guessed it – marmalade. The show was live and, of course, we had our disasters. One that sticks in my mind was a tennis shoe whitener. This consisted of a tube of white stuff topped by a little round sponge secured by a plastic cap. During the line-up break, the prop man left the cap off and the whole thing baked under the studio lights. When Ned tried to demonstrate the ease with which he could whiten his shoes, he produced streaks of white goo similar to toothpaste. The more desperately he tried, the worse it looked, and lines such as 'Look how smoothly it goes on,' and 'It takes no time at all' were no help. The result of these disasters was that we had to give numbers of free insertions to help repair the damage done to the reputation of the product.

I went from this to direct *The One O'Clock Show*. I approached this with some trepidation because I had never done a programme that ran more than 15 minutes. *The One O'Clock Show* was live and ran for 45 minutes. I sought the advice of Philip Jones, who was the only experienced producer on the staff. He placed three pennies on a table and said, 'Suppose these are the cameras.' He then placed a finger on each. 'When you move them about,' he said, 'don't cross your fingers and you won't get your cables tangled.'

'What about the booms and the sound?' I asked.

'Oh, don't bother about them. They'll sort themselves out.' The lesson took about three minutes, and is the only instruction I have ever had about how to produce television.

In each show were a couple of comedy sketches and a couple of band numbers, the boy and girl singers sang a duet and a number each, and there were three or four interviews with the public in the audience. The singers were Chris Langford, who was a young and pretty singer with a great voice, and George Romain, who sang well and played in the sketches if required. The overall presenter was Terry O'Neill, a multi-talented entertainer who sang, tap-danced, played a mean clarinet, was funny in the sketches and proved an easy interviewer. Helping him out in the sketches was Jack Haig, who later played Monsieur Leclerc for me in *'Allo 'Allo*. Other parts were played by Terry's wife and by Ann who, in no time at all, was appearing in admags with Kenneth Horne, in straight magazine programmes and in most of the shows that were being presented. In the afternoons we rehearsed the next day's show and prepared the camera script. At one time I was producing two admags and three *One O'Clock Shows* – five programmes – per week.

Every Monday evening I would go to see the star who was topping the bill at the Empire Theatre and tell them what wonderful fun they would have if they appeared on *The One O'Clock Show*, although we couldn't pay them more than a couple of bottles of Scotch. Most of the stars fell for it. This was the cause of one of my early encounters with Leslie Macdonell, who was the boss of Moss Empires. 'I pay them, and every week you use them for free,' he complained. I countered that I was giving his shows wonderful free publicity and he was doing better business. I also went with Terry O'Neill to the Turk's Head Hotel and filmed any celebrity who happened to be staying there. This way we managed to interview Louis Armstrong, who was recovering from whatever he had to recover from following the night before. He was nevertheless very complimentary about the trumpet playing of Humphrey Lyttelton, which I presume delighted the viewers.

Although Ann and I were both working, we were making only slow progress towards solving our financial problems. I was in the middle of planning a show when the garage that had supplied the Lagonda – on hire purchase, of course – rang and insisted on talking to me. 'Sorry to 'ave to do this, Mr Croft, but unless I get your very overdue monthly cheque on Monday morning, I'm coming up there to Newcastle, and if you don't give me the keys I'll 'ave my 'ooks on it.' The bank manager still didn't like property as security, so had lost his sense of humour about overdrafts. It took me ten minutes' talking to persuade the garage to wait another couple of weeks until my salary was paid in.

Bill Lyon-Shaw and George and Alf Black were keen to do situation comedy, so we embarked on *Under New Management*, which was set in a derelict pub in the north. It starred Glenn Melvyn and Danny Ross, who were well-known northern comics. Danny was an immensely likeable young comic who was wont to get his feet tangled in a most complicated way and, consequently, to fall over. When sitting he would wind his ankles inside the legs of the chair, forget he had done it, and fall flat on his face when he tried to get up. Glenn had a natural stutter, with which he got a lot of laughs. Ronnie Barker saw and admired Glenn and borrowed the stutter for his character in *Open All Hours* with David Jason. Glenn, however, was a less likeable character than Danny. A physically strong worker, he used to knock Danny about in the process of being funny, and the poor lad used to finish up black and blue. By way of compensation, Glenn was the 'brains' of the duo. The Blacks put Mollie Sugden into the show as Glenn's wife. At first this didn't please me at all because I didn't know Mollie or her work. I wanted to do my own casting, but I very soon came to love and admire her and later put her into *Hugh and I* and *Are You Being Served?* as well as *Up Pompeii!*

I cast Grahame Stark as an eccentric and secretive Irishman who entered the pub from time to time in a conspiratorial fashion, whispered a few inconsequential lines and made a hurried exit. I put Robert Raglan in as an incompetent policeman. Robert later played the colonel – Mainwaring's superior – in many episodes of *Dad's Army*. I well remember one sequence he played as the less-than-bright copper. He rushed into a telephone box and reported to his boss: 'A man has just held up the pub. I'm speaking from the telephone box opposite.' His boss said, 'Can you give a description?'

147

'Yes,' he said. 'About seven feet high and painted red.' The cast was completed by Jerry Verno as an inebriate – which, of course, he was.

The storylines were written by Johnny Speight, who was not very well known at the time. The scheme was that the stories would be sent to Robert Moore, who happened to be Mollie's husband. He would use them to write the complete script. Unfortunately, storylines were not Johnny's strong point, so the scheme didn't work. We would all sit round and read through the script on Monday. Having done that, we would say, 'Well, we can't possibly do that,' and jointly devise a new script, which Bob would write for the rest of the day and most of the night and all day on Tuesday. The principal contributors to this system were Glenn, Grahame and I. We would set it and make it work on Wednesday, give it a coat of funny paint on Thursday and do it live on Friday evening. Thus we did 13 programmes. A lot of comedy shows were done this way in those days. It was not very good for the nerves, and the result was never very original, but we usually managed to remember some funny material, so we got by. It was one of the happiest shows I ever did because four members of the cast were bridge fanatics. As soon as we stopped rehearsal, out came the cards.

A pivotal domestic incident happened about this time. Nicky and Penny were going to the local council school in Ponteland. One memorable night Ann was putting them to bed when Nick piped up, 'Mummy – do ye have to pit the leet oot?' Ann flew into the kitchen. 'That's it. They go back to London next week. They can stay with my mother and father and go to school in Hitchen.' The kids and Olive, Hoover, Mambo and cat accordingly went to Hitchen. Ann and I gave up the bungalow in the bog and went to live in a one-room flat with plastic furniture in the still dreaded Jesmond Road, with the cooker in a cupboard and the shared loo on the half-landing. It was a long way short of being a chic pad, but at least I had devised an ingenious scheme to get rid of all the puppies – I gave them away as prizes for the winners of quiz programmes and charged George and Alf Black £3 per pup.

One sad thing happened during our stay in Newcastle. Mother died. Her latter years had been very unhappy. She was much deluded, believing her second husband, Hugh Gough, was having her followed and that Olive and I were squandering her fortune. Of course our enforced stay in Newcastle meant that we were not able to see her or to help very much financially. She had failed to find a co-tenant to stay with her in her large flat in Burleigh Mansions, Charing Cross Road, so she was threatened with termination of her lease. She had gone to visit her cousin, Winnie Meldrum, and there she had a massive stroke. We went down to Bournemouth for the funeral in our as yet unrepossessed Lagonda, and Mother was laid to rest in the Parkstone Cemetery. It was a sad ending to what had for many years been a brilliant career.

I had written a lot of material for Bill Lyon-Shaw and the Blacks, so when I had an idea for a comedy show, they readily agreed to let me go ahead. I wrote it for Terry O'Neill and it was the first and only situation comedy with music. I called it *Sunshine Street*. It had a composite set consisting of Terry's flat, part of the street and one or two shops; an orchestra led by Dennis Ringrowe; six dancers; and the audience. It also had a separate area for the odd extra scene. As a live show it was a pretty hairy experience to produce, but the viewers loved it and it worked out to be a very good and unique format that I was never able to reproduce in later years.

One sketch stays in the mind. It was the beginning of the era of 'theme' restaurants. Terry decided to take his girlfriend to an 'Olde Englishe' restaurant. The waiter was Jack ('It is I – Leclerc') Haig, dressed as a Beefeater, who had just retired after 25 years waiting on the dining cars of British Railways. As a result he staggered everywhere as if on a train travelling at 70 miles an hour, spilling soup on the diners when going over the points. This was just the sort of material that Jack could handle impeccably, and he got gales of laughter.

The chairman of Tyne Tees visited us during this production. He was a dignified gentleman who walked with difficulty on two crutches. He arrived during an energetic dance number. The choreographer was Pat Kirschner, who was a principal dancer with the Festival Ballet. At the climax of the number she did a spectacular knee slide towards the chairman. Her skirt rose, leaving little to the imagination. The dignified chairman promptly fell off both his crutches.

I wrote 13 episodes of *Sunshine Street*, the Blacks paid properly, and commissions continued to come in for Palladium summer shows and pantomimes. Thus our financial troubles began to recede. I will be forever grateful to the Blacks and Bill Lyon-Shaw for starting my career as a television producer. The 18 months we had spent in Newcastle had proved invaluable experience and were exceedingly enjoyable, but Ann and I couldn't see ourselves as long-term Geordies, and we had a gorgeous house in Sussex. We now had renewed confidence in the future and decided to quit the north and return to our glorious Kent's Farm House. Here Ann gave birth to our third child – Jane. The date was 16 July 1960.

I proceeded to pick up a living from freelance writing and, strangely enough, singing. Fiona Bentley, a former stage manager and a good friend of Cyril's, was starting up the World Record Club and had obtained the licence to adapt a number of Beatrix Potter classics for inclusion in a children's record catalogue. The records were '45s' and made of coloured plastic – red, green, blue and yellow. The text was narrated by Vivien Leigh. I did the adaptations and Cyril and I wrote special songs. Fiona was a very persuasive boss and managed to recruit many stars to play parts on the records, including Cicely Courtneidge.

Cis was a bundle of nerves on the day of the recording, and her script was positively shaking in her hand as she sang and played the part of Jemima Puddleduck, but she gave a superb performance. I got Grahame Stark to play the fox and also Squirrel Nutkin and, when in any doubt, in order to save money I played the parts myself. We spread the catalogue a bit further, and I adapted *Aladdin* for Dickie Henderson and Norman Evans, *Treasure Island* for Sir Donald Wolfit, *Thumbelina* for Bernard Braden and *Ali Baba* for Dick Bentley. Ian Carmichael was supposed to do *Daddy Longlegs* with Anna Massey, but he got flu, so again I played the part. It transpired that Fiona was keen that I should not appear in the publicity photographs, but didn't like to tell me. However, I suspected what was afoot because I noticed that I was always on the edge of the pictures, which meant that I could be cut off with a pair of scissors in the finished shot!

During most of the years we were living at Clymping, Cyril Ornadel was conducting musicals for Jack Hylton. These included *Wish You Were Here, Call Me Madam, Pal Joey* and *Kismet*. Cyril was a man of enormous energy and, to enable us to write together, we had given him a bedroom next to my office at the top of the house. He would come down to our place after the show on Saturday night and, as further evidence of that enormous energy, he would be accompanied by his current and frequently changing girlfriend. At one time we had a young Frenchman helping us in the house. He would take up Cyril's morning tea and return to the kitchen to report laconically, 'This week, it is blonde.'

It emerged that the Gilbert and Sullivan catalogue was going to be free of copyright in Germany before it was released in England, so Fiona decided to make three of the operettas, including *The Mikado,* in Hamburg with the Hamburg Philharmonic. To my utter delight she cast me as Ko Ko, so off we all went to Hamburg for the recording. The orchestra being busy with their Philharmonic duties both day and evening, we started to record at 11 o'clock at night. Fine German sausages and steaming hot coffee were served to everybody at one in the morning, and the session went on until four. I received a bit of an accolade from the string section for 'Tit Willow'. After I had finished they all rapped their bows on the back of their violins. I thought they were giving me a German version of 'the bird', but I found out later that it was a very great compliment. Those playing on a Stradivarius are not expected to be too vigorous in their enthusiasm! When Fiona released the record she decided to call the orchestra the Westminster Symphony Orchestra. I can only report that they spoke fluent German to a man and munched knackwurst at one in the morning, which is not an activity much seen in Westminster.

Not being required for the other recordings, Ann and I spent a couple of nights sampling the delights of the notorious Reeperbahn. German husbands take their wives to these 'entertainments' and the most outrageous sexual acts are greeted with loud guffaws of laughter and rounds of applause. We thoroughly enjoyed ourselves.

We made records of several other musicals, including *Rose Marie,* in which I was very bad as Hard-boiled Herman. I was very pleased to do a couple of tracks in *No, No, Nanette* – the musical in which I had failed to get a job in the chorus just before the war. A notable recording was *White Horse Inn.* I pleaded successfully with Fiona to let me sing 'Goodbye'. If you ever get a chance to listen to the lyric, you can see that this was written as a comic song, but every singer gets so wrapped up in vocalising the tune that the comedy never emerges.

On the actual day of the recording the chap who was playing the leading role on the record lost his voice, so Cyril handed me his score and said, 'You're on!' I didn't know the song 'You Too', but by this time I could read music pretty well, so with one brief rehearsal I made the track. It was a duet with Barbara Leigh who had one of the loveliest soprano voices I ever heard. I had to persuade her to put an extra breathing space in a couple of times for my benefit, but the recording went well and the item is played from time to time on quiz shows when the quiz-master says, 'I bet you can't guess who the singer is.' They can't. The recording of the whole musical was made in two sessions of three hours. Seven minutes before the end of the second session, the musical director Johnny Douglas realised that they had not recorded the overture. 'Shall we go for it?' he asked the session musicians. 'Why not?' they answered. Go for it they did, and they made a faultless track. This is yet another illustration of the fantastic professionalism of session musicians at that time. It makes an interesting contrast with the weeks pop groups spend in the studio these days.

Deciding that we were not very skilled landlords, Ann and I decided to sell Wickliffe Avenue, and as it turned out, the tenants were prepared to pay a good price for it. The bank manager was overjoyed that he was no longer being asked for extended overdrafts with property as the security, and we were overjoyed to have the change from the mortgage in our account.

Cyril had undertaken to write *Pickwick* with Leslie Bricusse and, at about the same time, the BBC advertised for a couple of experienced television producers. Still hankering after directing my own material, I applied once more. While awaiting the inevitable board and interview we decided to go to New York to see some musicals and then to San Francisco and Los Angeles. In New York I could meet my stepmother for the first time, and in Los Angeles we could see Father's Hollywood homes and also try to sell the recordings of children's stories to Capitol Records.

New York greeted us with 16 inches of snow. The plane landed in an avenue bulldozed between piles of snow 10 feet high. Only public transport and taxis were allowed on the streets. Parked cars were completely buried next to the pavements. We saw *Camelot*, with Richard Burton, Julie Andrews, Robert Goulet and Bob Coote. Bob was a great mate of my brother Peter's and knew Father well, so it was very good to see him. Herta, my stepmother, took us round the Metropolitan Museum of Art and introduced us to some unspeakably ugly paintings. She seemed a nice enough girl and had looked after Father in a most devoted way. She had since married a professor of music from Yale who was considerably younger than me. He wrote books about the technical aspects of music. (If you understood the title, you didn't need to read the book.) Herta and I were from completely different worlds, and I can't honestly say that we got on.

San Francisco was warm and friendly. We hired the biggest convertible in the world – a Sunliner – that bristled with chromium and was a gloriously bright red piece of vulgarity, and automatic with it. I almost put Ann through the front window the first time I touched the brakes. We then drove down to Hollywood via Monterey and the imposing Big Sur, finishing up in an apartment hotel in Santa Monica.

As well as the parties, dinners and other social activities, we duly went to the circular building that housed Capital Records. There we were received by a typical hard-faced Hollywood executive who gravely listened to *Peter Rabbit*. Within a couple of minutes of unsmiling stony silence, I was suddenly seized with an urgent desire to be somewhere else. We offered to play him *Little Black Sambo*. 'In this country,' said the executive with a steely voice, 'Sambo is a very dirty word.' Thankful that we hadn't played him *The Flopsie Bunnies*, we left, found the nearest bar, and had two strong gin and tonics.

On our return to Kent's Farm House I was delighted to find that I had been summoned to the BBC the very next day. Expecting to have a polite interview, I found myself being taken straight into a BBC board headed by Eric Maschwitz with Tom Sloan at his side. Eric I knew well from *Belinda Fair* days. Tom's job was as a sort of unofficial assistant head of light entertainment, although I think he had the title of programme manager. His function was to 'work' Eric Maschwitz, who was a brilliant if rather erratic character. They were both exceedingly polite and, after asking a few routine questions, revealed that they had consulted George and Alf Black who had sent a glowing report, with a PS at the bottom to the effect that 'Having re-read this letter, we would like to point out that we are not related to David Croft.'

A week or two later I got a letter offering me the producer job at, as far as I remember, £1,200 a year. There were apparently nearly a hundred applicants and the other successful one was the radio producer of *The Show Band Show* – Johnny Stewart. I eagerly said 'Yes'. With a hell of a lot of experience and about 250 shows for commercial television under my belt, I was finally with the BBC.

16
Early Days at the BBC

Things happened very fast when I arrived at the BBC. I was given a long thin office in Television Centre overlooking the scenery block and, if you looked a bit further, London. It was the custom to allot secretaries on a permanent basis, so I was made the chairman of a special board to select one from the likely candidates. We interviewed several and I selected Eve Lucas, who became my loyal helper for many years. She knew the BBC backwards, having been secretary to the head of liaison, and her contacts among the secretarial mafia were impressive.

Frank Muir and Dennis Norden were running the comedy side of the light entertainment department. They were called 'comedy advisers'. They sent for me in high excitement and told me they had been nursing a new project that they were thrilled about, based on the life and background of university students. They had contacted a few writers who had attempted scripts, and the whole project was to go to air in four weeks' time. Not knowing the time it takes to mount a series at the BBC, I was not daunted by this aspect of the project. On the other hand, I did point out that my education stopped before I actually took the School Certificate and I had no knowledge of university life whatsoever. Frank and Dennis in turn were not daunted by this fact. 'You know comedy,' they said, 'and you're a writer. This is definitely writer's comedy. We're sure you'll make a marvellous job of it.'

Being new to the BBC, as I left their office I failed to hear their loud sigh of relief at having unloaded this particular turkey. Vere Lorrimer joined me as production assistant. He had spent his early career in the theatre, where he had run his own rep company. He had now been at the BBC for a long time and was one of the people passed over when I was selected to be a producer. Many years later he directed and produced *Tenko*. He was a great enthusiast and only slightly bitter that he had been allocated to me as my assistant. I thought it a pretty cruel stroke on the part of Tom Sloan. I later learnt that Tom was inclined to do that sort of thing. Together Vere and I embarked on the project.

First came the search for a star. A few weeks previously I had seen Brian Blackburn and Peter Reeves performing in cabaret at the

Embassy Club. I thought, and I still think to this day, that Brian Blackburn is one of the funniest people I have ever seen. He has had a good career as a comedy writer, but I think I was the only producer to believe in him as a performer. Perhaps I ruined his career in the process. I played him as an inadequate and not over-energetic student, with Peter Reeves as his sidekick and feed. I thought that the British public would prefer the show to be set in a redbrick provincial university rather than in Oxford or Cambridge. Redbrick universities were little known at the time, so maybe I was wrong about that.

With Brian and Peter I assembled a good cast of miscellaneous boys and girls. I was presented with four or five sets of writers who had made attempts at scripts, but they were distinctly ordinary. By the time we were ready to rehearse I had about three possible episodes on the shelf, and so, with high hopes and one hell of a lot of ignorance, we started on the series. Cyril wrote a signature tune that I decreed should feature six trombones and a rhythm section. I called the show *The Eggheads*.

The BBC had a system of assessing programmes at this time that lasted until quite recently. We would receive an estimate of how many million people were believed to be watching and, of equal importance, a figure known as the 'Appreciation Index', or AI for short. A good average AI was 60. The pilot programme for *The Eggheads* got 45, which at that time was a record low. Nobody said anything. True, at the bar of the BBC club a space of two or three feet would quickly develop on either side of me in case failure happened to be a communicable disease. Dennis Main Wilson, who was going great guns with some programme or other, winked at me sympathetically from time to time, but I was left to get on with it. Muir and Norden went on holiday.

After about six programmes, with the figures improving at a pace that would not have caused a snail to lose any sleep, I decided that something had to be done. I got together with Richard Waring. Richard was a fine writer and we had met when writing *The Bells of St Martin's* for Bill Lyon-Shaw at the St Martin's Theatre. Together we knocked out an episode that I thought would do a bit better. I recorded this on a dictating machine and then sent for Eric Maschwitz and Tom Sloan and made them sit down in my office to listen to it. Meaningful looks passed between them that I was unable to interpret as good or bad. They did, however, tell me to go ahead. After all, what had they got to lose? We wrote a couple of episodes that happily gained an AI of 65, so honour was satisfied. The critics, however, remained implacably opposed to the show – Peter Black in particular wouldn't leave us alone and even gave us bad mentions when he was criticising other shows that we had nothing to do with – so, after 11 episodes, we came off the air.

To give Eric Maschwitz and Tom Sloan credit, I don't think they blamed me for *The Eggheads*. The show was professionally produced and ran to time but wasn't particularly funny, though it had its moments. For my part, I learnt that it takes a lot longer than four weeks to stage a 13-episode series at the BBC.

My next assignment was *The Benny Hill Show*. Benny was one of the first big stars of television. I had written songs for him in his earlier programmes, produced by Ken Carter, and for his theatre appearances at the Prince of Wales, so I knew him quite well. We had socialised together with Cyril Ornadel. On one memorable occasion we were all going out and Benny didn't have a girlfriend. He proceeded to ring round from Cyril's flat in Weymouth Street, using his large address book. One conversation started, 'Hullo, my love angel – this is Sexy Benny! Oh – sorry Mrs Whiteley – is your daughter there?' She wasn't. The next candidate said she was washing her hair. The one after that was washing her friend's hair. Benny was less than successful with girls.

Benny's career had reached really great heights with Ken Carter, but it was now on the decline. It is difficult to say why. He was young, slim and still quite attractive, but his boyish charm was not working as far as the public was concerned. Dave Freeman, a large, unflappable comedy author of great experience, was writing the scripts and we met many times at his house to plan the show. A lot of fundamentally funny material was devised, with special film inserts that included a sequence where a model of an American battleship was bombed by the Japs. The hand of the man releasing the bomb was well in shot in true Benny Hill style. He received much assistance from the BBC's wonderful Special Effects Department and it was a big production with an orchestra and girls and singers. Eric Robinson was conducting every television show at the time, so I decided to hand the baton to Cyril, which wasn't very popular but nobody stopped me.

For some reason or other, Benny decided to play me up. He messed about during camera rehearsal and ad-libbed a lot during scenes. All comics ad-lib and you expect it. One interesting point is that most of them ad-lib in the character they are playing at the time. Dick Emery for instance, would never come out of character. Benny ad-libbed as Benny Hill. We got through six 45-minute shows this way. Much of the material was corny and some of it was funny. In later shows for commercial television Benny disposed of his writers and wrote all the material himself, borrowing liberally from this series. The upshot of all this was that Benny and I didn't get on. I talked to Jeremy Hawk, who played Benny's straight man in this show, as in many others previously. I said that I didn't understand Benny and nor could I fathom his sexuality. 'I don't understand him either,' said Jeremy. 'I think he buys cheap night-dresses for cinema usherettes and has them parade up and down for him.'

Tom Sloan was present at some of the rehearsals and said he admired the way I dealt with Benny, but all the same the series did not enhance my reputation. Not long after that Benny left the BBC and made a huge hit and a lot of money with ITV. By way of punishment I was drafted to *This Is Your Life*. I directed alternate weeks with Yvonne Littlewood under T. Leslie Jackson, who was the legendary producer of the series. I directed 'Lifes' for Kenneth Horne, Coco the Clown, Madame Rambert and several brave Englishmen and nursing sisters who had massaged polio victims from sickness to health.

I found the 'casting' of real-life characters fascinating. There was one very brave naval officer who became an MP. At an early age his father sent him to Spain to view the civil war and get shot at because it would be good experience for him. He then sent him on a wind-jammer to get some experience 'before the mast'. At the rehearsal of the subsidiary characters that we held the day before transmission I was fascinated to see what the captain of the wind-jammer would look like. I was expecting someone like James Robertson Justice. He looked like a grocer.

The MP had later failed to torpedo a destroyer and, having run out of ammunition, he rammed the enemy vessel with his motor torpedo boat, sank and promptly got himself captured. He then escaped from POW camp disguised as 'Captain Bugaroff' and we succeeded in finding the SS officer who recaptured him. The SS officer was even kind enough to look roughly like an SS officer. I had no idea what attitude the brave MP would take. It could be quite dramatic. The great moment arrived. 'Here is the very SS officer who arrested you on that fateful day and took you back into captivity all those years ago,' said Eamonn Andrews. Enter the German officer. He approached the MP, who stretched out his hand. 'How frightfully nice to meet you again, old chap,' he said.

To liven the show up a bit, Jackson the producer rightly decided to change the scenery. Instead of the large affair with a grand mid-set entrance, which they later reverted to, he decided to make a set appropriate for the personality being featured. Thus Madame Rambert had a ballet studio with barres and Coco the Clown had a circus tent. The ultimate came when we featured a brave Englishman who had been torpedoed in the south Atlantic. He had then spent weeks on a life-raft while, one by one, his fellow sailors dropped off into the ocean. For this we had two large back-projection screens. On each screen we showed moving pictures of the surging, rolling, foaming south Atlantic. The result was that on every monitor in the gallery I had pictures of people in front of an exceedingly rough sea. About ten minutes into the programme I didn't know where to look. I was feeling very, very seasick. The brave seaman was completely unmoved by the proceedings and not a shadow of emotion crossed his British countenance. I had in reserve a great device on the front of one of the circle cameras. It was an outside broadcast camera and had an amazing zoom that would take the shot from a wide angle to a tight close-up at the plunge of a lever. We also had a really great research team on the show. They had managed to find the captain of the submarine who actually torpedoed the sailor. The critical moment arrived. Eamonn Andrews made the announcement, and the submarine commander made his dramatic entrance. 'Zoom in!' I yelled from the gallery. The lever was plunged. We zoomed in on the sailor's face. Nothing! He remained totally unmoved.

The shows were all live. The professionalism of Eamonn Andrews was breathtaking. He had a large clock in his eye-line and somehow he brought every show out to time. It was a nerve-racking show to direct. Time after time I would cue the inserts that were all on film and required a ten-second run-up to get them running to speed. The contributors would then remember another gem that they had forgotten and I would be yelling, 'Hold telecine! Hold telecine!'

As soon as Nick was born, Ann and I had resolved that by hook or by crook we would send him to boarding school, first to Pat Cox at Durlston Court and then to Rugby. We had entered him for both places within a week or two of his being born. Parents have mixed thoughts about this form of education these days. In the early 1960s the trend was to take advantage of this system if it was possible to afford it. We couldn't afford it, but we decided to enter him just the same, with the blind faith that fate would somehow supply the wherewithal. The due time arrived and Nick was accordingly kitted out as I had been in the early 1930s, even down to my old trunk and tuck-box.

We drove down to New Milton in Hampshire, which was the new location of Durlston Court. We had viewed it several times before and knew it to be warm and comfortable with a far more benign atmosphere than I had experienced all those years before. All the same, memories of my first days at boarding school came flooding back, and if anything the feelings of a parent seemed worse than those of a young schoolboy. We kept up a wholly artificial veneer of cheerfulness for the entire operation until we finally said goodbye to the worried lad. Seeing his small figure through the rear window receding into the distance proved too much for the pair of us and, once round the corner, I stopped the car and we both collapsed into floods of tears.

I was still writing for the London Palladium pantomimes and summer shows, and also for Fiona Bentley for the children's records. However, my television career was not exactly zipping along, and I started to worry whether or not I had a future with the BBC. Having nothing to do, I followed Duncan Wood around when he started directing *Steptoe and Son*. Duncan was a great operator and I learnt a lot from him. He was the first to realise that television comedy lies more in the reaction of characters to a line than in the line itself. The show was written by Ray Galton and Alan Simpson. Television comedy owes more to them than to any other writers. They invented it, and their scripts for *Steptoe* were superb. Duncan cast Harry H. Corbett as the son and Wilfred Brambell as the father. I came to admire Harry enormously. Wilfred, although very successful in the part, was not a very likeable actor. He was a poor study and would fluff and change lines in a pretty chaotic way. Harry would alter his phrases on the spot and would gather a scene together and hand it back to Wilfred time after time. I never missed a rehearsal or a transmission and it was a most valuable experience for me.

A couple of propositions came up and Tom Sloan sent for me. The first was a show for Ted Ray. The second was a show for Terry Scott and Hugh Lloyd, which became *Hugh and I*, with a script by John Chapman, who had written a couple of very funny farces for Brian Rix at the Whitehall Theatre. I thought Ted Ray a very funny comedian, but he was nearing the end of his career, so I voted the Scott/Lloyd/Chapman project a more interesting challenge. I knew Terry from Clacton Pier and Hugh from Butlins. Terry had made a big success with Bill Maynard in *Great Scott It's Maynard,* but they both had egos big enough to sink the *Titanic,* so they were no longer keen to work together.

I got on exceedingly well with Terry Scott. He was a funny man and in my experience unselfish as a comic. He had a reputation for being difficult, but I found that he just wanted everything to be right and everyone to work their socks off to make the show good. I had no quarrel with that. Hugh was always a delight and a perfect foil for and contrast to Terry. Terry would work with enormous energy to achieve any object the plot required. Cut to a close-up of Hugh and you would see that bland countenance wondering what all the fuss was about.

I put Mollie Sugden and Warwick Ashton in as the couple next door, who had a startlingly pretty daughter in Jill Curzon. There was great conflict here as Terry's character fancied Jill and was forever trying to ingratiate himself, much to Mollie's annoyance. Vi Stevens, a lovely warm cockney actress, played Terry's devoted mum, and the next-door neighbour was played by Patricia Hayes. Her screen husband was the venerable character actor Cyril Smith.

I was keen to get a new sound for the signature tune that had been written by a brilliantly talented young musician called Wally Stott. I therefore got my friend Jock Cummings to play the theme as if on a xylophone but using gin bottles for the notes. He tuned these by putting different amounts of water in each. It was a hilarious session, but to be honest it sounded not dissimilar to a xylophone.

Terry and Hugh used to drive to rehearsal together, rehearsing their lines which, by the time they arrived, they both knew perfectly. Terry used to accuse Hugh of not working hard enough, but this was rubbish. Hugh worked quite as hard as Terry, but it just didn't look like it. Every Thursday after the final rehearsal we would go to Bertorelli's in Shepherd's Bush and reward ourselves with their delicious jugged hare for lunch. In all, over the years, we did about 80 shows together.

We had to make a couple of cast changes. The first was when Jill Curzon had to leave. I had heard a girl on the radio on a record with Mike Sarne called 'Come Outside'. She had the voice of a cheeky cockney character. I had no idea what she looked like, but her name was Wendy Richard. She came to see me in my office and I thought she looked smashing and I had her read Jill's part. She didn't have acting experience but I thought she was a natural, so I took a chance and gave her the part.

Terry was a bit awkward at first, but he soon realised that Wendy had something the audience liked, and as the weeks went by she blossomed.

Cyril Smith, who was a dignified and lovable actor, fell ill and died. He had been playing Patricia Hayes' husband, so this time, rather than try to reproduce the character, I brought Jack Haig into the show to play her brother. Terry didn't like Jack, but when they were on screen together the comedy positively sparkled. They were magic together, each one determined not to be outshone by the other. Pat Hayes on the other hand was a most painstaking and thinking actress who did wonderful work. She later won best actress BAFTA for her performance in *Edna, the Inebriated Woman*. To be frank, she just plain hated Jack and his haphazard and spontaneous technique. They never got on, and I had much difficulty in keeping the peace.

John Chapman's scripts were always solid and workable and we became lifelong friends. He introduced me to Arnold Ridley, who later played Godfrey in *Dad's Army*, and we jointly enjoyed finding parts for Fred Emney, another awkward and ungrateful old comic actor who was absolutely marvellous on the screen. Fred always smoked a cigar when working and I am convinced that it was the act of removing that cigar from his mouth and flicking the ash off with two taps of his fingers before delivering a line that gave him his wonderful timing. John wrote an episode in which Terry and Hugh went pheasant shooting on Fred's estate. Somehow they got themselves mixed up with a unit of the Royal Artillery and were caught by Fred while standing beside a 25-pounder field gun. Fred took out his cigar and flicked off the ash. 'Not very sporting,' he said.

By now the programmes were being recorded on tape with the use of Ampex machines. The tape was about 2 inches wide and went through the recording machines at 15 inches per second. To assemble the sections of the programmes we would run the tapes on the machines and I would yell 'Now' at the point where we wanted the scene to end. The editor was a highly skilled but nervous character whom I used to call 'Jittery Joe'. He would mark the spot where I had yelled with a chinagraph pencil, and then we would go through the same process to find the point where the new scene began. Next came the worrying bit. Jittery Joe would poise a razor blade above the marked place and say 'Are you happy?' and I would lie and say 'Yes'. The blade would then descend and cut the tape with the awful finality of a scene from *A Tale of Two Cities*, and I would offer silent prayers that we had struck in the right place. A sort of microscope thing would then be produced and Jittery Joe, having smeared an iron solution on the tape, would examine the magnetic patterns through the microscope. These he would match with the other part of the tape before making a very accurate cut in both bits. These would then be joined together with a special metallic strip. Finally, the join was run through the recording machine and with any luck it didn't make the picture fly all over the screen. All this took 20 minutes or so, with the result that about eight joins was the maximum possible in the three-hour editing session.

Rebecca, our fourth child, was born at Kent's Farm House on 23 January 1962. Ann received unbelievable attention from the doctors for reasons we could not fathom at the time. It transpired that she had been prescribed Thalidomide, but we were fortunate that she did not take it during a critical period in the pregnancy. To everyone's relief and delight, Becky arrived sound and healthy and very pretty.

Palladium pantomimes and various sorts of freelance work continued, but the BBC didn't pay too extravagantly, so we were still over-committed financially. Ann, still the avid reader of property advertisements, found a house in Cheyne Walk that was apparently to let in rather mysterious circumstances. When she investigated it turned out to be a substantial house on the Cadogan Estate that had been rather neglected. The whole terrace was due for very substantial and expensive refurbishment, but in the meantime the Cadogan people were anxious to prevent the place being squatted. The rent was virtually nothing and we could have it for a year as long as we paid the rates and cleared out as soon as the estate was ready to do the rebuild. It was too good a proposition to miss, and so, with the most enormous regrets, we left our lovely house in Clymping and moved into the once elegant but now tatty house next door to Lord and Lady Longford. Some rather nice squatters occupied the house on the other side.

It was a very different style of living for Ann and the kids, and the minute garden was a bit of a shock for the dogs. Hoover the Labrador broke through to the Longfords' patch accompanied by Mambo the mongrel, and they both proceeded to crap all over their garden. Bela, the mongrel belonging to Ann's mother, mistook our house and got himself into the Longford residence. There he commandeered the marital bedroom and refused to let anybody enter. There followed a highly embarrassing but hilarious encounter between Ann and her ladyship, during which Ann was forced to admit that the various turds could in no way have been produced by the Longfords' little Norfolk terrier.

The house was large and rambling, but we decorated the more dismal parts. On the first floor was a large drawing room with three big windows leading to a narrow balcony. We staged some good parties there. On the ground floor was a large dining room with a lift to carry food from the roomy kitchen. The kids had a great time shouting 'Cod and four penn'orth twice' to Olive if she was down below, or perilously pulling each other up and down in it. In this same dining room we attempted one or two elegant dinner parties. On one occasion we were trying to raise a little capital for a theatrical venture. Some of our posher friends had been invited. During the pudding course Ann accidentally knocked over the cream jug. She rang the bell for Adrienne, our current 'help'. She was a sweet, willing girl but scarcely the brain of Britain. 'I've had a bit of an accident, Adrienne,' Ann said. 'Do you think you could bring a cloth?' Adrienne hurried from the room, went into the downstairs loo and sped back with a wet lavatory cloth. She then proceeded to wipe up the cream with this Jeyes Fluid-impregnated article that filled the room with an antiseptic aroma that lingered on until well past the coffee and After Eight mints. Nevertheless, the whole house had a feel of faded Edwardian dignity that was quite attractive.

Ann had been fronting an interview programme in Birmingham, a type of show she did well. However, she had a couple of traumatic experiences when the person being interviewed was very verbose at the run-through but was struck dumb on the actual transmission. When Richard Stone invited her to join him as an agent she decided to give it a try. She set up a department to deal with the pop and advertising side of the business, which was growing considerably. She worked in one of the smallest offices known to man that also contained all the office files, but with her salary and the much-reduced domestic bills, the financial pressures eased a bit.

Cheyne Gardens was large enough to provide an office for my nephew Mike Sharland and his new writing partner Ken Hoare. Mike had spent a lot of his childhood with us. We had sorted out schools for him and Ann formed a very good relationship with him as a sort of deputy mother. She managed to find a little radio work for him and Ken, but after a while she received a phone call from Mike. He said that he had decided that the agency thing wasn't working out and he was going to leave her and get representation elsewhere. Ironically, during this conversation Ann, who was at her office, could hear our canary singing in the background and also the rattle of coffee cups being delivered to Mike by the ever-willing Adrienne. Mike grew into a good writer and an astute operator and go-getter in the difficult world of show business, and is now a very successful writer's agent. Over the years Ken Hoare has proved himself to be an inspired writer with a particular flair for involved plots.

Hugh and I, summer shows and pantos kept me pretty intensely busy, and Ann was likewise heavily involved in the pop world. When the time came for us to leave Cheyne Gardens, we decided to try to find a compromise between country and town living. Ann found a desirable residence in Cheam. We gave it a cursory look, taking in the small landscaped garden and the super kitchen, and bought it. The house-moving operation fell, as usual, on Ann's shoulders. On our first night in the house we were alarmed to hear trains very loudly from a nearby railway line that had somehow escaped our notice. Ann was in the loo at the time. I knocked on the door and called 'Tickets please', and we put the house on the market next day. It took five months to sell it at a very small profit. Ann next found a large house to lease in Lansdowne Road in Holland Park. We hurriedly viewed this as daylight was dying. It was on four storeys, and by the time we had climbed to the top the dying daylight was dead and there was no electricity connected. On sheer instinct we took it. I was in rehearsal on the day we moved in, so once again Ann handled the move on her own.

Our instincts had paid off. It was a big and elegant house with five bedrooms, a dining room and a large drawing room, with a study for me and a two-roomed self-contained flat on the bottom floor. It was a great place to work and only about ten minutes' drive from the BBC White City studios. If Tom Sloan wanted to see me, he never realised that I was at home writing pantomime because Eve, my faithful secretary, was able to say quite truthfully, 'He's just popped out for a minute but he'll be back in the office in a quarter of an hour.' It was to be our home for 17 years.

It was in this house that Ann gave birth to our fifth child, John. She was well acquainted by now with the way her body handled this particular process. The midwife was summoned at the appropriate time, but she chose to ignore Ann's prediction that the latest member of the family would arrive within the hour. Furthermore, the woman chose to leave, saying that there was plenty of time to spare. John duly started to arrive as Ann had predicted. I was present for once and was to be seen with the telephone in my right hand trying to contact the absent midwife while trying to shove the emerging John back with my left. He finally arrived as the midwife was climbing the stairs. It was 11 May 1964.

It was decided to give Dick Emery his own show. It was to be quite a big affair, with Gary Miller and Mary Millar doing production numbers with guest stars, singers and dancers, and with Joan Sims helping with the comedy. Una Stubbs was featured as the principal dancer. The musical side of the show was sheer joy, but Dick was difficult to handle. We would set the show on Monday. By Tuesday afternoon he had lost confidence in the sketches. By Wednesday he had metaphorically folded his arms and said, 'Make me funny, I dare you.' It was a struggle to achieve a show by Friday. An added complication was that Dick enjoyed singing in the show. He had a very good voice and put over songs such as 'What Kind of Fool Am I?' really well. Unfortunately Tom Sloan didn't like his voice, which he referred to as 'Dick's polite baritone', and constantly nagged me to cut it. I knew this would be fatal to Dick's morale, so I wouldn't cooperate.

Joan Sims was great fun to work with and a delicious giggler. Dick I used to refer to – not to his face, I hasten to add – as a 'senile delinquent'. For instance his agent, Mike Sullivan, booked Dick Haymes the famous American film star as a guest on the show. Before transmission Dick Emery invited him into his dressing room and they started to hit the vodka in a big way. By the time the show, which was live, was due to start, Haymes was decidedly the worse for wear. The repetitious eight-bar intro started for his first song, 'Look Down, Look Down that Lonesome Road'. My assistant, the excellent Harold Snoad, was not a particularly musical person, but by the time the intro had been played six times and I had yelled 'Get the bastard on' over the intercom, he realised that Haymes should no longer be standing at the side of the stage grinning happily. He placed his boot in the Haymes backside and gave a good shove. Haymes sang the rest of his act immaculately, while rubbing his rear end a time or two.

Being much concerned with pantomime I was given the television panto to produce. It starred Terry Scott as Mother Goose, with Norman Vaughan, Laurie Lupino Lane and Jon Pertwee, and was staged at the Golders Green Hippodrome. Norman was pure magic doing a spot with kids brought on to the stage from the audience. Jon Pertwee played Baron

Hardup or some such character. Like Terry Scott, he was a strong worker who was inclined to shove his fellow artistes about. Unfortunately he had scenes with Terry Scott, so rehearsals required a referee rather than a director. Another hazard was Kay Lyell – the most famous player of the Goose in the land. Kay was 80 if she was a day. In rehearsal she made her first entrance to music without the goose skin. She came from the side very, very slowly while the pianist patiently played the entrance music three times. Before I had a chance to comment and ask her if she could gee it up a bit, she came to me and said, 'I think I should explain to you that I can't move so quickly when I'm wearing the goose skin.'

The Mike Sharland/Ken Hoare partnership suddenly bore fruit when they evolved a script for a show called *Beggar my Neighbour*, which I produced. I cast Peter Jones and June Whitfield as a middle-class couple with social ambitions who were trying to better themselves, and Reg Varney and Pat Coombes as their common next-door neighbours who were blue-collar workers but always seemed to have more money. Pat was a tall, thin, gangling actress with a great sense of character and was a solid, reliable laughter gatherer. The characters gelled straight away and the show got off to an excellent start. The only difficulty I had was with Peter Jones. Peter was a sweet man and very creative. He had a wonderfully original, inventive and subtle mind. The difficulty lay in the fact that as soon as he had read about three pages of a script he decided how he would have written the remainder of it and wanted to alter it to his specification. Much negotiation then ensued. Reg was from the variety world, was a great user of props and had enormous natural talent.

Half-way through the series Reg acquired a 'dicky ticker', having had a minor heart attack. On medical advice a bed was provided for him in the rehearsal room, but every time he wanted to use it Peter Jones was to be found on it fast asleep. It was a happy and successful show. My assistant was Terry Hughes, a tall, handsome, immaculately dressed but not very experienced young man. The ladies in the cast could scarce take their eyes off him. On location filming he managed to lose half the unit somewhere in East Anglia. Flying squad police were seeking them from King's Lynn to Bury St Edmunds. Terry is now one of the most brilliant and respected television directors in Hollywood. He was responsible for *The Golden Girls*. He still recounts the tale of the strip I tore off him.

One way and another my career was beginning to move a little more swiftly when, to my enormous surprise, Tom Sloan sent for me and said that he was about to appoint a new head of comedy and he would like me to apply for the post. You could have knocked me down by merely throwing one page from the large pile of scripts on his desk in my direction. I thanked him for paying me this great and unexpected compliment at such an early stage of my BBC career and agreed that my name should go forward. I subsequently came to think that he was making up the numbers to lend some veracity to the BBC system of appearing to give everyone a chance to join in the competition. Anyway, I didn't get the job. It went, quite rightly, to my friend Michael Mills.

Michael was about to produce a television version of *The Mikado* re-written by Alan Melville. He asked me to take it over. This I was very keen to do because I loved it and knew it backwards both from my schooldays and from the recording we had done in Hamburg. It was to be the BBC's first big production in colour. Michael had booked Cyril Richard to play the Mikado and had contracted a couple of elephants to take part in the Mikado's parade to the town of Titipu. The elephants were hugely expensive, so I cancelled them and set about assembling a great cast. Hattie Jacques agreed to play Katisha, and Richard Wattis signed for Poo Bah. I was keen to approach Tony Hancock for Ko Ko. I talked to Tom Sloan about this. He agreed that Tony would be fantastic in the part, but said he would practically forbid me to book him because at this stage he was so unreliable. I decided to look elsewhere. Harry Worth was very popular with his show at the time. I met him and had him try out 'Tit Willow'. He sang in tune with a delightful natural baritone voice. I convinced him he would be marvellous in the part, which indeed he was. My assistant for the production was John Howard-Davis. As a child star he had played Oliver in David Lean's film of *Oliver Twist* and Tom Brown in *Tom Brown's Schooldays*, so he was well versed in film and show business. He was a superb assistant.

We filmed the Mikado's arrival parade in the film studio at Ealing. The whole stage was carpeted with sawdust, to represent desert sand, with one or two mounds to give the effect of desert mountains. It was a perishingly cold day, and the procession of horses with bare-chested riders, chimps, goats, a camel and a large puma all had to wait outside in the open air. We drew a line in the sawdust for the procession to follow and I told John to start the move. All went well until the camel reached a point 15 yards from the camera. There, for no apparent reason, the wretched animal veered off course to the left. His minder, who was a villainous-looking character dressed in long Japanese camel-keeper's robes, promptly socked his charge three telling blows on the head with his fist. The camel, unsurprisingly, went back on course while I shouted 'Cut'. John patiently explained to the minder that, although he was probably adopting the normal method of controlling camels, the British public would not be sympathetic to his technique. The procession very reluctantly went round to its starting point again to wait shiveringly in the cold for us to restart.

At the second attempt the camel and minder behaved beautifully, but the puma stopped in the middle of the set. Having reached the point where the lights were brightest and the heat was greatest, he then rolled on his back, wiggled his paws in the air and luxuriated in the warmth. He didn't respond to tugging on his lead, so I approached nervously. An unidentified noise was emerging from the puma. 'Is he purring?' I asked, knowing the animal was from the cat family. 'He is definitely not purring,' said the keeper. On these occasions the solution is always to call for a tea break, and this I promptly did. Cups of hot tea as usual solved all the problems and we got the procession in the can. I had a large orchestra conducted by Harry Rabinovitz in one of the small TV Centre studios and the show in one of the large ones. I recorded all the choral numbers so that we were not presented with chorus singers goldfishing their way through the score. All the principal artists' songs were accompanied live by the orchestra. We rehearsed with cameras for two days, so by the evening of the second day everyone had a chance to solve their problems. That evening we recorded the whole 90-minute show in a three-hour session. It was a triumph for everyone concerned.

I was still producing *Hugh and I* and *Beggar My Neighbour*. One of the *Beggar* scripts required an actor to play Reg Varney's brother. This was to be a character who was even more loud-mouthed and flamboyant than Reg. Ann had a client who she thought would fit the part. He was an actor who had run his own repertory company but was having great difficulty in finding work in television or in the West End. Ann had arranged a lot of auditions for him, but no work had resulted. He had finally come to believe that he had spent too long in rep. I remembered him because he had given what I considered to be a very good and professional audition for a stage musical by Bob Grant. Ann persuaded me to go to see him in a farce near town, so we proceeded to Watford. I saw him, liked him and booked him for Reg's flamboyant brother. His name was Jimmy Perry.

17
Don't Panic!

Jimmy was a good actor, although not easy to cast. He was a flamboyant character and very much the 'actor-laddie'. He suited the part of Reg Varney's brother and gave an excellent performance. After we had been rehearsing the episode for a couple of days, he had a conference with Ann. He confessed that he had been toying with an idea for a television comedy based on the activities of a small seaside Home Guard platoon. He had written a couple of episodes. The question was, did Ann think I would take the trouble to read them? Ann told him to give the scripts to me and she would make damned sure I would read them. The next day he nervously handed me a couple of episodes of a show called *The Fighting Tigers*. The subtitle read 'The Confessions of a Home Guard Sergeant'. I took them home and after a couple of days I got round to reading them. They were pretty rough but contained some genuinely funny scenes and I very much fancied the general set-up. It was a welcome departure from the usual TV comedy, which seemed always to be set in a living room with a sofa, two chairs and the next-door neighbours popping in. I told Jimmy that I fancied the general idea and would get Michael Mills to have a look at it. Michael was a great head of comedy with boundless enthusiasm. Forget budgets and technical problems. These were difficulties that could be overcome. Anything was possible in Michael's world. He too saw the comedy advantages of a little seaside Home Guard unit without proper weapons, or even ammunition, preparing to take on the might of the German military machine. He suggested that, since Jimmy was not experienced in television, we should write a pilot episode together.

Jimmy readily agreed and we started to devise a first episode. His original script did not cover Anthony Eden's speech and the actual formation of the Home Guard, and we decided that this would make a good start to the pilot. The leading part at this stage was that of the sergeant, who was a dynamic character, whereas the bank manager was a fairly conventional British officer and a bit of a silly ass.

Jimmy was keen for Arthur Lowe to play the sergeant. I thought Jon Pertwee would be good as the officer because I had used him in a similar part in *Hugh and I*, but unfortunately he was about to do something in America. I next approached Thorley Walters, but he didn't fancy himself in the part. Jimmy took me to see Arthur Lowe down at Windsor. He was playing an Italian character. I thought he was pretty ghastly but I had seen him in *Coronation Street* and in *Pardon the Expression* and *Kiss Me Kate* on stage, so I knew him to be a good actor. Michael then suggested John le Mesurier as the officer. 'You must use him because he suffers so beautifully,' said Michael. He further suggested that we should use John Laurie because it would be a good thing to have a Scotsman in the team. He thought he should own a shop that sold fishing gear. I was definitely in favour of Jack Haig as Jones, the butcher. I offered him the part, but he had been asked to do 26 programmes featuring him as 'Wacky Jackie' – one of his most popular characters. He went to ask Tom Sloan which job he should take. Tom told him that the Home Guard programme would probably run at the most for 13 episodes, so 'Wacky Jackie' won.

If all this sounds like pure chaos, that is because it was. Casting is a very difficult craft, and each new character that is put in place affects the others enormously. Also, we were still very flexible about the team that we should assemble, the characters at this stage being very indefinite and woolly.

I had known Clive Dunn for many years and had written material for him in summer shows. He was now the fairly obvious choice for Jones. At the same time, he had been playing old men in several well-known shows. I thought on balance it would be best to avoid putting somebody in the part who was so well established in the mind of the public in a similar role.

Some time before, Ann had taken me to see a reading of *Under Milk Wood* that had been produced by one of her clients. A small, dark-haired young actor played one of the parts and he was a natural. The audience took to him instantly and he got some wonderful laughs. We were both very impressed indeed by him. Ann tried to find out if he had an agent and, if not, whether he would like to come to her office with a view to her representing him. He replied that he wasn't an actor. He was the stage electrician and he was just standing in for the chap who should have been playing the part but who was ill. He had been present at all the rehearsals so knew the character in the piece. He had volunteered to read the part just to be helpful. He wasn't very interested in Ann's suggestion but was ultimately persuaded to come to see her, and she duly signed him up. His name was David Jason.

I used him a time or two in small parts in various series and in *Mother Goose*, the BBC's television pantomime. He came along to read the part of Jones and, of course, was excellent. All the same, with some reluctance, I decided not to offer him the part. I thought the task of changing a man in his twenties into a 70-year-old who would look right on camera in close-up would be too much for the make-up department – particularly on a daily basis when we were filming. I went for Clive Dunn. To my exasperation he said he wanted time to think about it because he was undecided as to whether he wanted to play another old man.

For Walker, the spiv, I was definite in wanting James Beck. I had cast James in one or two programmes and thought he had great talent. He was cocky and cheeky and just right for the spiv. Jimmy was disappointed because he wanted the part for himself. That was the main reason for him writing the script in the first place. He would certainly have played it very well indeed, but I wanted my co-author beside me in the box when the show was being shot. I was also keen to avoid a situation where members of the cast thought that one of the writers was giving all the best gags to himself.

I was keen to have Arnold Ridley for Private Godfrey, who was to be a very polite retired gentleman's tailor with a weak bladder. John Chapman had introduced him to me to play a similar part in *Hugh and I*. Bill Pertwee's work was familiar to me and he was my favourite to play the air raid warden. I preferred the idea of the warden being the antagonist to Mainwaring to our first idea, which was to have a senior officer whom Mainwaring would have been compelled to obey. The warden could be more insulting.

However, I was not happy with the thought of John le Mesurier as the officer and bank manager. John is at his best when terribly laid back. At the same time, he had been strongly suggested by Michael Mills. When the head of comedy makes a definite suggestion you have to have a very good reason for not taking any notice. Michael knew what he was doing, and John had appeared highly successfully in countless movies. Jimmy was still dead keen on Arthur Lowe, and he had run the repertory company in Watford and knew a good actor when he saw one. By some extraordinary miracle while pondering this situation we hit on the idea that maybe Arthur should be the pompous grammar school bank manager who appointed himself officer, while John should play the ex-public school chief clerk and sergeant.

Jimmy and I took Arthur Lowe to lunch so that we could meet him, get to know him a little and discuss the part. Arthur was a bit cagey about agreeing to risk another television comedy, especially if it was to be anything like *Hugh and I*. Before we had even got through the soup he confessed that he hated that type of programme. I explained that I had produced and directed all the episodes of *Hugh and I* and could assure him that my whole approach to this programme would be quite different. Arthur realised that he had put his foot in it and straight away became more sympathetic to the proposition.

The part of the sergeant and chief clerk was offered to John le Mesurier. He was reluctant. I learnt later that a strange stroke of fate intervened at this point to come to our assistance. John knew Clive well and phoned him up. 'What about this Home Guard thing?' said John.

'I don't know,' said Clive. 'What do you think?'

'I was ringing to find out what you thought,' said John.

'Well, are you going to do it?' said Clive.

'Well – I suppose I wouldn't mind – as long as you're doing it – are you going to do it?' said John.

'Well, all right – so long as you're doing it,' replied Clive. On dynamic exchanges such as this, one's success hinges.

The remaining principal part was that of Pike, the bank junior. This character was based on the real-life experiences of Jimmy when he joined the Home Guard as a boy. Ann had recently taken on the representation of a young actor called Ian Lavender. Pike was supposed to be about 18. Ian was 20 but had a very young face. It so happened that Ann had fixed a television play for him called *Flowers of the Forest*, which was being shown at the time that I was casting Pike. I saw it and liked him. He came to my office and read the part well, so I wanted to offer it to him. The fly in his particular pot of ointment was that Ian was represented by Ann. I went to Tom Sloan and pointed out that I didn't want to be accused of favouring my wife's clients. 'On the other hand,' said Tom, 'you must not be in a situation where you show disfavour – that wouldn't be fair to her actors. Just let me know, which you have done, so go ahead and book Ian.' This I did, which meant that the main casting was complete. It was at about this point that Michael Mills said he didn't think much of *The Fighting Tigers* as a title. 'What about calling it *Dad's Army?*' said Michael.

The Home Guard was first formed in the spring and our first day's filming was to be on 1 April. I figured that the trees and hedges would still be bare of leaves on this date, and might not look appropriate. Harold Snoad, my assistant, set about trying to find somewhere in the country with plenty of conifer woods so that we would not give the game away that we were filming at the wrong time of year. We settled on the country surrounding Thetford in Norfolk. Thetford itself had a couple of hotels that could accommodate the cast, and nearby was the Stanford Battle Area, where the War Department would allow us access to fields and woods for about £5 a day. The added advantage was that we could stage all sorts of explosions and fireworks without interference from the general public, who were not allowed in the area.

By this time Jimmy and I had written six episodes, so the series was taking firm shape. We had evolved an unusual way of working. We would meet for two or three days, either at Jimmy's flat, which was up 82 exhausting stone steps in Westminster, or at my house in Holland Park. We would talk, have coffee and set the world to rights, following which we would discuss the plots for a couple of episodes and take copious notes about possible scenes. We would then go our separate ways and each of us would write one episode. In this way each of us would feel personally responsible for the episode he had written. This is in complete contrast to the American way of working, where eight or a dozen writers sit round a table and throw ideas and lines into the pool. The head writer then tries to sort out the chaos, as a result of which he has a nervous breakdown. Nobody sees their work performed but, by way of compensation, some of them become very rich. Their system can work very well, but I don't think that way of operating suits the British temperament. Most of our best writers are rather private and inhibited people who work alone or in pairs and would find the method far too daunting.

It was at this stage that a serious crisis developed. Paul Fox was the controller of programmes and the all-powerful boss responsible for the BBC's output. He got wind of the imminent production of *Dad's Army* and expressed grave doubts as to whether we should be making Britain's Finest Hour the subject of a comedy television show. Top-level meetings were held and the whole future of the programme hung in the balance. I wasn't present at these meetings, but our corner was fought very strongly by Michael Mills, Tom Sloan and Bill Cotton. Paul began to waver in his opposition when Bill Cotton suggested a face-saving compromise. A campaign with the slogan 'I'm Backing Britain' had been launched to help the sale of British goods. Bill suggested that we write a prologue based on this slogan, which would give us a reason for a nostalgic look at our triumphant past. I think that by this time Paul Fox was bored with the arguments and had respect for the people opposing him. Bill Cotton's suggestion was approved and the programme was given the go-ahead provided the prologue was included.

Jimmy and I were happy enough to go along with this solution and promptly wrote a scene in which the team were all present at an 'I'm Backing Britain' dinner. It was taking place in 1968, which was 24 years or so after the Home Guard disbanded. This wasn't too bad an idea in the case of the younger members of the cast – the spiv and young Pike, for instance, who would now be in their mid-forties or perhaps 50 years old. We were, however, faced with making Jones, Fraser and Godfrey, who were in their seventies, into really decrepit, doddering old men in their nineties. One other disadvantage lay in the fact that we had already planned to include at the beginning of each episode a funny fake newsreel sequence narrated by E.V.H. Emmet, who was the well-remembered voice of *British Movietone News*. These bits depicted Jones turning signposts back to front and sticking spikes into fields to impale unwary parachute troops as they descended. As a result, the pilot programme now started twice, but I thought it best not to complain since the compromise had been so hard won.

The cast finally assembled for the first read-through. Jimmy and I were filled with a high level of excitement, but our enthusiasm didn't last long. Most of the actors were mumbling their lines as if they didn't want to commit themselves. Jimmy and I huddled in a corner at coffee time. 'I think we've got a right stroppy lot here,' said Jim. I tried to reassure him that my mother used to rehearse in this fashion so as not to reveal her performance to the rest of the cast until the actual first night, when she would produce the magic. Jim didn't believe me and neither did I.

We all arrived in Thetford on 1 April for the first day's filming. The weather was dire. It was dull and drizzling with occasional flurries of something between sleet and snow. Some time previously Ann and I had bought a very glamorous if ancient 1954 Rolls-Royce Silver Wraith. It had one great advantage as a family car. There was an electric-powered glass partition cutting off the back from the front. The kids could sing, fight and be sick to their hearts' content, and Ann and I could drive serenely in front. In this vehicle in coddled comfort sat Arthur Lowe, Clive Dunn, John le Mesurier, Jimmy Beck and I. Occasionally we would wipe the steamed-up windows to survey the dreary landscape. After about 45 minutes I could stand this no longer. I climbed out of the car and called to Harold Snoad, my assistant: 'It's definitely getting brighter. Get some light on to those trees in the background and we'll have a go.'

'But the snow's still falling,' said Jimmy.

'Never mind,' I said. 'It'll look like apple blossom.' It didn't. Thus we began the first day of filming a production that was to carry us through nine busy and mainly triumphant years.

The film schedule was constructed largely around Arthur Lowe's bowels. Arthur was not prepared to leave the hotel until he had 'been'. He was not able to 'go' until half an hour after ploughing through a considerable English hotel breakfast consisting of porridge, eggs, bacon, sausage, mushrooms, tomatoes and, if possible, kidneys. To avoid delaying the entire company, who were being transported on the location bus, Jimmy would wait patiently in the hotel car park to ferry him in his Beetle to wherever we were filming.

Arthur was never too sure of the words, particularly in the later episodes of the show. In the studio in front of a live audience this would be frustrating for Jimmy and me because he was prone to paraphrase lines. He would deliver something that made perfect sense but was not quite as good as the line we wrote. On the other hand, the fractional pause that was caused by the thought 'What the hell am I supposed to say next?' gave us that heavenly nanosecond of hesitation which is the hallmark of perfect timing. After three or four series, John le Mesurier and several other members of the cast rang me at home to say, 'Can't you make Arthur learn his ruddy part?' This situation was aggravated by the fact that Arthur would never take his script with him after rehearsals. He would place it in a drawer that he would close with great finality. Someone once asked him if he wasn't going to take it with him. 'Oh no,' he said. 'I don't want that sort of thing – not in my home.'

As a crafty way of counteracting this situation I decided to send him two scripts. I enclosed a note saying that I hoped he would find it convenient to have one copy to leave in the rehearsal room and a further copy to place under his pillow at night in the hope that some of the words would filter past the feathers while he slept. His only response was to say to Jimmy, 'David seems to be very grotty these days.'

We were never held up by John le Mesurier. He was always on parade on time, dressed and knowing his lines. He had a photographic memory. If he wasn't sure of a line he would often say, 'Don't tell me – it's at the top of the page about two inches down.' Perhaps as a result of his long experience of feature films, he formed close friendships with the electricians and prop boys, who worshipped him. He also had a profound effect on the make-up and wardrobe girls. He would sometimes sit alone away from the rest of the cast, only to be swiftly joined by one of the girls who would say, 'Are you all right, John?'

'How very sweet of you to ask,' he would answer, 'and how nicely you've done your hair this morning. It suits you so well swept behind your ears like that. And you have such pretty, tiny ears.' I once heard him say, 'There is one small thing you could do. Would you be a sweetie and wind my watch for me?' John was very popular with the girls. He was not quite so popular with his dresser. The moment I said 'Cut' he would undo his belt and send his webbing equipment crashing to the dusty ground, swiftly followed by his rifle. The armourer would leap forward to retrieve the rifle and inspect it to make sure no little pebbles had sneaked down the barrel to provide lethal projectiles if a blank cartridge was fired.

I never rated John very highly as an actor. I cannot imagine how he survived his early days in repertory. The mere thought of him playing a North Country character is too awful even to contemplate. He would have been a total disaster playing, for instance, Hercule Poirot. In my estimation, he was a behaviourist. As such, he could turn in an absolutely immaculate performance as John le Mesurier. I once overheard a remark he made to James Beck (Private Walker). 'You're far too versatile, Jimmy,' he said. 'You should always try to play the same character and, when possible, wear the same suit.'

Clive Dunn was a funny man and was one of the few actors who could be genuinely creative in rehearsal. He would frequently ad-lib around the script in a way that was quite hilarious. 'Keep it in,' I would

176

say, but he seldom remembered what he had ad-libbed. He had total recall of other things and would keep us all in fits recounting his early days in the army and in concert party.

John Laurie formed a close relationship with Ian Lavender. They would sit together poring over *The Times* crossword puzzle. John would usually have finished it by coffee time. 'What's the matter with your brain, boy? Use your brain.' John was a great Shakespeare scholar, having played so many of the roles. He didn't have much regard for Jimmy Perry and me. 'The trouble with you two is you're damned nearly illiterate,' he once said. On the occasions when we wrote him a small part he would threaten to phone in his performance. In the latter days of the series he was rather resentful that he was being remembered for the weird Scottish undertaker rather than for all the important parts he had played throughout his career. But he had a rare and canny ability to spot any comedy possibilities in his part and milk them to the full.

Arnold Ridley had had a most distinguished career in the business. He'd written *The Ghost Train* and many other plays. He'd directed plays and movies, and he was well known for the parts he'd played on radio and in television. He was in his early seventies and I was concerned that he wouldn't be physically up to playing the part. He came to see me and I explained that there was bound to be a certain amount of running about that I couldn't avoid requiring of him, but he said that if I was game to give him the part, he was game to try. In the event, we got a lot of warm laughs when the other members of the platoon had to help him get aboard Jones's van. During filming he was mostly to be seen walking up and down, flapping his arms like a penguin while muttering, 'Tell them to get on with it, tell them to get on with it.' I found him to be a dear old love and remarkably like his television character.

Jimmy Beck was on the fringe of a fine career. He was, as John had detected, very versatile. He was a good sculptor and could draw well. He could also do life-like impersonations. He was a great admirer of some of our more inebriated stars, such as Wilfred Lawson and Wilfred Hyde-White, and used to recount their drunken exploits with relish. Unhappily he was very confused in his private life. He was madly in love with his wife while being infatuated with his girlfriend, and I think this led to him drinking a lot more than we realised. When collecting a round of drinks he would be inclined to down an extra double before he made the delivery – a fact I should have spotted. His drinking never affected his work, however. He was very good company and on location we went around together a lot.

Ian Lavender was the only inexperienced member of the platoon, but he lost no time in falling into his character. In no time at all the long scarf appeared, and I got him to wear his hat dead straight, which always made soldiers look gormless. From the start he gave a totally believable performance of a very young mother's boy. Arthur took him under his wing and loved his scenes with him. Arthur used to enjoy doing things like stumbling off ladders. He would collapse into Ian's arms. Ian would then surreptitiously tip Arthur's hat off-centre and Arthur would rearrange his specs so that they were skew-whiff. He would then emerge and call Ian a stupid boy, which the studio audience found hilarious.

Right from day one Bill Pertwee gave a robust performance as the air raid warden that was just right for everyone to play off. I shall always be grateful to him for being a wonderful booster of morale whenever a bit of a crisis looked as if it was going to loom. Bill could always be relied upon to weigh in, saying everything was marvellous and everyone was excellent and weren't we all lucky everything was going so well. It always seemed to be Bill's lot to finish up falling into the river or sinking into the sea in a small boat, but I never heard him complain.

The verger (Teddy Sinclair) and the vicar (Frank Williams) became firm friends and always travelled together. Teddy was the most worrying driver I ever travelled with. He would hold long conversations with me if I sat beside him, only rarely looking where he was going. I thought I would get over this problem by sitting in the back seat, whereupon Teddy insisted on turning right round to talk to me. I first came across Teddy when he played a very short-sighted undertaker in *Beggar My Neighbour*. He mistook a lady's flower-decked hat for a small wreath, threw it into the grave and buried it with the corpse, to the horror of its owner. He was incomparable as the verger and was singled out by Alan Bennett for giving a memorable performance of the part.

The younger members of the platoon had to be taught foot and rifle drill. All the old soldiers immediately became drill instructors, so the beginners were positively overwhelmed with support, but they soon learned. It was one of the unavoidable features of the show that I had to say 'Fall in' from time to time. Actors – especially ex-service actors – definitely do not like to be told to 'fall in', so a sort of competition developed to see who could be last on parade. The winners were invariably Clive Dunn and Jimmy Beck. Arthur Lowe and John le Mesurier were not part of the line-up, so they didn't compete.

During the first week of location filming, when the weather completely closed in on us, I decided to film the closing captions in a large Nissen hut. The ever-ingenious scenic department managed to rustle up some black curtains for me, and each of the principal members of the cast pretended to be walking forward to their destiny. This entailed them marking time on the spot but, since I only shot them from the waist up, it looked as though they were marching. Back at Television Centre we superimposed this on top of phalanxes of marching Nazi troops, rows of tanks and various shots of German field guns, howitzers and bombers. I wanted this to illustrate the enormity of the task the Home Guard were undertaking and the bravery of our little squad in preparing to meet the Nazi hordes. I was delighted with the result.

Unfortunately, Paul Fox saw a rough copy of the first programme and had very strong objection to the end credits. I had unwisely included the explosion of a tank and also a stream of refugees in the sequence, and this I realised was perhaps an error of judgement on my part. I had a long meeting with Tom Sloan and Paul at which I agreed to exclude the two shots, but made a very strong case to include the rest. I felt very strongly that this was indeed what the series was about and graphically represented the task that these ordinary old chaps were taking on. Paul finally agreed the point, and I thought I had won the day – whereupon up piped Tom to say that if Paul wasn't entirely happy, of course we would do a different version. So I never got my chosen end captions, and to this day I regret it.

18
Dear Sexy Knickers

As soon as Nicky and Penny were old enough to toddle we made efforts to organise various family holidays. The first one was definitely a luxurious affair. We rented a large house on the isthmus between the sea and the harbour at Sandbanks in Dorset. Years earlier it was alleged to have been the home of the millionaire inventor of Fox's Glacier Mints. Every day at 11 o'clock a tourist boat used to pass us on the sea side and announce in a loud voice on the Tannoy that they were now passing the home of the millionaire inventor of Glacier Mints, and we would stand on our balcony and try to give a Glacier Mint millionaire wave.

Our tenancy got off to an exciting start when the heath around the house caught fire. Ann, in her very glamorous and diaphanous blue peignoir, tried to douse the flames with water carried in a child's bucket, while I did my best to beat out the conflagration with a broom.

After that, mainly due a shortage of the folding stuff, we were forced to make do with more ordinary holiday efforts. These varied from borrowing a shack in Jaywick from Ann's grandma to trying to fit a quart-sized family into a pint-sized coastguard cottage, camping van, caravan or tent. Aside from our ever-growing family, the happy band usually included Olive, Ann's parents, my brother Peter and his current girlfriend and his son, and occasionally the bewildered domestic help.

We became, through lack of money, enthusiastic Continental campers, carrying at one time no less than two frame tents with all the accompanying camp-beds, tables, chairs, wash-bowls and cooker. The frame tents were fiendish devices consisting of canvas bags full of metal tubes held together by devious corner bits with three or four sockets in each. The skill lay in fitting the right tubes into the right bits and then covering the whole shebang with an all-embracing blue canvas cover. We chose some really beautiful sites that had surprisingly been left vacant by more experienced campers, only to find at 4 o'clock in the morning that the winds had got up and were threatening to blow us into the sea, or that we had selected a dried-up river bed which was no longer dried up. The kids still have memories of their dad, wearing lemon-coloured silk pyjamas, trying to dig a gully round the tent in the blustering rain while their plimsolls sluiced away down the river flowing through their canvas bedroom.

Returning from one French holiday we decided to get a bit of 'Kulture for the Kids' by visiting the Château de Chenonceaux in the Loire. Proceeding gaily (in the original sense of the word) up the impressive tree-lined drive, I failed to notice a sleeping policeman. Had it been a real policeman asleep, I'm sure I would have seen him, but this was a concrete lump painted in faded white. The camper van lifted into the air, and the roof-rack carrying the two tents and most of the furniture bounced on to the bonnet and from there on to the ground. Another similar obstruction resulted in Rebecca taking her first flying lesson when she and the carrycot she was sleeping in went into free fall somewhere south of the Dordogne. It spent the rest of the journey wedged between the cooker and the sink, securely tied to the Calor gas lamp bracket.

At Weymouth, where I was staging a summer show for Bernard Delfont, we rented a coastguard cottage. It was perched on the edge of a cliff and had only two bedrooms and a sitting room. It must have had elastic walls, however, as it accommodated Ann and me, Nicky, Penny, Jane and Becky, Ann's parents, Peter and his son Michael, and Jenny the Siamese cat who, seeing the generosity of the room measurements, brought us a specially caught dead Weymouth mouse.

On arriving, we received a message that we were being joined by Ann's aunt and uncle from Rhodesia. We explained that we had no room, but her uncle said that we were not to worry because they carried a tent that they would put up on the lawn – which they did.

Weymouth was packed with incidents. One night we had a major power cut and I drove my Lagonda up the steps in front of the theatre so that the performance could continue lit by its headlights. On another occasion the theatre roof succumbed to a huge downpour and the organist, Neville 'Thunderfoot' Meale (he didn't play too quietly), was to be seen salvaging the bits of his Hammond organ while the water poured across the footlights and fell, Niagara like, into the orchestra pit.

On another occasion we took a cottage in Norfolk at South Winterton or North Summerton – I never remember which, but fortunately I knew at the time. Ann was supervising Cathy McGowan in a new TV show in Manchester and was to join me and the five kids after the evening performance. TV personality Katie Boyle pleaded with her not to travel until the next morning because her 'aura' was showing murky leanings. Ann ignored the warning, overturned her convertible and put herself in a ditch and into hospital. I was woken by a Norfolk policeman who informed me that 'Your woif has had a aaaacident and is in horspital but is quoit all roit.' The kids promptly all got mumps and Ann, bruised and brave, joined us four days later.

Some three or four years before *Dad's Army*, Ann and I were watching H.G. Wells's *Ann Veronica* on television and thought what a wonderful musical it would make. Ann took Frank Wells – H.G.'s son – to lunch at the White Elephant, and he agreed to let us have the musical rights for a couple of years to see what we could make of it. Cyril Ornadel and I set to work on the score. Frank started to write the book, and Ann and I became genuinely fond of him. He was an exceedingly civilised character and a bit of an eccentric. He drove a Porsche at breakneck speeds, altered the course of his garden stream according to any passing whim and taught me a lot about wine. However, it soon became clear that he was not a dramatist and the book was not going to be good enough. He agreed to allow Ronald Gow, who had written an earlier stage version, to rewrite the musical. This achieved, Cyril and I gave countless auditions of the score to artistes and producers such as Vanessa Redgrave and Wendy Toye, while Ann tried all possible sources to raise the money. After we had all laboured some four years or so, Ann finally came up with Ian Abrahams, who was the chairman of a television facilities company, and Dorothy Tutin, to my surprise, agreed to be directed by me. She was a *Dad's* enthusiast. We then set about helping Ian Abrahams to raise the money. I made a 30-minute black and white TV presentation fronted by David Jacobs, featuring most of the songs and telling the story. This was backed by an 11-piece orchestra, for which we got a special deal from the Musicians Union. One way or another Ian raised most of the money and a production was arranged over the Christmas period at the Belgrade Theatre, Coventry.

Arthur Lowe agreed to play the leading character role, and Hi Hazel, Mary Millar, Charles West, Peter Reeves and John Inman were added to the cast. Dorothy Tutin was very patient with me as a director. She was used to having the motivation for her lines clear in her head before proceeding with a scene. When once she said to me, 'Why am I saying this?' and I replied, 'Because it's funny,' she let me get away with it.

The show opened to an excellent and enthusiastic press. It felt good and we were pretty pleased with it but Dorothy became worried about her singing voice. She was magic in the part because she made such wonderful sense of the book and the lyrics, but she became rather obsessed with her vocal performance. After a week or two she said regretfully that she didn't want to come to the West End with it, so I had to release her. Mary Millar was covering Dorothy in the role and we decided to let her take over the part. Mary sang divinely and later was hilarious in *Keeping up Appearances* but she wasn't born to play Ann Veronica.

Donald Albury dithered about with us, half promising that we could take the show to the Piccadilly Theatre, but in the event after a couple of weeks he finally left it to his secretary to tell us that he had made other arrangements. Emile Littler came to the rescue, though as it turned out the rescue was somewhat akin to being saved from the surging sea by the *Titanic*. He ran the Palace Theatre at the time and he informed us that *Jesus Christ Superstar* was falling below its break figure and it seemed likely that we could move in there. In the event *Jesus* ran a further year or so and we were offered the Cambridge. This we were obliged to accept, although with marked misgivings.

We moved into the theatre on Sunday and opened on Thursday. When I told Bob Nesbitt this simple fact some months later he said, 'David – tell me no more.' The first night was a scenic disaster. Unbeknown to anyone, the lighting director had re-hung the lights just hours before the first night. Moving sets stuck. Cloths and borders failed to rise and descend. Arthur Lowe, meanwhile, was superb and attacked the audience like a tiger. Hi Hazel was also great, as was John Inman, but, as the showbiz phrase goes, 'It didn't happen.'

At the first night party at the Embassy Club Ian Abrahams was inclined to wait for the morning papers in the traditional Broadway supper-at-Sardi's fashion. Anticipating the result I said, 'Go to bed and get some rest, Ian. I think you're going to need it.' The press was vitriolic. When embarked on an enterprise such as this, one has to be pretty ruthless and single-minded. For a number of weeks I had ploughed through all opposition, determined to get my way. This is great so long as everything goes well. If it doesn't, you are right out in front to take the flak and it is no good looking around for someone else to blame.

Ian called a meeting at ten o'clock next morning. I went to it. The principal backers were all there sitting round a table. Looking back, they were quite polite. 'What happened, David? We trusted you. We thought you knew what you were doing. You seemed so sure.' What could I say? 'I'm sorry,' I said brightly. 'I got it wrong.'

The show should have come off that week, but we were committed to the theatre and its rent for five weeks, and heavy penalties would be due for the bars etc, so it was deemed better that the show should teeter on. The end of a theatre flop is a very sad affair. There is no market for old scenery. *Ann Veronica* finished up on the Thames mud-flats as a smouldering pile of ash. Some of the cloths were still on the pavement outside the Cambridge Theatre some months later as a sort of long, thin, flat and soggy memorial. Ann, having put years of effort into making *Ann Veronica* happen, was devastated. We all were.

As our fortunes improved and we had a bit more money, Ann and I and the family took markedly better holidays. On one such occasion we were both bound for the Hotel la Bouée at Cap d'Antibes for a few days. The hotel was beautifully sited on the Plage Garoupe and had been first introduced to us by John and Betty Chapman. Waiting for our luggage at Nice airport we bumped into Jeremy Lloyd and Joanna Lumley, who had just got married and were on their honeymoon. Jeremy and I had met a few times before when he was writing bits and pieces for *The Billy Cotton Band Show*. He had also written a lot of episodes for the comedy series starring Dickie Henderson.

When I returned to London I was sent for by Bill Cotton Jr, who was worried, as well he should have been, about a pilot comedy written by Jilly Cooper called, and I was never quite sure why, *It's Awfully Bad for Your Eyes, Darling*. Maybe it referred to the danger of watching too much television. Maybe it was the possible effect of too much masturbation. I was never quite sure and I never asked. It starred Joanna Lumley and Jeremy Lloyd and was about four girls who shared a flat. The show was very definitely on crutches and Bill asked me to look into it and to see if I could help.

Look into it I did, and wrote to Bill that the whole proposition was beyond redemption and the best thing to do was to lose it. I received a rather curt note back from Bill to the effect that the BBC had been a considerable help to me in my career and I should regard this as an opportunity to put a bit back. This was an unusual line for Bill to take, so I dutifully knuckled down and 'looked into it' more closely. Chatting to Jeremy, I concluded that at least we could do something about the first three or four minutes of each script in order to make the studio audience laugh and at least make the viewers aware of their existence. I didn't want to get involved with the actual writing, so Jeremy nominally took on the rehash. Jilly was a notable journalist, although unaccountably inclined to trumpet her belief in her extraordinary ability to attract the opposite sex. I thought that possibly she had something to say in the show, but it had fallen into the hands of a BBC script editor who had made the whole thing into a conventional sitcom. I was never able to obtain her original script, so I don't really know whether she was to blame.

It may sound pompous, but I didn't like the moral attitudes of the characters, who were prepared to sleep around with their boyfriends without any sense that what they were doing was unacceptable, for instance, to Mother. I didn't think the BBC should be depicting this kind of conduct as normal. The script editor hated what we were doing, so after about three programmes Jeremy and I withdrew our labour and the viewers remained unaware that a studio audience was watching the show. It died after six episodes.

During our sessions, Jeremy mentioned that he had written a script about his experiences when he was a junior assistant at Simpson's in Piccadilly. I read it and liked it, but he had given an option on it to one of the commercial companies. I said that if he could get it back, I would like to work on it with him and try our luck with the BBC.

Jeremy duly recovered it and we started to adapt it. Jeremy had written it entirely about the men's department. I thought it would have a much greater mileage if the main thrust of story involved the conflict that would arise if the ladies' outfitting department were to be thrust on to the unwilling gentlemen's clothing department, the men being forced to give up space and make room for the ladies. We swiftly made the changes and decided to set the whole thing in Grace Brothers, a small, old-fashioned department store struggling to survive.

The BBC were doing a series named *Comedy Playhouse* consisting of six or seven different comedy scripts. I persuaded Michael Mills to include *Are You Being Served?* in the next run. I quickly secured Mollie Sugden as the senior ladies' department saleswoman and Frank Thornton as the ex-service floor walker Captain Peacock. Arthur Brough, whom I knew from the time when Ann was in repertory at Folkestone, was available to play Mr Granger, the senior gentlemen's salesman, and I was sure he would be marvellous. I had seen John

Inman playing in *Salad Days* at the Golders Green Hippodrome and thought a lot of him. He could dance and sing and the audience loved him. I had used him in various shows, including *Ann Veronica* and one of the Roy Kinnear programmes where he had played a scene with a famous Scottish comedian. The Scots comic was getting huge laughs that he couldn't account for, little knowing that John was in the background of his shots doing some very effective mugging. John later told me that I had given him his first five jobs in television.

I fancied he would score as the camp Mr Humphries, although at this stage it was only a very small part. For Mollie Sugden's assistant I planned to have a young Jewish lady – hence the name Miss Brahms. It was quite usual to have a Jewish girl behind the counter serving ladies' underwear, and I thought it would open up a lot of Jewish humour. I wanted Sheila Steafel to play the part because she had a wonderful way with comedy, but it transpired that Sheila was not available. My next thought was to abandon the Jewish element and to go for Wendy Richard, although at first I was not keen to use her because she had played Mollie's daughter in *Hugh and I* and I feared the audience would be confused. Finally good sense prevailed and I booked Wendy. Trevor Bannister had made quite a name for himself in *The Dustbin Men* and he agreed to play the young Mr Lucas, provided he could share top billing with Mollie.

Jeremy and I thought the store should be owned by an incredibly ancient eccentric known as 'Young Mr Grace' – Old Mr Grace being so old that he didn't get about much. Young Mr Grace had a pretty secretary, a pretty nurse, a chauffeur and a yacht in the Caribbean. I had seen Harold Bennett play an old bishop in a Player's Theatre pantomime and he made me laugh a lot. After first checking that he was capable of learning and remembering lines – which he was – I engaged him. Larry Martin as the union-orientated odd job man, the bald-headed, big-eared Nicholas Smith as Mr Rumbold the manager, and Stephanie Gathercole as his secretary completed the cast.

Ever striving for a new sound for the signature tune, I sent out the highly skilled sound supervisor Adrian Bishop Leggat to record the sounds that could be heard in a store, such as tills opening and closing, lift-door bells and pings, and packages being dumped. These he very cleverly formed into a rhythm track. I then wrote a sort of recitative for the lift girl, which Stephanie recorded, saying things such as, 'First floor perfumery, gents' ready-made suits'. On top of this Ronnie Hazelhurst recorded a violin and trumpet obbligato. The result was a catchy sound, which we later realised was one of the first 'rap' numbers.

Money was short, and I was fortunate to get the about-to-retire James Bold as the scene designer. He had been the scenic department manager for years and knew the scenery stock like the back of his hand. The complicated set cost a mere £600. The BBC at this time was a very efficient organisation. A show would be staged in the studios ready to rehearse with cameras by 10.30 a.m. and would be performed in front of an audience at 8 o'clock that evening. By 10.30 p.m. the set would be struck and the scenery for the next show would be set and lit by 10.30 the following morning. Certain members of the organisation were, however, a little light-fingered to put it mildly. The set of *Are You Being Served?* was packed with suits, ladies' underwear, socks, gloves, hats, ties and everything you would expect to find in a department store. After the pilot show it was said that just one pair of gloves was returned to the prop store. To counteract this, when we came to make the series we tore the backside out of every pair of trousers, ripped one sleeve off every jacket and somehow made each article of clothing unusable.

The cast moulded together like magic. They were all seasoned theatre professionals and knew where the laughs were and how to handle them. Their precision, their control of the studio audience and their use of props was pretty to watch. The first programme went off like magic. All that remained was to convince the comedy department to make it into a series because the general feeling was that the show was a bit common and not quite the sort of thing the BBC should be doing.

I was leaning against Bill Cotton's doorway, chatting about programmes in general, as one was able to do in those days, when Dennis Main Wilson phoned through to say that he was doubtful whether he could deliver *Till Death Us Do Part* as promised. This would leave six nasty holes in the schedules. Opportunities like this seldom present themselves. Straight away I leapt in and said that Bill could have six *Are You Being Served?* shows if he gave the word. What's more, they were cheap and required no outside film effort. 'OK,' said Bill, 'but do we have to have the poof?'

'He isn't a poof,' I said. 'He's a mother's boy and he hasn't made up his mind yet. And without him, bang goes half the comedy.'

'Oh, all right then,' said Bill resignedly. 'Go ahead – but watch it.'

Over the next 12 years we did 79 programmes. 'I'm free' and Mrs Slocombe's Pussy became national institutions, and the programme became the BBC's biggest earner in the USA. To see the first forty or so shows is to be present at a master class in comedy playing. They were a joy to present. Jeremy is a near-genius when it comes to comedy, and wonderfully funny dialogue simply pours out of him. After a few weeks we were writing the scripts in three days or less. But as Jeremy said, it took 30 years to learn how to do it.

One of the great joys of *Are You Being Served?* was to be with Mollie Sugden and Wendy Richard once more. I had been with both at the earliest stages of their careers. Mollie was always a completely co-operative character with an incomparable sense of comedy. Moreover, she had no hesitation in playing a physical misfit who was prepared to be insulted by Trevor Bannister as Mr Lucas, and was happy to suffer any indignity if it helped the comedy. They were both marvellous to write for and direct.

Not long after the start of *Are You Being Served?* I inherited *Up Pompeii!* It had been devised and piloted by Michael Mills and scripted by Talbot Rothwell for Frankie Howerd. The original idea was to base the series on the tales of the Roman comic playwright Plautus. Talbot Rothwell wrote all the best *Carry On* films. Frankie wasn't entirely happy with the set-up of the pilot. He had three focuses of attention. He would address the camera for the main body of the script. He would react to the studio audience and chide them for making the script sound dirty or not paying attention, and this I promised him would always be on an eye-line above his main camera. He would also have to play scenes with the other characters. When we had sorted this out, the show worked like a dream.

I can't say I enjoyed working with Frankie. He was painfully slow to learn his script, repeating every line time and again, which was very boring. I once fell asleep during rehearsal, which was not a habit of mine. Frankie was also quite ruthless with his fellow artistes, and from time to time I had to get rid of really good professional actors because he didn't get on with them – and if Frankie wasn't happy with the other players, we didn't have a show. I had to lose Fabia Drake – she was giving a wonderful performance, but Frankie didn't like her, so she had to go. Frankie also had some odd personal habits. For instance, he was rather bald and wore a not very good wig. The make-up department had to pretend that this wig was his natural hair and plonk his stage wig on top.

None of the young call boys dared go near Frankie's dressing room just before the show because at this time he always became extremely randy. I finished up insisting that we had only girl assistants, who didn't have the same trouble. On a 'live and let live' basis I booked the odd male extra to whom he had taken a fancy, for two or three programmes. On one occasion when he tired of the poor chap, Frankie asked me not to have him in the cast any more and offered to pay his cancelled fees. His ad-libs were 90 per cent scripted and rehearsed. On the occasions when he went wrong he was quite hilarious in his efforts to put things right, and I begged him to flounder on until I stopped him because this could be some of the best comedy in the show. The cameramen were all ready for such an event and we shot it spontaneously until he found himself again.

And yet it must be said that when the studio audience arrived the great Frankie Howerd emerged. He played them as a master fisherman plays a trout. He had complete control. They loved him. He was magic. As soon as they left the studio he was rotten again. That most distinguished actor Max Adrian, whom I had known since *Tulip Time* in Hull when I was 11, was in the regular cast as the slave Frankie's master. I once asked him why he was bothering to be in a show like *Up Pompeii!* 'It's Frankie,' he said. 'I just find him wonderful to watch.'

Tragically, Tom Sloan's health deteriorated and he finally died of cancer quite young. He had been a good boss and a great help to me and I was deeply sorry to see him go. Bill Cotton had to busy himself reorganising the department. He sent for me to offer me the post of head of variety. This wasn't really my bag but I was a great admirer of Bill. I knew I would enjoy working with him and he would take care of me through the early stages. Ann was very keen for me to accept the job, but I had reservations. I had done quite a lot of musical and quasi-variety shows and knew most of the stars in this field, but my leanings were more towards comedy. To be pompous again, I thought *Top of the Pops* was encouraging the yob culture, but nobody would thank me for changing it, and I definitely did not want to give up writing, producing and directing. In the end, reluctantly, I declined, although I regretted forgoing a nice office with comfortable armchairs, and Ann would have liked to host the light entertainment parties. This particular cobbler finally decided to stick to his last.

19
Lessons in Laughter and Life Down Under

On 18 November 1969, Ann gave birth to our sixth offspring, Richard. This time she decided to undertake the whole process with a star gynaecologist and in luxury – if childbirth can ever be regarded as luxurious – in a private room in Queen Charlotte's.

Shortly before this event I had met the remarkable George Rockey, a Hungarian who had escaped his country after eluding Russian secret police during the 1956 uprising. Landing in Australia he met Peter Abels, a fellow escapee. They were totally broke for an hour or two, hired a truck and a few years later owned Thomas Nationwide Transport, which was the largest transport empire in Australia. George wanted to sponsor a television sitcom to be made in Australia starring Hugh Lloyd and a witty Australian comedian by the name of Ron Frazer – no relation to the British Ronnie Fraser. The nickel boom and the new nickel finds at the Poseidon mine in Western Australia were a suggested subject. He invited me to stay in his apartment in Sydney to visit Channel 7 and explore the possibilities.

I went to Sydney via Los Angeles. At Sydney airport I found a taxi driven by a Greek immigrant. I gave him the address of George's apartment. Once we were on the way he turned to me in the back of the cab, threw a *Sydney A to Z* at me and in a pronounced Greek accent shouted the only English words he seemed to know, which were, 'Find it'. This I endeavoured to do.

George was in Hong Kong so I had the free run of his magnificent pad which had sensational views over the harbour and lots of bottles of Dom Perignon in the fridge. I also had the use of an enormous new Mercedes with only 600 miles on the clock. I was too scared to drive the magnificent car out of the garage so Margie Bond, George's straight-talking assistant, who had a great sense of humour, drove me all around Sydney so as to get the idea of locations and the countryside. I spent some time at the studios at Channel 7. These were pretty good, though not large enough for an audience. The lighting staff were all very inexperienced and I realised that I would have to bring someone with me from the BBC. The company had invested in a camera system known as 'E Cam', which consisted of three very heavy cameras that shot on 35mm colour film but were started and stopped from a central gallery. In this gallery were crude monitors that gave a picture of roughly what was happening, and if you peered closely you could see whether the boom was in shot. As well as the technical problems, there was also no costumier in Sydney capable of supporting a situation comedy, no one used to making scenery and props, and none of the facilities that I took for granted at the pre-Birt BBC.

I had a conference with George in Hong Kong and advised him that there was every chance that he would lose his money. George was undeterred. 'Don't tell me how to spend my money, David,' he said. His enthusiasm was catching and I agreed to write and direct the show. Over the next year and a half I wrote and shot 13 episodes of *The Virgin Fellas*. The story concerned Hugh Lloyd, a Brit, who had been left a ranch in the remote outback by an uncle. On visiting it he found that it was inhabited by seven nubile 'nieces' who were untouched by civilisation, had had no education or contact with men, and were sitting on a nickel mine. I cast former Miss England Ann Sidney to lead the beautiful nubile nieces. I got unpaid leave from the BBC, went to Sydney three times to make the pilot and the series, and had an absolute ball. I was compelled to find out things about making television that I had taken entirely for granted. I filmed on location with a great cameraman and crew with the aid of lighting powered by a couple of dozen car batteries carried on a flat-bed truck. The lights could only be used for a total of two hours. The batteries then had to be charged overnight. The great advantage was that the battery truck could be brought right alongside the location because it produced no noise whatever. I never ran out of juice. I tried to use this method in England, but nobody believed it was possible.

Studio sound was a problem because the boom operators were the least regarded and lowest paid men on the team, so after two or three weeks secured themselves other jobs. Audience reaction had to be dubbed on after the completion of editing, so I equipped Australia with a tape full of *Dad's Army* laughs, which they probably use to this day.

Crises came thick and fast. We had a 'loo' strike because the ladies – quite rightly – refused to use the adjacent million square miles of bush as a lavatory and had to be bused every couple of hours to the nearest town to spend their pennies. Portable loos were ultimately provided. (I became fascinated with the million square miles of bush which consisted mostly of plants that would cost £6 each at Harrods.) Another crisis arose when the crew refused to work while they were being fed 'crook tucker' as my ace cameraman described it. On one occasion we waited for the best part of a day for a police car to turn up. The only one available had been promised by the local police. When it finally showed up the cops apologised for the late arrival, explaining that the car had been needed to follow up a smash-and-grab raid.

One of the most important locations was the ramshackle, decrepit corrugated-iron house belonging to a Mr Rasmussen. Nearby was a 10-foot mountain of empty beer bottles that had taken Mr Rasmussen years of joyous oblivion to assemble. The house was perfect for our purposes and had taken ages to find. To our horror, when we turned up to film, Mr Rasmussen had repaired it, painted it, mowed the grass and trucked away the bottles.

One day Hugh Lloyd looked particularly yellow and turned out to have jaundice, which necessitated a month with no filming. Ann came out to keep me company during the break. I met her in Fiji and we had a sensational South Sea Island week.

We were now a whole month behind schedule and I was contracted to be back at the BBC, so I had to leave the series as soon as it was in the can without being able to supervise the edit, but there was nothing I could do about that. John Chapman wrote a couple of episodes for me but otherwise I was fully responsible for the whole thing. Once back in England I persuaded the BBC to show it. They showed the first seven episodes and the critics gave it the 'Worst Comedy of the Year' award, which just shows that you can't win them all. Unfortunately the critics have never thought of an appropriate statuette to go with their award, so there is nothing to display on the mantelpiece. I would have thought that a small bronze turkey would fit the bill, or perhaps a little plastic bomb.

For some time Jimmy and I had been thinking around our experiences of the army in India and trying to devise the best way of putting them on television. We were pretty much set on the idea of basing a show on Jimmy's days with the Royal Artillery concert party. It would feature a group of lads desperate to avoid being sent up the jungle to fight the Japs, and a sergeant-major determined to thwart them. My problem was that I was very unclear about how to devise the setting. To be viable, a comedy show at the BBC studios has to be staged

above: Harry Worth as
Ko Ko and Hattie Jacques
as Katisha in the *Mikado*.

left: DC in the vice-like grip
of Jeremy Lloyd.

opposite top: Dad's Army. Harold Snoad (my production manager) bottom row, left next to DC. Paul Joel (designer) top left, with moustache.

opposite bottom: Some of the *Dad's Army* team on a Christmas shoot for *Radio Times.* They covered them with holly. 'They did not like it on 'em'.

above top: Blackpool, outside The Opera House and The Winter Garden showing *Dad's Army* and *Are You Being Served?* respectively.

above: A rare view of the back of the Queen (with Hugh Weldon) talking briefly to DC and Jimmy Perry.

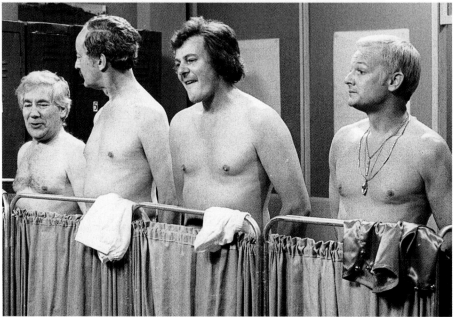

top: Come Back Mrs Noah (from left to right) Ann Michelle, Tim Barrett, Donald Hewlett, Michael Knowles, Mollie Sugden, Ian Lavender.

above: The episode that caused Mary Whitehouse to get her knickers in a twist, (from left to right) Alfie Bass, Frank Thornton, Trevor Bannister, John Inman.

above: Are You Being Served? (from left to right) back row: Frank Thornton, Trevor Bannister, Arthur English, Nicholas Smith. Mid row: Wendy Richard, Mollie Sugden. Front row: Arthur Bough, Harold Bennett, John Inman.

above: It Ain't Half Hot Mum, including Don Estelle, Mike Kinsey, Kenneth McDonald, George Layton, Christopher Mitchell, Stuart McGugan and Melvyn Hayes.

left: It Ain't Half Hot Mum. We thought Michael Bates would be too ill to do the series so he isn't in the picture.

left: Goldie Hawn presented us with the Writers' Guild award.

right: DC receiving the Desmond Davies Award at the London Hippodrome, 1981. (Left to right) Terry Scott, Frank Thornton, DC, Jeremy Lloyd, Jimmy Perry, Arthur Lowe.

below: Hi-de-Hi!

top: 'Allo 'Allo – cast and crew.

above: 'Allo 'Allo (from left to right) Kim Hartman, Richard Gibson, Carmen Silvera, Arthur Bostrum, Gorden Kaye, Franscesca Gonshaw, Vicki Michelle, Richard Marner, Sam Kelly, Guy Siner.

in front of an audience of 320, and the space available is 90 feet by 60 feet. The main set needs to be used for most of the scenes in the series. About 20 out of the 30 minutes need to be shot in the studio in front of the audience, and normally the budget runs to about 10 minutes of film on location.

The recording time allowed in the early television days was 90 minutes. Over-running was very expensive and I never did it. After about 60 minutes, the studio audience start to lose patience, so it pays to finish the main shooting by that time. Once they have seen the main entertainment, the audience doesn't mind sitting while the retakes are done. These days directors tend to ignore this fact and shoot endless retakes with ever-diminishing laughs from the punters. This makes actors uneasy and shifty-eyed, and the whole show can fall apart because of the director's search for technical perfection. Building an extra set in front of the audience can't be done in less than 10 to 15 minutes and must be avoided at all costs because the audience get bored. Demolishing a set that has been pre-built you can get away with.

In the early days a lot of work went into the task of making the audience feel comfortable. At the beginning they were plonked in the studio and seated on tubular steel rostra in an atmosphere more akin to a surgical operation than a comedy entertainment. I managed to get them cosied up a bit by surrounding them with curtains. This also helped the sound. Next I managed to get them lit in warm colours. Mike McCarthy, the brilliant sound engineer who did most of my shows, studied the sound problem. Originally the audience reaction was gathered on one centrally placed microphone. Mike hung about 16 microphones above them and balanced them like an orchestra. He also arranged a similar number of speakers hung just below the mikes so that the audience could hear everything perfectly and without the 'howl-around' that bedevilled us up to that point. A further vital factor was that Mike had an instinctive knowledge of when the audience was going to react and therefore wound up the fader to catch the moment. This was a skill possessed by very few sound supervisors. I'm sorry to bang on at such length on purely technical matters, but ignoring them accounts for much of the failure of current comedy.

We finally evolved a set that consisted of the concert party's living quarters in Deolali, which was a main Royal Artillery depot in India. With charpoys, the Indian term for beds, army kit and mosquito nets, it turned out to be very atmospheric. This occupied about a third of the studio. On the other side was the battery office with a veranda outside, which was a place where the punkah wallah and char wallah could operate. In the middle was a bit of parade ground. Another small bedroom-sized set could be squeezed round the back.

With all this sorted out at last, we could go ahead and plan the series. The first great problem was the complete dearth of experienced Asian actors. Today there would be no difficulty. I could name three or four Indian actors who could handle the role of the head bearer Randi Ram, and there are many excellent African actors. In 1972 it was a very different story. There were no shows that employed Indian actors. There was no fundamental background of shows in which they could learn the trade. There were a number of actors who could handle small or cameo roles but their technique was unsubtle to say the least. There was no one who could deal with a leading comedy part.

Jimmy knew Michael Bates, who had been born in India, served with the Gurkhas during the war and spoke the language. He had been more or less raised by a bearer like Randi. It was from him that he remembered the detail of an old school snake belt worn round the turban. Michael's family were still in regular correspondence with him and sent him money. Michael was ideal for the part of the bearer.

The next problem was to cast the sergeant-major. We ran through several ideas. Leonard Rossiter was flavour of the month at the time, so we finally decided to send him a script. He came to see us to discuss the matter. I got the message that he was in reception downstairs, so I thought I would personally go to meet him, greet him and bring him up in the lift. I went down and introduced myself, took him to the lift and pressed the fourth-floor button. Naturally I asked him what he thought of the script, and he remarked that he had read it and passed a comment that there was 'undoubtedly something there', though he thought the character fell into the trap of being a bit of a cliché. There was something about his attitude that I found patronising, and I had to suppress a desire to say 'Thanks very much for coming to see us' and press the ground-floor button there and then. However, I took him along to my office to see Jimmy, and we had a non-committal sort of idle conversation, following which I took him back to the lift and bade him farewell.

Jimmy had exactly the same impression as I did. We both knew that we had written a sensational part for any actor when writing the sergeant-major. I came to the conclusion that Leonard Rossiter had a much bigger ego than I was prepared to deal with, having a pretty big ego myself. I could visualise endless rewrites to satisfy him, and rewrites were not something we were anxious to undertake. A script must be true to the original concept of the writer, and we happened to be the writers. He played several notable parts wonderfully well afterwards, but I think I was right in believing he was unsuitable for a team show. The function of the actor is to interpret, not to mastermind rewrites.

We next met Windsor Davies, having seen him in a police series playing a crook. He read the part for us. We suggested that perhaps he should play it as a Welshman, which he was. The part fitted him perfectly and he relished it and made it his own immediately. He was completely unselfish in his relationships with the other actors and was a perfect member of the team from that day forward. Windsor was an interesting character. He had begun his career as a schoolteacher. He could write well and with great humour. I once read an article he had written on rugby – a favourite topic of his, being a Welshman. He had a fine, untrained bass-baritone voice that he used later on records with 'Lofty' Don Estelle when they climbed to the top of the hit parade with 'Green Grass'.

We were in little doubt about Donald Hewlett for the colonel. I knew him well and he had a delightful light touch with comedy. Michael Knowles had played a silly-ass British officer a couple of times in *Dad's* and we thought him ideal for the captain.

A leading light in Jimmy's concert party had been a Jewish bombardier who was a great go-getter and Mr Fix-it. George Layton fell into our laps and we took him on. John Inman was obvious casting for Gloria, the female impersonator but he was well established in *Are You Being Served?* Melvyn Hayes had featured in a couple of Cliff Richard films. He seemed very suitable and agreed to play the part. Dino Shafeek had played for me in *Hugh and I* and was eager to play the char wallah, and Babar Bhatti came to see us and looked ill-nourished enough to play the punkah wallah, although in real life he ran an excellent Indian restaurant.

Don Estelle had swum into my ken by claiming to be a very good friend of Arthur Lowe. In fact he had met Arthur once for about 15 seconds, and Arthur wasn't sure he even knew him as well as that, but he had a heavenly tenor voice and was about 5 feet 1 inch tall. He was

195

a marvellous comic figure, whose physique didn't remotely match his exceptional voice, so I hired him to play Lofty. In the show we never took his lovely voice seriously. The general reaction was to throw curry and chapattis at him, and as a result everyone felt sorry for him, so it all worked a treat.

We needed a tall, good-looking lad to play Parky, the rather thick new arrival, and Chris Mitchell was perfect. His father had played many times for me. I thought of Stuart McGugan to play the Scottish strong man who could tear the telephone book in half with very great difficulty. He had the distinction of being a very good actor. Jimmy had used John Clegg in rep and we agreed that he should play the intellectual undergraduate La-de-dah Gunner Grahame, who was the concert party pianist. He couldn't play the piano but he pretended very well. The other two members of the party were Mike Kinsey, a great and lovable character who played Nosher, the food-obsessed paper tearer, and Kenneth Macdonald who played Gunner Clark and was a great enthusiast. He has done some very good work in *Only Fools and Horses*, but we could never find a proper character for him in the show. He was just there playing a bit of a nutcase who occasionally made very realistic bird noises.

The first pilot programme in January 1973 went very well with the studio audience and featured probably the smallest riot ever experienced by the British in India. There was no room in the studio for a proper full-scale riot mob, and we couldn't afford one anyway. I made do with about ten shadowy figures in the foreground, but the result didn't bear examination. I was present at the odd riot in India and they are extremely frightening affairs. Police and troops are usually heavily outnumbered and very scared, so ghastly mistakes can easily happen. The remainder of the show was a good pilot and served to introduce the characters and the general thrust of the plots, as any pilot should.

Once we got the go-ahead for the series we had to find a suitable location for the filming. England is a bit short of Indian scrub country and doesn't have a lot of jungle. I seriously thought of doing some of the show at Kew Gardens, but it didn't prove very practical. I had shot in a sandpit near King's Lynn for a sequence in *Dad's Army* that was supposed to take place in the Sudan. This was OK for the North-west Frontier, where the concert party was supposed to be giving a show.

There were woods in the district, so we plumped for King's Lynn for all the location filming. The woods themselves were pretty thin, being mostly conifers, so we strung washing lines between the trees and hung tropical leaves on them. This, reinforced with lots of tropical pot plants, made us an impenetrable jungle about 20 yards square. We could shoot on this from various angles for half a day or more because one tropical leaf looks very like another and, provided we could keep out of shot the actual pots that the plants were growing in, the illusion was very good.

At the start of the first day's shooting the cast looked remarkably like actors wearing tropical uniforms. By the time they had been sprayed with glycerine and water to represent sweat and had tramped through our jungle and crossed a 3-foot deep stream, they were exhausted and all collapsed to the ground. Surrounded by equipment and rifles, they had a smoke and now looked remarkably like real soldiers. I found that I couldn't take close-ups too early in the morning because the cold air made their breath visible, which rather spoiled the tropical illusion. We tried sucking ice cubes, which I had read was the classic cure used in the film industry, but it didn't seem to work very well. It proved easier to take the close-ups later in the day.

Most of the cast were unknowns, and it was very refreshing to feel their energy and the atmosphere of sheer enthusiasm. They all felt that they were on to a success and were looking forward to the experience. They all turned up on time, 'fell in' with no trouble at all and this time there was no competition to be last on parade.

Mike Kinsey was a perpetual source of amusement to us all. He was very severely accident-prone. I was explaining this fact to a journalist one day. He had asked the standard question beloved of all journalists which runs 'Has anything funny happened while you've been doing the show?' To answer 'The script' seldom seems to satisfy them, so we are all used to racking our brains to find something that will transfer into print. On this occasion I was telling him about Mike's affinity with disaster when there was a resounding crash. I looked round and there was Mike in the middle of one of the caterer's tables, which had collapsed under his weight. There he lay, festooned with spaghetti bolognese and chilli con carne. The journalist got his copy.

Mike was a constant source of joy. His accounts of his early attempts to make an honest buck or two were never told as funny stories. They were related in a flat voice as absolute fact. As a private detective he lost his quarry because his car wouldn't start: he had forgotten to put petrol in it. At a first attempt as a trainee taxidermist he had tried to stuff an elephant. Trying to build a do-it-yourself conservatory he had cut each piece of glass just a little too small and finished up with a mountain of small bits.

It Ain't Half Hot Mum was a happy show and we all had great fun making it. The whole cast rightly felt that they were personally involved with its success and they used to give us a lot of input, especially during meal breaks and at dinner at night. Between January 1973 and 1981 we made 59 episodes. A particular feature of this show was that three of the actors were going through marital trouble. There was a telephone just outside the rehearsal room. Every time we passed it, one of them would be standing red-faced shouting such vocal gems to his lawyer as 'The bitch! How can she say that?' or 'She's not going to have a penny more' or 'That's bloody ridiculous.' If they were called to the phone, the answer was 'Tell her I'm not here'. Aside from this, we all had a great time and the programme was going steamingly well.

Our happiness was marred when dear Michael Bates got a virulent form of cancer. He fought this off for a couple of series but when Jimmy and I went down to see him whilst he was holidaying on the Isle of Wight, it seemed impossible to us that he could endure even one more series. I moved the setting of the show to a small jungle compound in Burma so that we would create a new atmosphere and we wouldn't feel Michael's absence so deeply. The ploy didn't work because, to our amazement, Michael did find the strength to play one more series. I booked a lookalike to appear in the long shots and to 'run' for him, but Michael preferred do everything himself. A deeply embarrassing situation arose because, being sure that Michael wouldn't be with us, I agreed to a picture for the front cover of *Radio Times* that would feature Windsor Davies, Melvyn Hayes and Don Estelle without Michael Bates. Michael was understandably furious but, although nothing was said, I think in his heart he knew the reason. I never tried to replace him. We carried on for several more years without him, but to us the series was never quite the same.

Having grown tired of trying to make Norfolk conifer woods look like the Burmese jungle, we decided to move to the Farnborough area, where we could use places like Frensham Ponds to give us more usable vegetation. Our first day's filming was near to the airfield, where we chose to shoot in a War Department area. After about half an hour an infernal din started up in a nearby field. Agricultural workers are not very well paid, and the standard solution is to send an assistant with a £20 note to the source of the noise, at which the well-disposed operator will usually take a long break or fake a breakdown of his tractor. The source of this particular noise was a new type of army tank. It was surrounded by a great posse of senior officers and the intention was to test the engine to destruction. No amount of money could stop it. This was a truly desperate situation, so we had a coffee break, which is the standard procedure in desperate situations. We were faced with moving to a new location for the next three days. By the time we had found a new area and moved to it we would have lost a day's filming. I was about to order the unit to 'up sticks' when silence fell. My assistant went to make polite enquiries. The engine had destroyed itself.

It was about this time that the tabloid press started to flex its muscles. A headline appeared to the effect that 'Dad's Army Dave' had been guilty of an indiscretion that he 'didn't ought to have done'. The girl in question was described as a 'James Bond Lovely' on account of her appearance in one of the movies. She was quoted as describing the association as 'a purely physical relationship', which didn't help. The article was followed next day by gleeful telephone calls to enquire whether Mrs Croft had left home. Very fortunately, being of an exceptionally tolerant nature, she hadn't. It is all in the press files, so there is no point in trying to pretend it didn't happen.

I had some very fine assistants during *It Ain't Half Hot Mum*, and I was able to give their careers a good boost by letting them direct cameras. Prominent among them was Bob Spiers, who was the studio director in an elaborate sequence set in Deolali railway station and on the train when they were bound for the North-west Frontier. Studio directing requires a cool head because time is short. Moreover, five or six cameras and three or four sound booms can become wondrously entangled if you don't plan the whole operation meticulously. Bob was a notably cool operator and went on to do fine work in Hollywood. John Kilby was another assistant who became a good director, as did Phil Bishop and Ray Butt. Phil was very fit and hardy and I found it very off-putting when, on a frosty morning, he would turn up wearing shorts and a singlet.

Make-up presented an unusual problem. British troops in India never sunbathed. They therefore acquired a strange pattern of suntan. Their arms would be coloured as far as their rolled-up shirt sleeves. Their faces would of course be brown, they would have a small triangle of tanned flesh where their shirt remained open at the neck and by contrast, the rest of their bodies would be very white. I still have visions of Jill Hagger, the beautiful and super-efficient make-up supervisor, and her team dealing with a great queue of walk-on artistes who had to be browned up and made to look like soldiers in Burma. One of our great difficulties was to persuade actors that troops had severely short haircuts. They used to appear on the first day of rehearsal having had their personal barber give them a light trim. 'This is all right, isn't it, Dave?' would be the universal cry, to which they would get the reply, 'It's coming along very nicely but it needs to be just a touch shorter.' They all had a clause in their contracts stating that they would be required to have a very short haircut, so we won in the end.

We were able to cover some important and unusual events in the programme. The end of the war in Europe left the troops in India absolutely unmoved. They still had to deal with the Japs, which was a very daunting prospect as it was thought it would undoubtedly take several years. The other features that we were able to exploit were the return of troops to England and the process of demobilisation, which I have never seen covered in any other programme. Return to England and demob were unique and emotional experiences for the troops, and gave us the opportunity to write a couple of funny but very poignant episodes. All the boys, keen as they were to be out of the services, faced an entirely unknown future, and characters like the sergeant-major faced the end of the most exciting and memorable time of their lives. A feature of this last episode, which I found out about recently, was the inclusion of an unusual walk-on actor – Jonathan Ross made a fleeting appearance as a squaddie queueing up to get his demob gear. I can't say I recognised his talent or, for that matter, him, but at least it was no handicap to his later career.

Although it was only a comedy show, *It Ain't Half Hot Mum* covered a very important part of our imperial history – a period not touched on by any other programme. Unfortunately we came up against the early stages of political correctness, which has meant that the programme has not recently received repeats. The attitudes of the officers and soldiers were an honest version of the attitudes of the time. Warrant officers thought that anyone prepared to put on make-up, dresses and prance about on the stage was a 'poof'. British soldiers regarded any Indian as a 'native'. 'Quit India' came readily to the lips of any Indian who had not, like Randi and the char wallah, sold out to the British. Our show wasn't just a funny programme. It was founded in truth and deserves a place among our classic comedies.

20
Good Morning Campers

During the 1970s our lives had much in common with that variety act where a man spins about twenty plates on the end of sticks and rushes about, always arriving just in time to prevent any of them stopping and falling to the floor. The only difference was that Ann and I were an act where two people kept about forty plates going.

Ann was going great guns with the agency business, where her main energies were directed at the careers of Cathy McGowan, David Jason and the pop singers and writers David and Jonathan. I had *Dad's Army, Are You Being Served?* and *It Ain't Half Hot Mum*, which were being filmed in the spring and autumn so that the actors would be available to do summer shows and pantomimes. I did the school run in the mornings, Ann the collection in the afternoons. We shared the various destinations for half-term visits, sports days, speech days, school plays, for which we were usually a bit late, carol concerts and nativity plays. Holidays both at home and abroad were inserted into the schedule. Ann faithfully gave what is now known as 'quality time' to all the kids, particularly to the young ones.

My value and efficiency in these operations was marred by my complete inability to find Liverpool Street Station, which was the required rallying point for the school train. I was usually capable of getting within sight of the Tower of London, at which point the ministry in charge of directions was wont to abandon me entirely and ply me with useless destinations such as Bank and St Paul's.

Way back in 1968 we had decided that the kids needed country air for their weekends and holidays, so we searched for a country cottage. While on location for *Dad's* I realised that property in the Norfolk/Suffolk area was one-third cheaper than in Sussex and Hampshire, so we started combing that part of the world for a suitable house. We visited some fifty likely and unlikely cottages in the £5,000 bracket, which was all we could afford. We finally plumped for a farmhouse on the Duke of Grafton's estate near Bury St Edmunds. It was a bit of a wreck. Water ran down the inside and outside walls, and it was heated by one small anthracite stove. Moreover, it was a lot larger than the cottage we had in mind, but it has proved to be an ideally flexible home which over the years has coped with our family whether large or small.

As I write this I can see the field where the girls made their cross-country course for their ponies, which they rode bareback and fearlessly like little cowboys. The dining room looks out on to the lawn where Ian Lavender tumbled around with the kids on the back of the revolving 'horse' we had hired for the village garden party, and where Bill Pertwee taught the boys to keep wicket. Every season in the dining room itself we had a party for *Dad's Army*, at which Arthur Lowe loved to pretend to be the drunk butler and John Laurie made impish and occasionally manual passes at the girl from the Seychelles who was helping us in the house.

In London, despite the feverish activity, Ann still contrived to stage elegant little dinner parties. We referred to these as 'After Eight Mint Parties', and one such was given to help David Jason get into the business of television commercials. Paul Lee Lander was a leading casting director for commercials, so he was a principal guest. David Jason hired a dinner jacket specially for the occasion. We discovered that Fortnum & Mason could deliver grouse to the door that were ready to be popped in the oven. This meant that Ann could arrive home about 40 minutes before the appointed time, spread the pâté on the toast for the grouse and prepare the 'pud', after which she could rush upstairs and make herself beautiful in time to sail downstairs ready to receive guests as if she had been doing nothing all afternoon. On this occasion Ann got herself stuck in the traffic, so she arrived home a bare five minutes before the guests.

At this time Scotch was the popular drink, so I kept things going with VAT 69 and witty conversation. Unfortunately I didn't pay attention when I was refilling the glasses and mistakenly picked up a bottle of Courvoisier cognac, which looked roughly the same as VAT 69. In a very short time the party started getting distinctly 'high'. From there it progressed to giggly. The slightest attempt at humour was received with a wave of hysterical laughter, and for some reason or other David Jason started blowing raspberries. This proved to be catching, and in no time at all the whole dinner-jacketed assembly was blowing raspberries. Ann was meanwhile preparing a rather nice 'pud' consisting of stem ginger and Cointreau topped with Chantilly cream. We had a remarkable machine powered by a compressed air bulb, which turned single cream into a gorgeous fluffy Chantilly. I suddenly remembered that I had mistakenly bought double cream, which didn't 'Chantillify' the liquid but instead turned it into shower of pea-sized pellets that flew in all directions. Amid appreciative giggles I said, 'Any moment now Ann is going to appear at the door covered from head to toe in lumps of cream and tell us that dinner is served' – whereupon Ann appeared thus attired to a positive gale of laughter that would have done credit to a Ray Cooney farce. I don't think David Jason ever made any commercials, but he did pretty well on the whole.

In the midst of all this frenetic activity and not long after the start of *It Ain't Half Hot Mum* – on 10 September 1973 to be precise – Ann gave birth to our seventh offspring, a fine 12-lb boy called Tim. As usual in such cases, Ann gave Tim a few extra names on the way to register his birth. By the time she got home she was able to tell me that he was called Timothy Edward Alexander Luke.

Richard Stone thought that the time was ripe for a stage version of *Dad's Army*, so he conspired with the well-known impresario Duncan Weldon to bring this about. Jimmy and I were keen that this should not be a rehash of material that had already been seen on television, so we contrived to write a sort of saga of *Dad's Army* sketches and wartime memories – particularly musical ones. We assembled a workable script and talked most of the artistes into joining us. John Laurie thought he was not fit enough to cope with eight shows a week in the theatre, so we had to find a substitute, but all the rest were keen to take part. I heard John Laurie answering the telephone to a member of the press who enquired why he was not going to take part. John could be a man of few words. 'Mind your own fucking business,' he said.

We opted for a sort of military band sound and persuaded Duncan Weldon that he could afford 11 musicians in the pit. I was very lucky to get Josie Stewart as my musical associate. She was a brilliant musician and had been invaluable in *The Mikado* and *Iolanthe* on television. Sheila O'Neil took on the task of doing the dances, which was a formidable one because most of the cast didn't know their right foot from their left. Poor old Arnold Ridley knew the difference but had difficulty in making either of them work. We started rehearsals at the Richmond Theatre because it was owned by Louis Michaels who was one of the backers. Roger Redfarn was responsible for the overall staging.

Rehearsals were a fascinating experience. We had John le Mesurier singing 'A Nightingale Sang in Berkeley Square'. He was very reluctant to do this, but once we had settled him in a key that was very close to his speaking voice he took to it as if he had been doing it all his life. In the event his performance of the song was a notable theatrical experience. So too was Arnold Ridley's performance of 'Lords of the Air', which was most moving, though for me half the entertainment lay in watching Ed Coleman, the musical director, trying to keep pace with him.

We opened at Billingham, in County Durham, which has a rather nice theatre close to an exceedingly ordinary hotel. The fiendishly uncomfortable bed contributed to some of the sleepless nights I spent trying to rejig the running order and cut the parts of the entertainment that didn't work. However, the customers loved the show and by the time we took it to London to the Shaftesbury Theatre it was in pretty fair shape.

We had a couple of public dress rehearsals, and unfortunately Clive Dunn rather fell apart through nerves during the first of these. Bernard Delfont laid about him with his blue pencil and as a result Clive lost a very stylish piece of material that I am sure would have served him very well had it remained in the show. It was a Victorian song that Jimmy dug up called 'Too Late', which we were going to combine with a depiction of the famous painting of General Gordon being killed at Khartoum. Bernie was adamant that it had to come out, so we couldn't save it, but I think Bernie was wrong.

In the second half we featured a scene based on popular radio shows, and Arthur Lowe was great as Rob Wilton, as was Bill Pertwee as Max Miller. Ian Lavender revised a number called 'When Can I Have a Banana Again?', and Joan Cooper – Arthur's wife – joined Pamela Cundell to impersonate the well-known wartime cockney duo Gert and Daisy. The highlight was Arthur Lowe and John le Mesurier playing Flanagan and Allen in 'Home Town'. The show went down a storm and the business was enormous. Unfortunately, when term-time started and the kids all went back to school, the attendance dropped dramatically. I think everybody thought the show would run forever and they would wait until the children came home for the holidays before they came to see us. The obvious solution was to go on tour and find the public that way, and this worked very well. My lasting memory of the show concerns Arnold Ridley. For a dressing room he had a tiny cupboard just below the stage. In it was a broken-down armchair about as old as Arnold. When not actually on stage he would be poured into this chair like a blancmange. Wardrobe assistants would take off his trousers and replace them with different ones to play the next scene, following which he would be manhandled upstairs and levered on to the stage. No word of complaint ever passed his lips.

In 1976, shortly after the show opened in London, I had a quick heart attack. I attributed this to the extreme difficulty of teaching John le Mesurier to cross the stage on the same foot as the rest of the cast during 'Home Town'. I finished up in the Royal Free Hospital in Hampstead, in a delightful room with views all over London. A few floors below me was Harold Bennett, the young Mr Grace from *Are You Being Served?*, recovering from some bladder infection. He was one of my first visitors. It took him a long time to make it to my floor because he had to pause on each of the intervening levels, get out of the lift and spend a penny. Another visitor was Dino Shafeek, the char wallah from *It Ain't Half Hot Mum*, who arrived bearing three large round melons for my consumption. These were carefully placed in a cupboard by the bed. Every time it was opened they fell out like giant bowling balls, sped across the ward and skittled any passing nurses to the ground. I was particularly touched when Arnold Ridley staggered in to see me.

To hasten my recovery Ann and I took ourselves to Jamaica. It rained solidly for the first three days, which was frustrating but very restful. On our return our daughter Jane informed us that she had been taken into hospital with appendicitis, insisted on going to the Royal Free, had undergone the operation and returned home before we got back. She gave the surgeon strict instructions to make the scar small. She didn't tell us because she didn't want to bother us. She was 14. Truly her mother's daughter.

Bernie Delfont fancied *Are You Being Served?* as a summer attraction for the Winter Garden, Blackpool. Jeremy Lloyd and I quickly wrote a play that regrettably did not include Trevor Bannister or Arthur Brough. Bernie's budget didn't run to adding them to the Blackpool cast, and Arthur Brough wasn't too fit anyway. It was a rather elaborate production for a summer show, having two full sets. We played twice nightly, which was hard work for the actors. Roger Redfarn again staged it, and we opened on the Wednesday in Blackpool next door to *Dad's Army* at the Opera House. It grossed more money in the four days than *Dad's* did in the week.

Blackpool is an honest-to-goodness fun place. Everybody goes there to enjoy themselves. The play was broad comedy and from the first minute was exactly what the audience wanted. Gloriously long queues developed at the box office from the next day forward. I didn't believe him, but Bernie said that the season achieved 95 per cent capacity audiences. Jeremy persuaded me to visit the fortune-teller Gipsy Lee. She said that I had not had the recognition that perhaps I deserved, but not to worry – success was just around the corner. It was, two big theatres full of it.

Herman Rush, a dynamic American television producer, was impressed with the success of *Dad's* and thought it would stand a chance if he were to concoct an American version. Jimmy and I went over to Los Angeles to see the production of the pilot programme. It proved to be a profound, although not unexpected, cultural shock. Mainwaring had been turned into a Jewish tailor, well played by Lou Jacobi. Wilson, his side-kick, was a character of Italian extraction named Nick Rosatti, played by Clive Norton. They chose the episode featuring the German submarine commander and crew. Since the Americans have not been introduced to the delights and subtleties of fish and chips, and the importance of salt and vinegar, Walker's scene with the U-boat commander was concerned with ordering corned beef or salami sandwiches, which is not quite so funny. It was staged at the ABC studios with electronic cameras, which was a fairly new experience for American comedy. To me, after spending so long producing shows for the BBC, the outstanding feature of the production was its great inefficiency. The whole operation was slow and plodding, whereas I had expected some sort of Hollywood magic. The most noticeable feature was that the scenery didn't touch the floor by about 1½ inches. The gap was filled in the outside set by placing boxes of artificial flowers in front of it. The whole proposition of transferring the show to the USA was pretty hopeless, and in the end died a natural death. America was never threatened by an invasion, so the perilous situation of the Home Guard and of the country itself simply did not exist. Jimmy and I stayed at the Beverly Wilshire Hotel and enjoyed the whole experience immensely. We were wonderfully well treated, and Artie Julian, the writer of the American script, referred to us as 'the publicity-hungry Limeys'.

Jeremy and I were keen to do a show set in the year 2050 which was to be called *Come Back Mrs Noah*. It was to be set in Pontefract, where the UK had established a space exploration complex. Mollie Sugden as Mrs Noah wins the Housewife of the Year competition and her prize is a visit to a spaceship. While she is there, it spontaneously goes into orbit. What followed speaks volumes about the flexibility of the BBC at that time. I thought the idea was very vulnerable to duplication so I went to see Jimmy Gilbert, who was then the excellent head of comedy. I told him that we had an idea for a comedy show and I wanted to do a pilot, but the idea was so hot that I didn't want to tell him what it was. To his eternal credit, he didn't protest or ask for a script. He told me to go ahead and do it.

I included Ian Lavender, Donald Hewlett and Michael Knowles in the cast. Gorden Kaye had played a one-line part as a stroppy soldier in *It Ain't Half Hot Mum* and he had made two or three telling appearances in *Are You Being Served?* I thought he had a lot of talent, so he was included in the cast as a BBC presenter on a *Tonight* type of programme. The show was technically very sophisticated. Seeing it today you could say that I had definitely bitten off more than I could chew, but the show was very funny indeed. The special effects boys had a field day in making futuristic gadgets. These included an automatic mechanical hen that produced eggs and of course egg-laying noises at the touch of a button. As it was in development, it slung them forcibly from the hen's backside against the wall, where they broke. The laugh was enormous. The everyday needs of the rocket crew were provided through the use of a computer. They were delivered through a trap after endless key-pressing. Requests for a cup of tea usually produced a bored-looking goldfish in a glass bowl. Once in orbit, gravity ceased to exist, so Mollie spent a lot of time floating around the cabin using her scent spray as a propelling device.

Everyone liked the pilot, so Jimmy Gilbert told us to go ahead with the first series. It presented us with the opportunity to do some marvellously original comedy, and in this we were backed up by the inventiveness of the special effects department, who revelled in the chance to create some zany devices. Jeremy and I still think of it as one of the funniest things we have ever done, but the figures were disappointing. This was due partly to scheduling and partly to the runaway success of Kenny Everett, who was against us and in top form. The show was never repeated and is not even seen on UK Gold, the excuse being that the channel has no room for a six-episode series.

At home I still watch it from time to time when in need of a good laugh tonic.

Dad's was made into a film by Columbia Pictures and also went on the radio, with about sixty of the scripts adapted by Harold Snoad and Michael Knowles. By 1977 we thought that all the juice in that particular orange had been extracted. Filming for the last series was a bit of an ordeal. John le Mesurier was very ill indeed. In spite of all the make-up department could do, he looked awful. I remember getting all the available light and making a sort of 6-feet square Riviera for him, to warm him up a bit. Arnold Ridley had somehow ripped a cartilage in his leg and he was brought up to the location in a large limousine. By the time I went to greet him he had slid to the floor, and as I opened the door he smiled bravely at me from the prone position. I shook him warmly by the hand. John Laurie saw us from the steps of the make-up caravan. 'Look,' he said. 'Look – look – they're pumping him up.'

I couldn't resist directing the last studio show and it was a very emotional night. There were lumps in throats and eyes being surreptitiously wiped all round, and I remember thinking that none of them would ever be well enough to work again. In fact, they all went on to do other things and survived for many years.

With *Are You Being Served?* and *It Ain't Half Hot Mum* going strong, it seemed that there was time for Jimmy and me to plan a further series. We both knew the Butlins Holiday Camp scene very well indeed. Jimmy had spent his holidays from RADA as a Red Coat, while I had produced the professional show there for a number of years. It seemed to us a very good field for a comedy show. There had been several previous attempts at the subject, but the people concerned simply didn't know the background. Their approach was usually to treat the holiday camp as a sort of POW camp from which the holiday-makers were trying to escape. We knew that Billy Butlin specialised in giving his campers a thoroughly good break. They would return year after year simply because they had the time of their lives. We thought the stories would lie with the staff, who were all failures but with burning ambitions to succeed in show business or in their own particular field. Bill Cotton thought I was out of my mind to try another series on the subject, but he gamely gave the go-ahead. One of Bill's great assets as head of light entertainment was that he knew just what he *didn't* know and had confidence that his producers would deliver the goods. Most of us were well grounded in show business, which of course is barely possible for present-day producers.

The star of *Hi-de-Hi!* was to be a university professor who thought that he was being stifled by the academic world and that life was passing him by. John Quayle was our first choice for the part, and it was more or less arranged that he would do it, but it transpired that the National Theatre would not release him. We started to ask round the agencies, and the result was that Simon Cadell walked into the rehearsal rooms where we were meeting likely actors. He read the part and Jimmy, to Simon's bewilderment, read the part of his mother. He was obviously ideal for the role and I engaged him, thus acquiring not only a fine actor and star but also a lifelong friend and a son-in-law, because he married my daughter Becky. The second lead was to be Ted Bovis, the camp host. We saw one or two leading actors for the part. I rather fancied Ronnie Hilton who had played a summer season for me at Bridlington, but when he read for us I came to the conclusion that he wasn't quite experienced enough as an actor. That very night Jimmy saw Paul Shane in *Coronation Street*. He thought him a likely candidate, so Paul came down from the north to see us. He was a natural actor and a very experienced comedian. He had won the Comic of the Year award for about five years for playing the northern clubs. Tougher audiences than these cannot be found. He fitted the part perfectly.

We were fairly flexible about the characters that were to be in the show, but obviously we needed some of the sort of people we had both encountered at Butlins. There had to be a head Yellow Coat, for instance. Jimmy had used Ruth Madoc in his rep at Watford. I had seen her in *The Man from La Mancha* in the leading part that she took over from Joan Dinar. She was very Welsh and seemed ideal. When I had first seen John Inman in *Salad Days* at Golders Green, he had Barry Howard as a partner, and I always had a guilty conscience about separating them because Barry too was very talented. We decided to play him as half of the ballroom dancing act. He had a wonderful long face with a bored, superior look that fitted the part perfectly. The other half was Diane Holland, who had been the girl who was thrown about by the Ganjou Brothers, a top-line adagio act. Adagio dancers usually number two strong men and one slim girl. One of the men flings the female right across the stage or circus to be caught, with an unconcerned expression on her face, by the waiting partner. Diane had a permanently unconcerned expression and a faded quality that was very funny.

We needed a wildly enthusiastic younger man to play the budding camp comedian. Roger Redfarn had introduced us to Jeffrey Holland for the stage production of *Dad's Army*. Whenever we required an actor to play a small part, Jeffrey would volunteer even if it meant doing an impossibly quick change of costume. This was exactly what we wanted for Spike, the camp comedian. We dreamed up a lovely character for Mr Partridge, the children's entertainer and Punch and Judy man. We thought he should be an alcoholic and a man who hated kids. I hadn't met Leslie Dwyer since he played Blinky Bill with Mother in *The Belle of New York* at the outset of the war. He had played in countless movies since then, and we were lucky enough to get him into our cast.

Felix Bowness had been an invaluable asset to many of my shows as the 'warm-up man'. He had an unusual capacity to burble on for anything up to ten minutes without ever being embarrassed or embarrassing. He engendered a relaxed and friendly feeling among the audience during pauses caused by costume changes or retakes. Listening to him up in the gallery, we frequently wondered what on earth he was going on about. When you were actually in the audience you were totally absorbed in what he was saying. I think it all stemmed from the fact that Felix is a thoroughly nice and likeable man who had been our loyal supporter for year after year. I remember the cast of *Are You Being Served?* remarking on Felix's meandering style. He was away one week and Michael Barrymore, early in his career, did the warm-up, during which he stood on his head for minutes on end and tried to make funny gestures with his feet. Next morning the cast wrote a notice in the rehearsal room saying, 'Come back Felix, all is forgiven'. Felix was pretty passionate about horse racing, so we played him as Fred Quilley, a jockey who had lost his racing licence for pulling a horse. He got himself a job in charge of the camp riding school, with horses that had been retired from pulling milk carts for the Express Dairy.

Richard Stone pleaded with us to agree that before we finished casting we would see a girl who he thought had a load of talent but had so far failed to find the right place for herself in the business. Accordingly, a breathless Su Pollard arrived at the top of Jimmy's 82 steps dressed as a cross between the Pied Piper and a bag lady and proceeded to bombard us with a not-too-brief résumé of her life story.

She appeared to be dressed by Oxfam, but even Oxfam don't sell odd stockings, so I think it was all carefully thought out. When she left I remember saying that we would have to find something for her. 'Cinderella, but she can never go to the ball.' We tailor-made Peggy, the chalet maid, for her. She was a remarkable actress and she made herself into a star. I came to have great admiration for Su as an actress. She is completely devoted to her character, whatever it may be. I think she could be wonderful in any part she is physically suitable for.

All we needed were some Yellow Coats led by Nikki Kelly, Rikki Howard and the Webb Twins, and we were ready to go. Knowing Butlins Clacton camp so well from having been there during the war, and later produced shows in their nasty concrete theatre, I was keen to do the filming there. To our surprise we encountered total opposition from the Rank Organisation, who had acquired the Butlins empire and were earnestly trying to lose the Butlins image. They had actually issued an edict to the effect that the well-known catchphrase 'Hi-de-Hi!' was never to be used. They had rebuilt the old-fashioned chalets into two-storey suites and were going for a self-catering type of holiday. In the event, we weren't too upset about the Clacton camp because the pool was too close to the road and the traffic noise would have been unacceptable.

Warners Holiday Camp at Dovercourt in Essex welcomed us warmly and we were there for eight happy years. Our first visit for the pilot programme, however, was anything but warm. It was in October and, for budget reasons, we stayed in the camp chalets. They were designed for summer occupation and there was no heating. At night we were all freezing. The cast bore it all with great fortitude and as many blankets as we could muster. I was particularly worried about Leslie Dwyer, who was elderly to put it mildly, but to our relief he failed to get pneumonia.

In the event, we made a great pilot programme and the studio audience lapped it up. A series was commissioned without delay. It was one of the happiest shows we ever produced. With the exception of Ruth Madoc, nobody was seeking a divorce, which released the rehearsal room telephone for normal use. The presence of Simon Cadell in the company made everyone try to perform up to his standard. All the cast were at the outset of their careers, which meant that the general tone of the conversation was mainly concerned with

212

what means they could adopt to avoid paying too much income tax. Simon and Paul Shane, who came from opposite ends of the business, got on remarkably well. Simon was mad about good food. Paul was used to downing a large number of pints of Newcastle Brown ale, but now turned his attention to red wine. He soon realised that he couldn't consume it in pints and had to think in terms of glasses. He referred to the carafes it was served in as 'them giraffes'. Simon and I spent our leisure in the pursuit of good food and good wine, which Harwich and Suffolk provided in abundance.

One of the hazards of this particular activity was that Su Pollard was always keen to join us. After a day's filming, far from being exhausted, she would be filled with energy and absolutely glorious enthusiasm. This evinced itself by a marked tendency to dance on tables while producing an ear-splitting whistle with the use of two fingers and her pretty teeth. If we wanted a quiet and civilised evening we would say to Su, 'Are you going out tonight?' If she said 'Yes', we would enquire where she was going and then book somewhere else. She was also incredibly short-sighted. If she put her specs down on a table, she could only find them by imitating a helicopter at a height of 10 inches from any likely surface. She would then hover to and fro until they came into view.

We were a big organisation when filming at Dovercourt because we had to give the impression that we numbered about 600 campers around the pool. We managed this by hiring about 60 walk-ons and moving them about, if necessary in different costumes. I remember telling one chap with a beard that if he wanted to be with us for more than half a day, he should forthwith shave himself, which he did. Somehow the programme generated a sort of holiday atmosphere and was enormous fun to be associated with. All in all, we did 58 of them.

21

The Operating Theatre and
the French Resistance

Gorden Kaye had first come to my notice when he appeared in *It Ain't Half Hot Mum* as a stroppy soldier. I had given him a couple of more showy parts in *Are You Being Served?* These he had played with gusto, not being in the least daunted by the presence of all the famous and experienced TV stars around him. I thought it was well worthwhile creating a series for him. Jeremy and I wrote *Oh Happy Band* with him very much in mind for the leading role. It was a story set in the present day in a village community that was getting together to prevent itself being obliterated by the building of a huge new airfield. The centre of the resistance was the village brass band, conducted by Gorden Kaye.

This series was planned before the disastrous management restructures by John Birt that led to focus groups, committees and hopelessly cumbersome decision-making. Jimmy Gilbert was able straight away to give me a date in September 1980 to make a pilot. Preparations and casting proceeded with speed. We included the incomparable West Country comedian Billy Burden in the company. Tony Simpson also joined us. I had first met Tony when I was about eight years old and he was a young actor with Mother in *The Maid of the Mountains* at the London Hippodrome. He was now an old, bearded character actor. John Horsley, whom I had long admired as a light comedy player, joined us as a rich landowner who was secretly in favour of the airfield, and Jonathan Cecil played a local schoolteacher.

Two or three weeks before the production date, a very awkward situation developed. Some sort of strike was threatened at ITV. Gorden Kaye had contracted to do a show there, so found himself in a position where he could commit to our pilot but would not necessarily be available to do the series. This of course was not acceptable, so on the Wednesday before going into rehearsal on the Monday I found myself without a leading man. Either I had to cancel the programme or find a new star. Cancelling programmes is an expensive pastime and leaves one with a terrible sense of having achieved absolutely nothing at all. I had a deep think and made a few telephone calls and finally unearthed the fact that Harry Worth was available. I liked Harry very

214

much and had enjoyed working with him in Titipu, so I jumped at the chance of using him.

We made a good pilot and Jimmy Gilbert agreed to go ahead with the series. It was a fair enough programme and the main cast and particularly the band and musical side were attractive. However, I thought the balance of the programme was not going to get us anywhere in the long run. Our idea was that Gorden Kaye would be a devious and scheming character surrounded by well-meaning, bumbling idiots. Harry Worth proved to be a well-meaning, bumbling idiot surrounded by a lot more well-meaning, bumbling idiots. We tried restructuring the scripts to give the scheming and devious part of the character to Jonathan Cecil, but this was not a feature of the original character and it was also a bit foreign to Jonathan's nature, so it didn't quite work out.

Nevertheless, we got some good comedy out of the series. It was quite well received by the public and Jimmy Gilbert was prepared to go ahead with a second series, but rightly or wrongly I thought it had nowhere to go from the story point of view, so we decided to pull it. It was a pity for many reasons. The Aldershot Brass Ensemble who provided the brass band were a delightful and enthusiastic bunch of musicians who made a gorgeous, warm sound. Gorden Kaye made a one-off appearance playing a recording engineer when Billy Burden was singing 'Leanin'. Billy had a rich baritone singing voice and invariably had tears streaming down his face by the end of the number, which was both funny and moving. Harold Bennett played a vicar and used his immaculate timing to very telling effect. For some reason or other Harry Worth accused me of trying to get him to play the part like Arthur Lowe, which couldn't have been further from the truth. In the last memorable episode we had the band trying to get into the *Guinness Book of Records* in order to gain publicity for the village cause. Their ploy was to become known as the only band that had played at a height of 500 feet in hot air balloons. This entailed me being in a helicopter at six o'clock on a sunny morning filming half a dozen huge hot air balloons gently rising out of the mist. John Chapman's son Mark was the cameraman, and it was far and away the most beautiful scene I ever shot.

Despite the early withdrawal of *Happy Band* I was still firmly of the opinion that *Are You Being Served?* was nearing the end of its useful life. Plots were getting far-fetched or else were thinly disguised rehashes of previous shows. The programme was still getting good audiences, and the new head of comedy – Gareth Gwenlan – was keen that it should continue, but I was gradually backing away from the wish to carry on writing it.

Jeremy and I had for some months been discussing new ideas for a replacement. One such was that selected members of the cast should take a holiday in Young Mr Grace's yacht and become shipwrecked on a Robinson Crusoe island. Having thought about the plot for a few days, we started to write it, but in the event it didn't seem to gel and, having got only to page 18 after two days, we thought it best to consign our efforts to the waste-paper basket. A similar fate befell our next effort. I can't even remember what it was about, but we had been nourishing the idea for some months.

Jeremy went home and lay flat on the floor for a couple of hours thinking about ideas, which he was inclined to do in desperate situations. Next morning he came to my house and said, 'Why don't we take the mickey out of those films and TV shows about the French Resistance and all those sinister Germans and Gestapo characters with duelling scars down their cheeks – *Enemy at the Gate,* etc?' I thought it a sensational idea and within two and a half days we had the pilot script finished. Ann read it, laughed until tears rolled down her cheeks and said that she thought it was a winner. Jeremy, who was sitting nearby, said, 'That's the kiss of death', because Ann was usually rather less than enthusiastic about our efforts.

Jeremy is a most remarkable writing partner. As I've said before, wonderful comedy simply pours from him. We couldn't get it written down fast enough and the pilot script stayed intact until it was on tape in the studio. We did half the casting as we wrote with, of course, Gorden Kaye in the leading part as René, the café proprietor and very reluctant member of the Resistance. Jack Haig – 'It is I, Leclerc' – had played for us many times in *Are You Being Served?* I'd had my eye on Kim Hartman ever since producing *Ann Veronica* at Coventry. She was a student there, quite enchanting and ideal for the blonde German Helga. I saw Kirsten Cooke in rep at Croydon and thought her ideal as leader of the de Gaulle side of the Resistance.

Richard Gibson was a quirky bit of casting. He looked incredibly youthful to be a Gestapo officer. Until that time he had played mostly teenagers. We made him Heinrich Himmler's godson, who had got himself into the Gestapo by influence and was rather struggling to subdue his soft heart so as to fulfil the role. For the two maids in the café I tried to book Amanda Donahoe and Mary Stavins, the latter having just finished her stint as Miss World. However, they hadn't got the right union card and Equity, the actors' union, was quite inflexible and refused to let them appear. Amanda became a big star in Hollywood, so she triumphed in the end, but it is very frustrating when union officials take it upon themselves to decide who has talent, usurping the role of the directors, who stake their reputation on making the right choices.

Vicky Michelle had worked for us in *Mrs Noah* as a most realistic robot, and Francesca Gonshaw looked gorgeous and had a great and very liquid French accent that splashed all over everyone when she pronounced an 'R'. I was happy to engage them. Guy Siner was new to me but I thought him ideal as the young captain of uncertain sexuality who seemed to fancy René. Guy played the part for the entire run of the series and always gave a well-studied performance of great subtlety. Sam Kelly was introduced to me by Gorden Kaye. Good actors are excellent judges of other good actors, and Gorden's faith in Sam has been justified time and time again. He makes laughter out of the simplest lines merely because he is so true to his character, and he has that rare ability to say his lines precisely at that magic nanosecond – which is inadequately called 'timing'. Richard Marner I had seen struggling in the ferry-based soap *Triangle*, but he made a great hit as Colonel von Strohm. Rose Hill was our first choice for Edith's mother, the old bat upstairs. She had appeared a couple of times in *Dad's* and had always scored in any comedy part. She had her own particular pace when playing the role, and her relationship with Jack Haig was sparky to say the least. On one occasion, when Rose had taken her time to deliver her next line, Jack was heard to say, 'I could have eaten a bloody ham sandwich in that pause.'

I loved Jack Haig's work and always found him hilarious. It is, however, true to say that Jack could whinge for England. When I first knew him in Newcastle he was becoming increasingly deaf, and finding it impossible even to hear his cues from other actors. Later he underwent a marvellous operation called fenestration, which entailed more or less replacing the eardrum. On coming round from the anaesthetic, he is reputed to have yelled for help. The worried sister rushed into his room. Jack was sitting up in bed with his hands clapped over his ears. 'Nurse! Nurse!' he shouted. 'For Gawd's sake shut the window. Those bloody birds are deafening me.'

Jack and Rose were an ill-assorted couple. Rose used to make elaborate notes on her script as to precisely how she would phrase each line and sometimes each word. Jack would be reluctant to rehearse at all. Despite this, they played some great scenes together.

John D. Collins, whom I had first used as a bewildered waiter in *Hugh and I*, had played many excellent comedy cameo parts for me, so I had no hesitation in booking him as one of the idiot RAF officers. Nicholas Frankau, son of director John Frankau, was the other. Finally we cast Carmen Silvera as René's wife, who couldn't carry a tune in a bucket. Carmen really was tone deaf, and this complete inability to hit a note became a major feature of the character of Edith. All the customers in the café rushing to put cheese in their ears every time she threatened to sing was one of the gems of the series. Carmen played the love of Arthur Lowe's life in 'Mum's Army', which is probably my favourite *Dad's* episode. She trained as a dancer in her early days, which reinforced my conviction that a lot of dancers rarely listen to the music. Once their cue arrives, they count the beats with the inexorable precision of a time bomb.

As with *Mrs Noah*, I thought the *'Allo 'Allo* idea was very hot and there was a great danger of somebody tumbling upon it. I was therefore very keen to send out a pilot to establish our ownership, so to speak, even though I knew that my schedule wouldn't allow me to do the actual series for 18 months. Accordingly, we made a pilot on 11 September 1982 – four days after I officially retired from the BBC. The night before the first rehearsal I practically had kittens. I suddenly realised that I had not checked to see if Gorden had a good French accent. I needn't have worried. Gorden's contribution to the show was immeasurable. He has an unerring instinct for comedy and added enormously to every scene, for which I am eternally grateful.

It was quite the best pilot we ever made, and the audience lapped it up. As they left the studio, there were smiles all over their faces, which is one of the best rewards you can have when doing a comedy show.

Duncan Weldon decided that *Hi-de-Hi!* was very suitable as a subject for a summer season. He booked the Pavilion, Bournemouth, and Jimmy and I got busy constructing a suitable entertainment based on the series. We enjoyed writing it. We were both well aware of what the summer show audiences were looking for and were determined to give it to them. At the same time we felt sure that we could aim a bit higher than the ordinary variety format. We made the general thrust of the show the attempt by the various members of the staff at 'Maplins' to escape from being on the holiday camp staff into the professions at which they had all failed. Simon Cadell held the whole show together, and Paul Shane was in his element playing in front of a big audience. Su Pollard triumphed as Peggy, particularly when she sang 'Look for the Silver Lining'. We didn't have to tweak the show much after the first night, and it played to spectacular business twice nightly.

My heart had now been playing up for some time. A doctor had performed an angiogram on me. This involves shoving a little tube through an artery in the arm, pushing it near the heart and then squeezing out a sort of dye that allows those who understand the whole business to see how the heart is performing. Before going ahead with the procedure, the doctor asked me if I wanted a running commentary explaining what he was doing. I declined this luxury because I had no ambitions to be a heart surgeon, so, as a substitute, he decided to sing 'Blue Moon' – fortunately in tune. The operation takes about 40 minutes, so he got through quite a few choruses. The upshot of this investigation was that I was urged to have a heart bypass operation. It was early days in the history of this operation and I was not a little scared. The rate of success was about 80 per cent, which I thought was not quite good enough.

Tomorrow's World demonstrated a less serious operation named 'angioplasty'. This involved sticking a tube into an artery somewhere around the crotch and sliding it up into the arteries feeding the heart. On the end is a little balloon that the doctor then inflates to widen any obstruction that he encounters. After a lot of thought I volunteered for this one.

The next scene in this saga sees me in an operating theatre in Guy's Hospital, lying on my back with arms outstretched and strapped in a crucifixion type posture because this particular doctor makes up his mind whether to go crotch or arm at the very last minute. I can't say I was happy about being in this position. The history of those who have hitherto assumed it is not very reassuring. There was no 'Blue Moon' this time. This doctor preferred to confine himself to commenting on his progress to his assistant. Like some sabre duellist, he concentrated on the cutting and thrusting. His first remark shortly after he inserted the long, thin catheter tube was worrying. 'Damn – it's kinked,' he said.

'Try another one,' said the assistant. A few more fumblings followed.

'Damn, that one has kinked as well.'

'Do you think it's a bad batch?' said the assistant.

'Give me another one.' Silence ensued, so I supposed that all was well. The next thing I remember is the surgeon pounding my chest with his fist and saying reassuringly, 'Just getting the circulation going. You passed out.'

'Did I really?,' I said. 'Well, I think I'm going to pass out again.' I woke up some time later in the intensive care ward, having died for quite a few seconds. It seems that I have an 'irascible heart', as the surgeon put it.

The surgeon said that there was absolutely no chance of this mishap occurring again, so I let him have another go a few months later so that he could complete the job. It did happen again and I died once more – this time in the Harley Street clinic, which at least was much more comfortable. There was nothing for it but to go for the full bypass operation. This was scheduled to take place a few weeks later, by which time I had started to film another series of *Hi-de-Hi!* By way of a farewell, Simon Cadell arranged that the cast should buy me an exceedingly expensive present – a case of Chateau Lafite 1962. As a bizarre afterthought Felix Bowness asked if it could be bought on sale or return, which eased the tension at a tense time.

The brilliant surgeon Donald Ross, who looks very like Arthur Lowe, did the operation. They don't hang about in hospitals these days, which is just as well considering how much it costs. They yanked me out of bed and sat me in a chair the morning after returning from intensive care, and I was back home within ten days. *Hi-de-Hi!* was still in the studios, and I was keen to visit and tell everyone that they weren't going to get the wine back, but Ann wouldn't hear of it. It was only seven weeks after the operation that *Hi-de-Hi!* was due to transfer to the Victoria Palace. It needed sharpening up after its season in Bournemouth. Jimmy said he would do all the shouting and running up and down the aisles if I could just manage to be there, so between us we restaged the show. If we had any worries as to whether it was suitable for a London audience, they were quickly dispersed. The first night was a huge success. The show was just right for the coach trade that had enjoyed *The Crazy Gang*, and it was a great joy to be in the audience with them.

I was now free to write and plan the long delayed *'Allo 'Allo*. Jeremy and I set to and wrote a first series of eight programmes. Fortunately the cast were all available and eager to get started. For a while we were concerned that by making a comedy featuring the German Army, especially the Gestapo, we were running the risk of being taken a little too seriously and that people might come to the conclusion that it was not a fit subject for a comedy series. I had a contact in the SAS who in turn was still in touch with former members of the French Resistance. Through him I let them have a couple of tapes of the pilot programme, to which they found no objection. A former inmate of Buchenwald concentration camp thought it wonderfully funny. A close relation of 'White Rabbit', the famous Resistance leader, was of the opinion that he would have found it hilarious. One way or another it seemed that the balance of opinion was on our side.

As was the case with *Hi-de-Hi!*, we were working with a cast of actors who were mostly at the beginning of their careers. They were all wildly enthusiastic. An unusual feature of rehearsals was that instead of congregating in corners for chats or going off to make phone calls, they all sat and watched each other play the scenes and laughed at the funny bits. We based our filming operations in Swaffham, Norfolk, because it was near to Forestry Commission land. The Ministry of Defence, who had been so helpful in the early days of *Dad's Army*, had become impossibly expensive having been spoilt by an American film company, who paid them £1,000 a day for months on end. Trust House Forte rates had also escalated, so the Bell Hotel in Thetford steadfastly refused to do a deal that we could afford on our budget.

The tabloid papers thought they could get a few meaty stories out of us, so we were infiltrated by several of their reporters. I was a bit worried when I heard Jack Haig confiding in one of them. 'I've been known as a dirty comic for years,' he said, 'but I could never have got away with some of the stuff in these scripts.' Martin Dennis, who directed a lot of episodes in the latter days of the series, used to call it 'self-cleaning pornography'. In fact the series attracted quite a lot of criticism when it was first shown. The *Radio Times* published a number

221

of letters both for and against the programme. Fortunately a large majority were for. Paul Fox, who by now was a senior executive with one of the ITV companies, led off in the press to the effect that the BBC should be ashamed to be so insensitive as to allow it in their schedules. By and large, however, the public took to the show readily and the ratings quickly soared.

As the series progressed it displayed many features that were unique from an administrative point of view. In the first place, many of the actors compared notes about the salary the BBC booking department was offering them. Actors usually guard the secret of the money they get very closely indeed, and will generally drop only exaggerated hints about the size of their salary. The '*Allo* lot rang each other up and had truthful chats. The bookers were not used to that kind of thing and didn't like it.

In addition, the make-up department was in conflict with some members of the cast. Jack Haig said he was not going to be made up by some girl who had only been in the business five minutes when he had been doing his own make-up for 50 years. Rose Hill thought that she should have a different make-up when she was in long shot from what she had in close-up. The girls in the show were a little wary of that particular department. I had insisted on a make-up trial some days before we did the pilot. The result was that they made our beautiful girls look like dogs. The main reason for this is that, when asked to do a show set in the past, the department rushes for period pictures and faithfully reproduces them. I wanted more of the Hollywood approach, where the girls look glamorous. This they ultimately gave me.

In the hotel it was discovered that one of the actors had a double bed to sleep on. The result was a large and impossible level of demand for double beds. We negotiated round all these pitfalls, but there remained an element of tension with some of the cast. To enhance the atmosphere of secrecy and conspiracy in the stories, we decided that much of the action should take place at night. I am dead against filming at night, however, and trying to play comedy when it is cold and dark. Actors find it difficult to be funny when half frozen at two o'clock in the morning. We therefore concentrated on the technique of filming 'day for night'. Hollywood westerns quite blatantly put heavy blue filters on the lens and carry on regardless. I had the help of Max Sammet, a great cameraman, who shot many shows for me from *Dad's*

Army onwards. He was an incredibly fast worker, which suited television filming well because we couldn't afford a relaxed schedule. He also specialised in 'day for night'. The main secret of this technique is to avoid seeing the sky in the shots and to use any sun as back or side lighting. This, combined with careful printing, gives a great effect. The only time we came unstuck was in a sequence where the two airmen were inside a pantomime cow costume following a herd of real cows through a narrow opening between two copses – quite a normal event in *'Allo 'Allo*. The result on the rushes was various degrees of blackness heaving against an even blacker background. We did a reshoot with a herd of Herefords that had white patches on them.

One of the most successful characters in the show was not included in the cast in the first series. This was the English policeman, played by Arthur Bostram. He had played a very small part in *Hi-de-Hi!* as Su Pollard's boyfriend and had a long, mournful face that was great for comedy. He was the character who spoke atrocious French. I suppose the inspiration for the part came from Ted Heath, who spoke the language with a broad English accent. We weren't sure whether the public would get the joke, but from his first entrance, when he said 'Good moaning', the audience fell about. He played the part throughout with his own intense sincerity that added greatly to the comedy.

After we had done a number of series Mark Furness approached us to do a stage version. Mark had put on *It Ain't Half Hot Mum* at the Pier Theatre in Bournemouth to record takings and had followed it up with a tour to major towns and a further summer season in Scarborough. He was convinced that *'Allo 'Allo* would catch the public fancy, but I didn't think he had a chance of solving all the salary and billing problems with the cast. Mark, however, was a tireless negotiator and he persisted. I helped to solve the salary problem by suggesting to the cast that they should all take a percentage of the gross takings based on their BBC salaries. This would have been too clumsy an arrangement in the past, but the advent of calculators made the computation of, say, $2\frac{7}{8}$ per cent of £27,583 a simple matter. I don't have a calculator, so I can't tell you the answer. A percentage deal also meant that if we played to poor business, the proposition would survive, and if we packed out, everyone would make a good deal of money. Such a deal would have saved *Dad's Army* during its London run at the Shaftesbury. To everyone's surprise, the cast welcomed the deal. Jeremy and I quickly wrote the play and Mark booked our opening date at the Alexandra Theatre, Birmingham. The set presented a great problem because we had devised no fewer than 17 scene changes. Peter Farago. who was directing the production, went through several different versions and, with his typical Hungarian ingenuity, finally came up with a set that allowed a fast, seamless show.

The opening was a night that I will never forget. As Ann, Jeremy and I approached the theatre we saw a spectacular traffic jam as the customers arrived. We then noticed that many of the audience were dressed as French policemen, waitresses, Resistance girls, German soldiers, Gestapo officers ... in fact all the characters from the show. When the curtain went up, the first funny line, instead of being politely received, got a belting great laugh. The evening continued like that, with so much laughter that we added 25 minutes to the running time.

We played practically every big theatre in the country to capacity. There wasn't a seat to be had from Monday onwards. I went to see the show at the Hippodrome, Bristol, and boxes that were normally full of dried flowers were packed with people. They could see little of the show because these boxes mainly faced the auditorium, but they seemed to be having a high old time.

Bernie Delfont brought us to the Prince of Wales Theatre and we played to standing room only. I heard two well-known critics on the first night talking to each other in the stalls aisle. 'Will they never learn?' one of them said. Since we had well over half a million in bookings, I don't know what he meant. There were of course those who sincerely thought that the show was trivialising the awful tragedy of the Holocaust, so in deference to his Jewish friends and relations, Bernie himself never came to see the show.

We broke to do another series for the BBC, following which Mark Furness booked us into the London Palladium. It was standing room only again. After a further series for the BBC, we played another season at the Prince of Wales, followed by a second visit to the Palladium. We didn't outstay our welcome until Mark rather rashly booked us into the Dominion, Tottenham Court Road. The Dominion has a vast, cavernous auditorium and is suitable only for very big musical spectaculars. It was also a bit tired decoratively before the big Disney shows arrived. The theatre management did their best to make it look less careworn, and painted the lavatories a lurid red. The paint was not quite dry for the first night, so a lot of the lady customers had red paint in unusual places. We were not a hit there. Perhaps the most remarkable thing was that we played all these enormous theatres with just one piano backstage and one accordion in the pit.

Among my most persistent memories is the dress rehearsal at the Palladium. Richard Marner as the German colonel lost his voice, so the assistant stage manager spoke his part from the wings while Richard went through the acting motions and mouthed all the words. The effect was ludicrous. The other memory is of Jack Haig. I had been exceedingly fond of Jack ever since our days in Newcastle. We had a lot of laughs together. I understood him, he was a great comedian but he was dead awkward. He had struggled for years with slender success in all the lesser variety theatres in the country. To see the sheer joy on his face when he first stepped on to the stage of the Palladium made me forgive all. The Palladium is the Mecca of all variety performers, and Jack had made it.

22
Hollywood Calling
and Birt at the BBC

In 1976 an American producer called Herman Rush decided that *Are You Being Served?* might stand a chance of success if it were adapted for an American audience. He wasn't far wrong because the British programme has performed consistently well on the Public Service Network. Unfortunately, the BBC doesn't do very good deals with these stations and, as a result, it doesn't pay well. Herman commissioned his writers Bill Idelson and Sheldon Bull to do an American version. The episode they chose for the pilot was 'German Week', which we thought was a good idea. Jeremy and I departed for Hollywood because we were co-producers and co-writers and they wanted us there for the planning and casting. We arrived to find that there were several hiccups in the project and it was a few weeks before the pilot got the all-clear. The go-ahead was due largely to the help of Gary Marshall, to whom I took a great liking. He was the writer and producer of *Happy Days* and *Laverne and Shirley* – both huge successes in America – and he later directed the film *Pretty Woman*. He was immensely talented without an ounce of bullshit about him, which is a great rarity in Hollywood.

The writers confessed that they didn't like the script they had written and suggested that we should rewrite it nearer to the original, which we proceeded to do. The show was to be produced at Paramount Film Studios. We were given a very large, sparsely furnished office and two secretaries. It had a large drinks machine that dispensed every type of sweet drink, including one that tasted like fog. We discovered that we were the only production at Paramount, occupying one of the 34 empty studios, which was a bit eerie. We were the only occupants of the 'commissariat', which was American for 'canteen'. They made very good clam chowder. We went to see the boss of Paramount, who I think was called Gary Nardino. He had a sumptuous, book-lined office with a sumptuous outer office where we were offered guacamole dip, crackers and coffee by his sumptuous secretary. We were ultimately summoned to the presence of Nardino, who was practising his putting on the luxuriously thick carpet. He was charming and welcoming and quickly told us that he wanted us to take $50,000 out of the budget. I pointed out that this could only be done by playing the show without any scenery or alternatively without half the cast. He said that nevertheless $50,000 had to be saved. We next suggested that, by way of a small economy, we only needed one secretary. 'We already got two secretaries,' said Nardino. 'Don't give me problems.'

Casting was a revelation. Fairly important actors are allowed to drive through the very imposing Paramount gates and park near the offices. They are called 'drive ons'. Less important ones who don't have powerful agents have to park in the streets near the studio and walk on to the lot, which can be quite a step. They are called 'walk ons'. Together with the American writers, Jeremy and I auditioned dozens of actors and actresses for days. I enjoy casting but I found it very bewildering to be in a position where I knew nobody and therefore was obliged to meet these actors of very variable ability. Some of them were great and some absolutely dire. Mr Humphries – John Inman's part – was particularly difficult. One candidate was a young man who had done well in the Comedy Store Club. His name was Robin Williams and he didn't stop talking and doing an act for ten minutes. I thought he would be very funny but would sabotage the whole production. I turned him down and thus prevented myself from becoming a millionaire. I favoured a retiring young man, who I thought was a very good actor and would be deliciously camp. In the event, we had a character called Alan Sues whom Jeremy knew from his days on *Rowan and Martin's Laugh-In*. He turned out to be funny but completely undisciplined and chaotic.

Gary Marshall went on holiday the day we started rehearsal, so the show was directed by Jerry Paris, who everyone said directed by the seat of his pants, whatever that meant. A feature of this approach was that he didn't read the script before the first rehearsal. The seat of his pants became an important asset because he sprained his ankle badly, and acquired a motorised wheelchair, which he sat in all day and whizzed about the studio like a blow-fly.

The first read-through was attended by a myriad people and was a sort of party with wine and lavish refreshments. Every day we authors assembled to do rewrites, following which a new and different-coloured script was produced and distributed next day. I had very little patience with this process. I pointed out that we were producing not necessarily better or funnier lines – just different ones. We knew the strength of the comedy from the British version and it all worked. A crisis soon developed when Captain Peacock refused to slap Mrs Slocombe's face in the traditional German dance because he would lose the sympathy of the audience. Mrs Slocombe didn't want to slap Peacock's face because it was unladylike. On the Thursday, which was the day before we went into the first of two days' camera rehearsal, the cast asked if it was OK if they learnt the script.

The three cameras were enormous 35mm Mitchels that had to be reloaded every ten minutes. They were mounted on Pathfinders, which were the type of trolley I used at Tyne Tees Television. They were not motorised and were therefore pushed by elderly Hollywood studio operators – and very good they were too. The cameras were directed not by Jerry Paris but by a mysterious man I never saw. He didn't have monitors to see the result, so I have no idea how he operated. I think he must have given secret messages to the cameramen. The wigs fitted about as well as cow-pats, and the mechanical props didn't work. For reasons of economy, our sets had to be made to the same dimensions as those of *Happy Days* because they had to fit under the same lighting gantries. The result was that Mr Rumbold's poky little office became about the size of a large drawing room. (Mr Rumbold was Young Mr Grace's nephew, young and with a crush on Miss Brahms.) I was not impressed by Hollywood's efficiency.

Gary Marshall returned from holiday in time for the audience show. He did a sensational warm-up. Peacock and Slocombe gave rather bad-tempered performances. Tom Poston, who was cast by Gary as Young Mr Grace, was very funny, and Lorna Paterson as Miss Brahms was charming. She did well in movies later on. In fact the show went very well. The audience reaction was similar to the one we were used to in London and the laughs came in the same places as they did in England.

The recording, with endless retakes, went on until one o'clock in the morning. Had it gone on a minute longer, everyone would have been on triple time. It was judged by all concerned to be a great success. The next day we came up against the hazard of Gary Marshall's dad, who was one of the co-producers and dead against the whole proposition. Gary is a family man. His sister was one of the stars of *Laverne and Shirley* and a big comedy star. His mother often plays the piano for warm-ups. His dad – Tony – could not, in my opinion, hold down a job as commissionaire outside the Odeon. As he was a co-producer, we came up against him in the post-production process. His opening remark before we viewed the various takes for editing was, 'I suppose we'd better see all this crap.' He punctuated the next six hours by saying, 'What will they make of this crap in Detroit?'

Paramount was so convinced of the success of the show that they commissioned us to write four more scripts so as to be ready to go ahead when the network, which was NBC, gave the word. This we happily did, using my apartment as a working base. The flat had three main features. The first was the provision of two balconies looking out from two sides of the four-storey building. The second was mirrored ceilings in all the bedrooms. This was not a good idea. The sight of middle-aged me in a waking-up state was more than I could bear. I had to take great care to sleep on my side and to be exceedingly cautious when getting out of bed in case I should accidentally catch sight of myself. If you should be thinking of adopting this decorative feature – don't. The third feature was an ice-making machine that lurked in the kitchen. It made great heaps of ice that from time to time burst open the doors of the wretched device. I was forever emptying mountains of ice into the sink or down the loo.

On our return to England, we gave a small dinner party on the day we were to hear if the show was going to series. Herman Rush was one of the guests. Also with us was Richard Waring, who had also made a pilot for another network. About ten o'clock in the evening the news came through. Both shows had been rejected. Jeremy, Richard Waring and I all collapsed into hysterical laughter, and Herman couldn't understand what had got into us all. We had one of the best evenings that I remember. Sadly, the wife of the ancient owner of NBC was dying at the time. I believe that with one of her dying breaths she croaked, 'Whatever happens, don't let *Are You Being Served?* go to series.' I visited Hollywood about 18 months later. My name was still on my car parking space at Paramount.

Towards the end of *Hi-de-Hi!* I again fell foul of the tabloid press. This time it was the *Sun*. It happened during a printing strike and I understand Kelvin McKenzie, the editor, got out the edition with his very own hands, and in fact practically single-handed. He unearthed an 18-month-old story that I had been having an affair with Nikki Kelly, who played Sylvia, one of the Yellow Coats in the show. Being very short of a story, he spread the article all over the front page and right across two centre pages, and twice featured the same picture of me in a borrowed top hat looking a prat. Ann was, understandably, not best pleased and threatened that if it ever happened again she would go out and buy a Ferrari. I am relieved to be able to report that we still haven't got a Ferrari.

Troubles rarely come singly, so at about the same time, while Ann and I were on holiday in Barbados, we got a telephone call from Peter Farago, who had obviously drawn the short straw. He informed us gently, and with great tact, that our beloved house in Honington had ever so slightly burnt down. There was very little point in rushing home before it had time to cool off. When we returned, it was to discover that very serious damage had been done owing to a malfunctioning of a flue from the boiler. There was nothing in the house that did not have to be dumped or cleaned.

The insurance wasn't large enough to cover the cheapest estimate for a rebuild, so Ann donned a hard hat and hired the labour and material for the task. She achieved the rebuild in six months.

'Allo 'Allo was still going strong. We got a very good bite from America, with the prospect of a syndicated showing that would make Jeremy and me quite rich. Gareth Gwenlan, the BBC's head of comedy, was keen on the proposition and we agreed to write and produce 26 programmes that year. I couldn't face the prospect of these being cut down from 30 minutes to 22 for the USA, so I persuaded Gareth to accept 25 minutes. In the event, we wrote all bar two and we produced them all in the large studio and a specially adapted warehouse in the BBC studios at Borehamwood. Martin Dennis, Susie Belbin and Richard Boden, all at the start of their careers, directed for me.

Jimmy and I judged that *Hi-de-Hi!*, although still doing well in the ratings, was due to expire, largely owing to the departure of Simon Cadell. His university professor, who wanted a change of lifestyle, and the impact of holiday camp down-to-earth reality on his character, provided the original thrust of the story. With the arrival of David Griffin as the squadron leader in search of a good time, the main idea of the original show underwent a major change. The show was still very funny, and David Griffin's character worked well, but it was not in accordance with our original conception. At the same time we were very conscious of the popularity and skills of the *Hi-de-Hi!* stars. We therefore put our heads together to devise a new vehicle for their talents.

I was very keen to try a 50-minute duration, still in front of an audience. It would need very slick organisation, but if the BBC could be persuaded to give us two days' recording, I was sure my team would be able to achieve it. The important thing was that it would give us a good opportunity to develop characters and scenes more thoroughly. We favoured an *Upstairs, Downstairs* setting pitched in the late 1920s, a very interesting time of social change that saw the decline of the aristocracy and the growing influence of the left wing.

Gareth Gwenlan, the ever-flexible head of comedy, was intrigued by the concept and prepared to back us. We kept the idea secret from the cast but decided that Donald Hewlett and Michael Knowles, who had played the colonel and captain in *It Ain't Half Hot Mum*, should play Lord Meldrum and the Hon. Teddy, the leads upstairs. Paul Shane, Su Pollard and Jeff Holland should be the butler, maid and footman downstairs.

We finished the pilot script for *You Rang, M'Lord?* in a week and were very happy with it. The extra 20 minutes meant that we were able to flesh out the characters and give everyone really meaty parts. Other roles emerged for members of the family and for the staff downstairs. We gave Lord Meldrum two daughters. There was Miss Poppy, the spoilt 'bright young thing' whose only thoughts were for clothes and men, played by Susie Brann. Then there was Miss Cissy, who was a member of the Communist Party and a bit of a tomboy. This character gave us a chance to touch gently on lesbianism, which was not understood by Lord Meldrum or the staff. The lovely Katy Rabett managed to balance this character beautifully. Angela Scoular was his lordship's complex mistress, and Mavis Pugh played his very eccentric aunt who insisted on throwing her breakfast at Ivy, the maid.

I had been impressed by Perry Benson playing a small part in *Hi-de-Hi!* and he made wonderful comedy out of Henry, the boot-boy. Mrs Lipton, the cook, was played by the homely, warm Brenda Cowling. She had played Godfrey's girlfriend of old in *Dad's Army*. Mabel, the daily who slaved away for threepence an hour and was grateful to be given fish heads, fitted Barbara New like a glove. Bill Pertwee was a regular visitor as the conservative local policeman. Other regular characters were John Horsley, playing Sir Ralph, the husband of his lordship's secret mistress, and Yvonne Marsh, who was the Hon. Teddy's long-suffering fiancée.

We set the first scene on a battlefield in France during the First

World War. David Buckingham, who had done such magnificent work in *'Allo 'Allo,* designed an awesome war-torn area for us, covering several acres. When we were ready to shoot on it, there were smouldering fires, charred trees, shell holes and ruined buildings. It was really very depressing to be on and it looked absolutely authentic when it was filmed.

We were due to record the pilot programme at Television Centre. Unfortunately, we hit a very bad period when the BBC was plagued by strikes, go-slows and walk-outs. When I arrived at the studio, the sets were barely standing. We rehearsed and recorded as they were completed. When we arrived on the second day for the public show, the audience seating had not been set and only the hall staircase was standing. The drawing room, dining room and kitchen had yet to be built and dressed. Nothing was to be gained by abandoning the recording, so I went ahead, determined to get all we could. It was far and away the most difficult day in the studio I have ever had.

Having created the problem in the first place with the go-slow, the scene crew worked like maniacs to get the show on. Once again, we rehearsed each scene as it was built, as often as not without the props. The actors were well versed in everything they had to do and I had done a very careful camera script. I didn't dare ask the crew to keep quiet, and the din was such that during the dress run we could barely hear the dialogue. It culminated in the audience seating and rostra being set during our final run-through. I told Mike McCarthy to record the cacophony and I sent the recording to Paul Fox to demonstrate the sort of conditions we were trying to work in. I never received a reply, and I doubt if he ever played it.

When the audience arrived for the recording, Felix Bowness did the warm-up as if nothing had happened and the actors bravely played their parts. It was an excellent performance but, for instance, the walls of the dining room, which should have been festooned with oil paintings, were completely bare. There was no question of doing the show again so, in that condition, it went out over the air. The paucity of the set dressing didn't affect the laughs, and Gareth went ahead and ordered the series. With the invaluable help of my long-term assistant Charles Garland and the able direction of Roy Gould, we started production.

Charles was a multi-talented character who had started his career in a military band, had been a successful restaurateur and played an excellent piano. He was a great administrator. Roy had been my assistant on *Hi-de-Hi!* On *'Allo 'Allo* he seemed to spend his life trying to string together fragile onions in order to hang them round the countless necks of escaping airmen. He had a very good idea of where the camera should be aimed in a comedy situation – which is close to being a lost art.

The show was meant to be a piece of major entertainment to go out on a Thursday at eight o'clock, to be followed by Anne Robinson's programme about viewers' likes and dislikes and then the news. The controller of BBC1 in his wisdom elected to send it out on Saturday evening. A Saturday show it was not. The ratings were good, but the Saturday audience was looking for a more robust entertainment like *Hi-de-Hi!*

'Allo 'Allo was still going very strongly and the cast was enormous fun in rehearsal, largely led by John D. Collins and Richard Gibson. Practically every lunchtime we would assemble on the balcony of the canteen on the top floor of the rehearsal rooms. One of us would have bought a toy glider for no more that a pound or two. John would imitate a trumpet and sing the tune of 'The Dam Busters March' and the glider would be solemnly launched, usually to nosedive and crash. The actors from other series looked on in bewilderment.

Jeremy and I had long had the feeling that although *Are You Being Served?* was past its sell-by date, there was good mileage to be found in a further series for the cast. They were a great laugh-gathering team and when we had a hilarious farewell lunch in 1984 I had given them a sort of promise that it was not the end. We would find something further for them, and accordingly, about ten years later, we did. We plumped for a story that started with the reading of Young Mr Grace's will. His ancient solicitor revealed to the remaining staff at Grace Brothers that the pension fund had been plundered. Funnily enough, this was pre-Maxwell. All that remained was a run-down country hotel. The series, to be called *Grace and Favour*, would cover the efforts of Humphries, Slocombe, Peacock and Rumbold to run the place for profit.

The pilot worked very well indeed. It was produced and directed by Mike Stephens, who had done a lot of good work on the later series of *'Allo 'Allo*, and was one of the BBC's best. Wendy Richard was delighted to get a bit of fresh air after months and months in *EastEnders*. To play the drab Pauline they don't make her up – they make her down. She looked as glamorous as ever as Shirley Brahms, and the readjusted relationships, now that they were all no longer subject to the hierarchy of Grace Brothers department store, were fun to play. Wendy, Mollie Sugden, John Inman and Frank Thornton had always been wonderful mates and they revelled in being together again. Mollie and John milking a cow is a particularly happy memory. Two series of *Grace and Favour*, totalling 13 programmes, were produced and went well in the ratings.

Mark Furness decided to take the stage version of *'Allo 'Allo* to New Zealand. Ann and I used this as an excuse for a round-the-world type of holiday that took us to Auckland via Singapore and Fiji, and after that to Sydney and the Barrier Reef. We booked ourselves into Castaway, which is a remote island off Fiji. This involved boarding a microscopic three-seater plane from Fiji piloted by a very young, bronzed and muscular Australian. Despite the size of the cramped plane, he politely went through the full air-hostess routine, saying over his shoulder, 'Welcome aboard flight 387 from Fiji to Castaway,' and then repeated the chat about seat-belts, the flotation jackets under our seats, 'To be used in the unlikely event of us coming down over the water', and finishing with the information: 'The emergency exit is on your right side and the handle to get out is just under your right elbow.' We made a bumpy landing 40 minutes later on a gleaming white beach. Our luggage was unloaded on the sand and the plane took off, leaving us under a couple of palm trees. As the pilot waved us goodbye he said, 'There'll be a speedboat to take you to the island any minute.' Sixty minutes later we were still on the deserted beach with all of our luggage, no phone and no one to complain to, and I declared that I had lost control of the situation, which for some reason sent Ann into hysterical laughter. After another half-hour I detected a small boat with a tiny white bow-wave heading towards us and we were rescued. A friendly Aussie, also bronzed and muscular, apologised for being late and took us to the romantic island where we stayed in a grass hut, accompanied by quite a lot of insect life, about 10 feet from the gently lapping Pacific. If there was any doubt about the island being romantic, we slept on a bed that pitched us both firmly together in the middle of the sagging mattress. It was a notable break.

In Auckland the scenery for the show was reported to be at sea somewhere off India, so New Zealand Television very efficiently built us a new set for the opening. The necessary number of New Zealanders were persuaded to get off their backsides, where they were mostly watching *Dad's Army*, and the show was deemed a resounding success.

We all returned to England for a further series and Mark booked the show to play in Sydney. This time Ann and I went to Singapore, where we hired a car to drive up the coast of Malaya, past Jahore Baru and Port Swettenham, where – save for the intervention of the atom bomb – I would have waded ashore with 4 Brigade against the Japs.

Meanwhile, back in England, Gorden Kaye had set off by car to Hammersmith on a windy day to collect traveller's cheques for the trip. A sudden gust of wind caught an insecure advertisement hoarding, which flew through his windscreen striking him on the head and nearly killing him. In our large, luxurious and empty hotel in the Malayan jungle, we were completely unaware of all this. When I hadn't received any messages or mail for two or three days I went to the front desk and investigated. There had been, indeed, no mail for David Croft. When I probed further, it transpired that I had registered as David Croft OBE and was therefore on the records as Mr Obe – not an unusual name in the east.

Peter Farago came post-haste to Sydney to find a replacement for Gorden, which sounded like an impossible task. However, he succeeded in booking Max Gillies, an excellent and well-known Australian actor, who not only filled the vacancy extremely well but learnt the part in a matter of three days to be in time for the original opening date. Sadly, in spite of the great job being done by Max, the customers didn't rush to book for the show without Gorden Kaye, so the business, although good, was not sensational.

Ann and I came back the pretty way. We had heard that the most fabulous hotel in the world was on the island of Bora Bora. We accordingly arrived there via Tahiti having booked the best 'basha' they had. The room was in fact pretty sensational in that it was only about 20 feet from the edge of the sea. The site narrowed behind the 'basha' so that the road was only the same distance from the back of the place. Dozens of Bora Bora youths put-putted by on their mopeds most of the day and night, shattering our Pacific Island peace. One of the advertised advantages of this resort was alleged to be the absence of telephones. One of the results of this was that the guests had to walk 150 yards, often in the pouring rain, if the not very efficient bedroom staff had forgotten to fill the ice bucket or provide tonic to go with the gin. All

235

the meals were buffets accompanied by 'leis' and flowered hats. Although we were booked in for a week I engineered our escape after three days by fast speedboat to Tahiti.

Here the hotel was a large, tourist-orientated affair, which was acceptable, though a little like a fabulously expensive Butlins. Our room was on stilts over the romantic lagoon. They were supposed to deliver our breakfast by canoe, but the management apologised for being unable to do this 'due to mechanical failure'. I assumed this was caused by woodworm in the paddles. I suspect that miscellaneous drainage was discharged into the romantic lagoon because I got an ear infection that wouldn't go away until I went to see a specialist in Harley Street.

By now the rot had begun to set in at the BBC. I suppose the trouble originated during the reigns of the chairman 'Duke' Hussey and his predecessors and the various teams of governors of the corporation. Despite having the largest propaganda machine in the world at their disposal, they failed to persuade the public or the government of the day that public service broadcasting needed a very large increase in funding. It should probably have been around the order of 40 per cent. If this seems a large amount, think of the millions who pay a much greater sum to Murdoch and Sky Television. From time to time he and his company still add over £2 to the monthly bill – a per month charge of £41 or more. Would the public not have been willing to gradually add £20 or £30 to the annual licence fee if they were getting the sport they wanted and some of the feature films?

Lacking the increased revenue, the BBC tried to make economies. Michael Checkland as director general seemed to be making cuts in a responsible manner, but there was still an eagerness to jump on any electronic bandwagon that happened to be rolling, so the resources were spread thinner and thinner. Then along came the Demon King John Birt to join the BBC pantomime and cast his evil spell over the whole future of broadcasting. He introduced hordes of management consultants. We would see the more junior members of these teams dressed in suits and ties, and wearing very worried expressions, going around, perhaps for safety, in groups of six or eight, all with clipboards nestling firmly under their arms.

There is a popular theory that a properly trained businessman can move into any business and run it successfully. I am convinced that this is utter rubbish. I believe that unless you understand most of the processes that the business is based on. you are heading for a large-scale disaster. This is particularly true of the entertainment industry. Demon King Birt and the lesser demons in the form of his senior management team, were obsessed with all the paraphernalia of business management, such as focus groups and critical paths. The departments were all required to divert their attention away from the programmes that they had been producing ever since television began and towards inventing business plans. James Moir, head of the light entertainment group, who was a brilliant producer and later became the controller of the fabulously successful BBC Radio 2, created a business plan that ran to 43 pages. This became a departmental obsession and achieved absolutely nothing. Programmes were almost forgotten.

'Total costing' was introduced. At first blush, it was obviously a good thing that the BBC should have a close idea about the cost of running each department. Extravagance and waste could be detected and eradicated. However, the process was carried to ridiculous extremes. At one end of the scale it resulted in the cost of borrowing records from the comprehensive BBC record library rising to £16 a go, which meant that it was cheaper to send somebody off to Woolworths to buy the album rather than to borrow it. The same applied to the book library. At the other end of the scale, it resulted in the studios being so overpriced that producers began to notice that independent studios appeared to be cheaper.

Hand in hand with this madness went a scheme called 'producer choice'. This was devised so that producers were completely free to obtain studios, scenery, make-up, special effects, camera crews – in fact everything they required to produce a programme – from anywhere they wished. This in spite of the fact that the BBC actually owned the studios, having paid for their construction years ago out of the licence fee. The staff for all these facilities were being paid anyway. Furthermore, the money for all this was actually going out of the BBC into the pockets of the independents. All these BBC services were grossly and, I believe, deliberately overpriced. The consequence of all this palaver was that the BBC was given the ability to make itself redundant and sack itself. If resources could be found elsewhere, the producer's budget dictated that he should use them. The internal facilities fell into disuse through being too expensive. The producers could be blamed rather than the management.

The new accountants were overjoyed by this. Their departments burgeoned. Administrators proliferated. Programmes were almost forgotten as budgets became an absolute priority. Every few weeks they were scrutinised and scrutinised again, and we were asked to save another 5 per cent. Those of us who had only common sense to aid us were completely mystified. Sinister signs such as the selling of most of the car park at the rehearsal rooms became noticeable. The rehearsal rooms themselves were later taken over to provide offices for the bureaucracy. Shows now have to find church halls to rehearse in and the artistes have to lunch in pubs, which means that during their breaks they have to deal with fans and members of the public instead of chatting to each other about their scenes.

Maggie Thatcher's decree that 25 per cent of the BBC's output should be provided by independent producers didn't help matters. Comedy shows that were costing £175,000 per episode to stage in-house were costing £250,000 by the time the independents had added their overhead and profit. When we complained, the management were too frightened for their jobs to do anything about it. The Demon King triumphantly announced all the millions that were being saved and put into programmes, but our budgets were still being rejected and cut.

Brilliant people and irreplaceable producers left the organisation and roundly denounced the Birt innovations as being disastrous, but he remained unshiftable. No fairy queen flew in to wave her magic wand and save the situation. Eloquent and probing articles were written in the press but nobody in authority took any notice. The Demon King was unstoppable.

In 1996, when the rumblings about 'producer choice' were reaching thunderous levels and failure was obvious to absolutely everyone, Birt had his next scheme ready. He sprang this as a surprise even to his most senior colleagues. This entailed splitting the producing arm of the BBC into two sections, one to be called 'Production' and the other to be called 'Broadcast'. To this day I don't think anybody is clear how this was meant to work. Thankfully, before Greg Dyke was cut off in his prime he had started the process of gently demolishing this particular lunacy and he was also chipping away at 'producer choice'.

The interesting thing is that throughout all these manoeuvres the chairman of the governors, Christopher Bland, condoned and agreed with all of them. He agreed when they were made and he agreed when they failed and were reversed. He is now in charge of British Telecom, so we will all watch with bated breath the progress of that massively debt-ridden monster.

Of course morale dropped to an all-time low as a result of all this. Everyone was looking over their shoulder to see where the next blow would fall. Few senior people dared to criticise the course that everything was taking in case they lost their well-paid jobs. A wonderfully creative organisation, brimming with devoted and talented people, was slowly being demolished.

Amongst all this mayhem it became clear that the third series of *You Rang, M'Lord?* was at risk so I made a flying visit back from my summer holiday in Portugal. Had I not fought for it there and then, I don't think we would have made the series. In effect, the BBC was no longer concerned with what went out on the screen, but had become budget obsessed.

We escaped from much of this by shooting the show in the Lew Grade studio, which the BBC had bought at Elstree. Nobody would make the journey from White City to Borehamwood to interfere, so we were able to carry on normally and happily with our ace crew. Some of the 50-minute shows were recorded in front of the delighted audiences in an hour and a quarter.

When it came to the fourth series, an even tougher battle was fought on our behalf by the head of comedy, who was my old friend Robin Nash. Then came for me what was the last straw. It had been the custom to repeat all comedy shows a few months after the first showing to increase the audiences for the next series. I suddenly realised that the last 39 of my shows had not been repeated. In the new atmosphere at the BBC it was time to go. After 30 very happy and triumphant years, and at the ripe old age of 70, I decided not to renew my contract.

23
The Clipboard Pantomime
and *Oh! Dr Beeching*

When *You Rang, M'Lord?* was done and dusted I was sent a script by Roger Miram, who was a veteran Australian broadcaster. He had devised many successful formats for Grundy Productions and was a long-time personal friend of Fred Grundy. Roger had spent time during the war in the Western Desert as a cameraman attached to the Australian forces with the Eighth Army. He was keen to do a series for television in Australia, and his outline involved a couple of Aussie rankers who got separated from their unit in Libya. The title, which I thought was a great one, was *Which Way to the War?* I needed another Second World War series like I needed a large cavity in the cranium, but the idea was well presented and I sent him a deservedly encouraging reaction.

Grundy Productions, who had achieved great success with *Neighbours*, were interested in getting involved in further productions suitable to be shown in England, so they sent over Don Reynolds, an excellent producer, who spoke my language and was a thoroughly competent person whom I liked enormously. We got on like the proverbial house on fire and he wanted me to go to Australia to discuss the matter in Sydney with the Grundy moneybags and to advise them about the whole project. I loved Sydney, as did Ann, and we were more than willing to go to see my old associate Margie Bond and our many friends, particularly if Grundy were prepared to pick up the tab.

The firm treated us handsomely and we spent three wonderful days at the rebuilt Raffles Hotel in Singapore, where they gave us the 'Charlie Chaplin Suite'. I don't know if Charlie ever stayed at Raffles. If he did, he certainly didn't stay in the Chaplin suite because it wasn't built until well after he had departed this world. However, they had dug up a lot of photographs that adorned the walls of the very large rooms, and the little tramp would surely have approved of the air-conditioning.

Ann and I spent a glorious ten days in Sydney. We visited Roger Miram in his extraordinary house on a cliff-edge at Mackerell Beach. Every evening he blew his bugle in a chaotic version of 'The Last Post' from his fabulous balcony that commanded views of the beautiful estuary. The wild parrots that abounded didn't seem to mind Roger's far from tuneful serenade. He was a most remarkable character and full of talent. I met all the Grundy executives. They were a nice bunch and very businesslike. To give them their money's worth, I did an outline of the show that I visualised producing. The result, predictably, was that they concluded they could never finance the show for production in Australia because they couldn't get their money back. I then gave them a rough idea what it would cost to make a pilot in England, and after going rather white and thinking about it for a few days, they said they would let me know.

Ann and I returned home via Hong Kong, where we spent three more stunning days at the President Hotel. Not long after we got back to England, Don Reynolds got word that the company was prepared to go ahead and make a pilot. I explained the general idea of the show to Jeremy Lloyd and we soon had the pilot script prepared. I didn't fancy returning to the Birt-led BBC because they were becoming obsessed with youth-orientated near-obscene subjects to the exclusion of family programmes. We managed to sell the idea to the ITV network, so we were able to go ahead with preparing a production and casting. I asked Roy Gould to direct for me, as he had done so successfully with *You Rang, M'Lord?*

Charles Garland and I found a grand location for the outside filming. It was supposed to be an Arab fort in the heart of the Western Desert. We found a vast sandpit in Norfolk where we could practically shoot in a 360-degree arc, and I soon assembled some young and unknown actors, including some great-looking girls with a lot of acting talent.

Don Reynolds had previously booked a very luxurious holiday in the Caribbean, and understandably but unwisely decided to be away for a fortnight just before we started shooting. It is never a good thing for an executive to turn his back on an organisation when the knives are being sharpened. While he was gone, a palace revolution took place at the British end of Grundy, and a new executive appeared who, with a few deft strokes, inserted himself between Grundy and Don Reynolds. I had no time whatever for this particular character, who had no regard for the worth of a show but only for the cost. We were thus saddled with two bosses, and a lot of administrative mistakes were made, the excuse always being that each thought the other one was taking care of the matter.

We shot the show in one of the BBC's studios with a great BBC crew. Duncan Brown did the lighting and there isn't a better lighting artist in the industry. The sound was handled by Mike McCarthy, who is the best in the business. The studio set was the interior of the old fort and it looked sensational.

We made a lovely pilot, with very realistic location shots that looked great, and got a wonderful reaction from the studio audience. The ITV network chiefs were very enthusiastic and it got a good audience figure when it went out over the air. However, my unfavourite executive at Grundy was less than keen to go ahead with a show he hadn't originated, didn't understand and thought Grundy couldn't afford, so we didn't go to series. A few months later the country celebrated the sixtieth anniversary of the Second World War, so I think the network regretted their decision.

The fact that I had done a pilot for an ITV company caused a bit of a stir among the bosses of the BBC. I was invited out to lunch with Will Wyatt and David Liddiment at Marco Pierre White's new restaurant at the Hyde Park Hotel. Will could perhaps be described as the Baron Hardup of the BBC pantomime. He was a very senior member of the Birt organisation but tried his best to be helpful and sympathetic to the Cinderellas of the outfit, who were the wretched producers and writers. He became the chief executive of the department named 'Broadcast' and was about the only person it was possible to talk to who understood that the BBC was expected to produce some programmes in return for the licence fee. Everybody else seemed to be entirely absorbed in reorganising the systems and in building their own particular empires. I never met anyone who knew precisely what 'Broadcast' actually was responsible for because this was part of the vast organisation that John Birt set up to cover the disaster of 'producer choice'. David Liddiment was the head of entertainment – they had dropped the 'light' from 'light entertainment' – and could be cast as Buttons, the Baron's page.

The lunch was opulent, and Will and David were very complimentary and flattering and also keen to know why I had deserted the BBC for ITV. I explained that my last 39 shows had not been repeated and that the present disastrous comedy output led me to believe that they were no longer seeking my type of family programmes. This they both vehemently denied, practically crossing their hearts and hoping for their instant demise. Knowing the difficulty that some writers had experienced in getting the go-ahead for the production of a pilot programme, I pressed them to tell me frankly if anybody any longer had the authority to say 'Yes' to a show. Buttons David immediately said, 'Yes, I do,' and Baron Hardup Will nodded in agreement. 'Without reference to any third party?' I asked. 'Definitely,' said Buttons, and the Baron again nodded. I then told them about an idea I had been developing concerning the staff of a small country railway station who were fighting for survival during the era of Dr Beeching's swingeing cuts. 'Wonderful,' said Will. 'I like it,' said David. 'Let me have a script as soon as you can.'

I was able to float this idea because several months previously I had been approached by a remarkable broadcaster named Richard Spendlove. Richard was on BBC Radio Cambridge for about 20 hours a week, including a four-hour stint on Saturday night which went out all over the southern counties, East Anglia and the Midlands. He had been a railway man, signaller and stationmaster for 30 years. After retiring, he hosted *The Richard Spendlove Show*, a chat show that had the highest ratings of any similar show on the BBC. He got in touch with me to do a comedy television show based on his experiences. I fancied the idea but at this stage didn't want to get involved with writing it. He made a couple of attempts but, not being a comedy writer, they didn't amount to much. I suggested he should try to work on the basis that the new stationmaster should be Geoffrey Holland, that the porter, who had no ambition to advance himself, should be Paul Shane, and the girl in the ticket office should be Su Pollard.

He immediately came up with a much improved script. Richard had total recall and a fund of true stories that could be the basis for scripts for the series. I got on to Jimmy Perry and suggested we should all collaborate. Jimmy came up to stay with me for a few days and we knocked out a possible pilot, but it transpired that Jimmy was not interested in a series about the railways and didn't in fact like trains. I therefore went ahead with Richard and we prepared a new script to submit to Liddiment.

I have always found it exceedingly difficult to read and visualise a comedy script, and I think most people have the same trouble. With *Oh! Dr Beeching* I decided on a new approach to the problem. I thought it best to take no chances with Liddiment, whom I didn't know too well, so I prepared a tape of the dialogue on my dictating machine. This entailed me doing vocal impersonations of all the parts. I don't count this among my talents, but since we were concerned only with sound, at least I didn't have to do the faces. The advantage of this system was that I could be present with Liddiment for the 35 or 40 minutes that the entire presentation took. It could be without preamble and place him in exactly the same position as a viewer who hadn't even bothered to read the *Radio Times*. A pilot programme, after all, should be entirely self-explanatory. I could also ensure that no telephone conversations took place to interrupt the session by the simple expedient of asking the secretary not to put anyone through, with the possible exception of the Demon King or Baron Hardup.

Of course, it is a bizarre scene – a bit like several grown men sitting round a table listening to Rory Bremner's parrot. Liddiment paid attention politely and smiled in most of the right places without actually breaking out into paroxysms of laughter and falling on the floor. At the end he said we could go ahead and make a pilot, which counts as a good result.

With Charles Garland as my fellow producer and Roy Gould as director, we swiftly assembled a production team, including Mary Husband, who would be taking care of the costumes, and Jill Hagger, to look after the make-up. John Bristow designed a great set. We searched for a suitably small railway station and Charles finally found one on the lovely Severn Valley line near Kidderminster. The four cottages with their little gardens, where the principal members of the cast were supposed to live, had to be mocked up on location in a space adjacent to the station. John Bristow built a façade that looked remarkably realistic, even at close quarters. He had very little space to play with, so just a few feet behind the front doors the ground fell away to a 20-foot drop, which made life exciting for the actors. As far as rolling stock was concerned, I personally auditioned eight steam engines and rows of carriages from the Severn Valley Railway's large supply before we finally settled on a suitable train. Finding an engine small enough to be on a branch line yet with a driving platform large enough to take a cameraman and camera plus a sound man and his microphone was no simple task. To drive the great machine, we engaged Ivor Roberts, who had played the foreman in Lord Meldrum's rubber goods factory in *You Rang, M'Lord?* He had a gorgeous 'Hovis advertisement' North Country accent, just like my grandma, and became bosom pals with Richard Spendlove, who spoke the same lingo. I persuaded Perry Benson – the boot-boy in *You Rang* – to join him as the fireman and trainee driver with the heavy touch on the brakes. In reality, Perry became a skilful train driver who could stop the heavy assembly of engine and carriages right on its mark.

A serious hiccup developed when Liddiment rejected our budget. I went for a meeting with him in his austere office. This was a stark affair sparsely furnished with only a large boardroom table and eight bum-unfriendly chairs. In a mere fraction of the time it would have taken to develop haemorrhoids, he explained that we were £20,000 above the normal in-house figure which he was expected to spend on shows by the totally inflexible, all-powerful John Birt accountants. I argued that without that £20,000 I would be unable to stage the show that I had promised at the aforementioned expensive lunch followed by my Rory Bremner parrot tape outlining every word of the script. Liddiment took the point and said that he would see what he could do and, to his credit, the budget was approved.

Location filming was complicated. On previous occasions, when not satisfied with a take, I simply said, 'Let's go again,' and a few minutes later take two was in the can. With *Beeching* it often entailed backing up the train. This was not as simple as I thought it would be. All sorts of safety procedures came into operation, phone calls to the signallers had to be made, lines cleared, green and red flags waved and lamps shown. This took 20 or 30 minutes, so we moved the train as little as possible. On the other hand, the sight of this great steam train with smoke billowing from the chimney was simply great and was very much what the series was all about.

Roy Gould and Charles Garland finished the filming on schedule and the rehearsal and studio went swimmingly. The studio audience lapped it up. I think the fact that they knew the main members of the cast helped. The pilot programme received an audience of 10.5 million when it went out, setting a record for a comedy pilot that has not been broken in the past ten years. Liddiment was delighted, but unfortunately he did not have the power to order a series. Unaccountably, the controller sat on the tape without viewing it for 11 weeks. At long last he gave us the go-ahead for the series so we quickly started preparation and the writing of eight further episodes.

I was keen to involve other writers because it seemed to me that it would be a popular move in the entertainment department to veer towards the American method of working without actually getting involved with a tableful of writers chucking lines and ideas into the pool. They would send me a one-page outline of their idea to make sure there was no duplication, following which I would tell them to go ahead.

In this way I got scripts from John Stevenson, an experienced writer from *Coronation Street*, who was keen to try his hand at audience comedy. The writing pair Paul Minett and Brian Leveson had a great touch with comedy and fitted into the organisation admirably. And I was helped, of course, by my friend John Chapman, who had come effortlessly to my rescue in practically every series I ever became involved with.

The first series received viewing figures of between six and eight million and an audience share of 30 to 40 per cent. These were good figures for a show placed in a competitive spot. The *Dad's* days of 13 and 14 million were of course long gone. Soon after we started the series I met Liddiment in the corridor near his fourth-floor office. He confided in me that, like everyone else, he was disillusioned with the BBC and was about to leave to take a very important job at ITV, more or less running things there. His move was hardly surprising because he was at the BBC at the worst possible time, when the Birt reorganisations were devastating the output, but it was a blow for me. Paul Jackson, the son of T. Leslie Jackson, for whom I had worked on *This Is Your Life*, was appointed to take over. Paul knew the business well enough, but somebody somehow managed to pull the plug on his authority, which gently drained away until he and the head of comedy were completely powerless figures. Neither of them even had the authority to commission a pilot programme, and that is the situation we find ourselves in today. Paul left the BBC and went to Australia.

Following this blow, Michael Jackson, the controller of BBC1, went to Channel Four to run things there. He liked the show and went so far as to thank me personally for bringing it to him, but with his departure I lost my last ally at the top. He was replaced by Peter Salmon, who was a charming character, but both he and Geoffrey Perkins had very little sympathy for standard family comedy. Peter, like all new controllers, was keen to start fresh schedules and to search for shows with youth appeal. As a result, I could never get *Beeching* repeated – an essential element in building a new series – which makes a grand total of 58 of my most recent shows unrepeated. Furthermore, I could not get the go-ahead for the third series. What was even more damaging was the scheduling. The programme was rarely shown at the same time for two consecutive weeks and suffered from being cancelled at the last minute. Eventually *Beeching* was allowed to expire after 19 programmes.

During the Liddiment reign, Jeremy Lloyd and I had been attracted to an item in the papers that related the story of a plebiscite held in one of the obscure countries in the Soviet Union. The majority of the population had voted for a return to the monarchy. We thought this a great basis for a comedy show and we wrote a pilot called *Here Comes the Queen*, with Mollie Sugden and John Inman in mind for the leading roles. They were to play a motherly figure and her brother who ran a Scotch wool shop in the north but who turned out to be the heirs to the obscure throne. It was a worthy successor to *'Allo 'Allo*. It would also have been suitable for June Whitfield and Sam Kelly. Liddiment liked it, but since I was busy with *Beeching*, the matter was not urgent, so I asked if he would prefer that I deal with his newly appointed head of comedy – Geoffrey Perkins. When the time came to further the matter, Jeremy Lloyd and I went to play my tape to Geoffrey who, to my alarm, proceeded to take copious notes. We always pack a programme, particularly if it is a pilot, with loads of content. This makes for a great pilot with plenty of twists and turns to make the customers laugh and hold their attention. Geoffrey considered we were overloaded and that the pilot contained enough material for the first four episodes.

To his credit, he paid us to write a new pilot, but I think the whole operation was staged to disguise the fact that he was in his position with no power and was not able to authorise a pilot. The proposition hovered around for a few months and then gradually got forgotten. Unfortunately, having accepted payment, we could not sell it elsewhere or even take it to Liddiment at ITV because the BBC had the rights for two years. I don't think the controller ever even heard of the programme.

I was left to reflect ruefully on the time when Jimmy Gilbert had commissioned a pilot when I wouldn't even tell him what it was about! That talented producer Ernest Maxim, who was responsible for so much of the success of Morecambe and Wise, once said to me, 'I think we had the best of it, Dave.' By God he was right.

24
I Had the Best of It!

So where are we now? *This Is Your Life* was brilliant. It was carefully and thoughtfully prepared, concentrated mainly on the show business side of my life and ran for 45 minutes. The edited programme ran to 30 minutes. Understandably, it didn't quite cover the last 24 chapters. That would have made the programme run for about six days. One or two viewers might have got bored. And what have I left out here? Acres of stuff – particularly about my witty and tolerant wife who has advised me and guided me through the last 50 years. My loyal and loving family haven't fared too well either. I have scarcely mentioned my daughter Penny, who wrote three very successful series of *Life without George* for the BBC, starring Simon Cadell. In the meantime she has had programmes commissioned in Hollywood, a tough world but one where talent is still valued and recognised. She married Peter Farago, who directed the record-breaking stage version of *'Allo 'Allo* and she produced one of our ten grandchildren.

The beautiful Jane married John Sims, who is a handsome, brilliant and extraordinarily kind man. He is a much-admired figure in the commercial property world. They have produced two lovely daughters and a son. Becky married my best friend Simon Cadell, who died of cancer after a very dignified and courageous fight. He was wonderful company and a dedicated and thinking actor who I feel sure would have become one of our theatrical knights. They produced two of our grandchildren. Her present partner and husband is Chris Butler, who is a brilliant musician – a rare phenomenon in the music industry in which he is a leading figure. They have produced a further three of our grandchildren.

My eldest son Nick is recording and writing songs and has produced numbers ten and eleven. All the grandchildren arrived at different times and I haven't here recorded them in their correct order. Son John is a very talented recording engineer who designed the sound for enormous musical shows in Germany and Italy, where the auditoriums seat 5,000 people. He recently married Serena Crichton, a beautiful and talented teacher and doctor of music. They live in a lovely old house 15 minutes drive from us in Suffolk. Son Richard manages the European side of John Sims's huge commercial property empire. He is married to the beautiful Georgie Deaville, and they have produced grandchild number 12, who is called Zak. Son Tim works for Merrill Lynch as a very highly skilled computer systems designer.

Not included are the countless hilarious holidays we have all spent together, the schools, the carol concerts, the half-terms, the chicken-pox, the exams, the ponies, the Guide camps, the cricket and football matches, the sports days and all the paraphernalia of childhood – oh – and I left out my second triple heart bypass operation, which didn't go too well. Eighty per cent of all this has been coped with and masterminded by the tolerant Ann. The result is an extraordinarily close family who enjoy each other's company. Hardly a week goes by without some combination of the family getting together to share experiences, to help each other and, above all, to laugh.

Which brings me to my final point. Countless times I am asked the same question by people of all ages in all walks of life. Whatever happened to comedy – particularly to television comedy – and what happened to the BBC? In its heyday during the 1970s, 1980s and early 1990s the BBC was undoubtedly the finest programme-producing organisation in the world. It was full of dedicated and talented programme people – largely from the world of the theatre – most of whom could pick up a telephone and sell their services to rival organisations at the drop of a hat. Hugh Weldon used to say that we all had a blank cheque in our pockets that we could cash in at any time, but probably only once. I was never tempted to move. It was important to me to be able to do good work, to allow that work to grow naturally and to be permitted to fail.

It was a large organisation and, as with any big conglomerate, there was a lot of waste and extravagance. But everyone was well aware that the sole object of the whole shebang was to produce quality programmes on the air and on the screen. A critical number of the staff and senior management were programme makers. They realised that the only reason for their existence was so they could entertain or divert Joe Public when he sat down and said 'What's on bloody telly?'

Inexperienced executives were hired, mostly from the commercial world. It is my experience that producers don't necessarily become good until they are in their late fifties. These were regarded as too old and were cleared out. None of the producers whom I trained, including the young ones, are there any more. The new wave produced programmes to be admired by their contemporaries and not by the public. Everyone was terrified of being labelled old-fashioned. Writers discovered that unless their scripts contained coarse language, yobbish attitudes and gross sexual licence they would be regarded as old hat. Editorial judgement ceased to exist. Family viewing went out of the window. The industry is making it damned difficult to bring up kids. Why should coarse and yobbish behaviour and language be tolerated at any time? Does television really intend to alienate its audience, or are they still trying to build up the figures? Do producers not realise that if a programme is offensive, at least half a million people will not bother to watch next time the series is shown? The 9 o'clock watershed is a joke. Kids have televisions in their bedrooms. The watershed should be at about 11 o'clock, by which time there is a chance that the kids can't keep their eyes open any longer.

As a result of all this, senior executives have started to mistrust the judgement of heads of departments. Controllers ask to read scripts before scheduling anything. In comedy even to this day a script has to be approved by the controller of BBC1 or BBC2, the controller of entertainment, the genre controller and the entertainment commissioner, as well as the head of comedy. Each of these people will chuck in their four pennyworth of suggestions, which the wretched writer and producer will be obliged to take notice of.

One of the most important ways of building a programme is to have it on at the same time on the same day every week. This is an absolutely fundamental principle of successful scheduling. An overrun of international or even Olympic tiddlywinks should not be allowed to throw the whole thing out of kilter. This is one of the main features of the soaps such as *Coronation Street*, *EastEnders* and *Neighbours*. The viewers don't want to have to plough through the *Radio Times* or the newspapers every time they turn on the set. My programmes have recently been screened at ten o'clock on Tuesday, then Thursday and then Wednesday in consecutive weeks.

Coupled with this, the scenery construction department has been closed, the scenery design department has been closed, the wardrobe department has been closed, and the make-up department has been closed. The dedicated rehearsal block, consisting of three studio-sized rooms with sprung floors for dancing and a dozen studio-sized rooms for ordinary rehearsal, has been taken over entirely for offices. We are left with hundreds of people looking at computer monitors and turning out paperwork. The ability to service in-house programmes has ceased to exist. Shows are now back to rehearsing in church halls and in rooms above pubs. Greg Dyke spent his time at the BBC battling with an organisation that was like a miniature version of the National Health Service and, had he not been compelled to resign, it would have taken him the rest of his time as director-general to rebuild it. What is exasperating is the fact that all this vast bureaucracy is required to turn out no more programmes than they did ten years ago.

I found Greg to be a flamboyant but rather likeable character. He was approachable and very concerned about what was going on at producer level. On one occasion he asked me to lunch at his suite in Broadcasting House. I expected to be dining with a dozen or so fellow writers, but when I arrived I found that I was the only writer invited. Greg and I were joined by Lorraine Hegessey who is the controller of BBC1 and Mark Thompson who was next in line to Greg. I was not a little overawed.

By the time we got past the soup and on to the seared scallops it was clear that they wanted to know what I thought was wrong with comedy. I took a deep breath and told them: return the power to the writers, producers and heads of department. By producers I mean the blokes who are going to commission the writers, find the cast, handle the actors and deal with the script. When a pilot has been produced it should then be up to the controller to decide whether to commission a series and when to schedule it. In my opinion, there is no evidence that Greg or any of them took any notice.

I have been exceedingly lucky. I have had great comedy writers to work with and a host of terrific actors and technicians to help me. I was lucky enough to be able to work without interference at perhaps the greatest entertainment-producing organisation in the world at the time when they were doing their best work. All this plus Ann, the best of wives, and a lovely family has combined to give me a great life. In return I have been able to give quite a lot of people in the world a good laugh.

I have indeed had the best of it.

Index

252

256